LISTEN

Article 12 of the United Nations Convention on the Rights of the Child (UNCRC, 1989) articulates every child's right to have their voice heard in matters that affect them. Yet acceptance of this right is sometimes slow, and there are barriers to effective implementation.

This vitally important book aims to accelerate acceptance of this right by bridging the gap between theory and practice, empowering adults to act as advocates and facilitators of children using their voices within our homes, schools, and wider communities.

Divided into thirteen chapters, *Listen* invites readers to connect the concept of 'child and student voice' meaningfully with the development of all children's physical voices and modes of communication. Topics explored include, but are not limited to:

- Current research on student voice, including an examination of public speaking within primary schools
- Advocating for a school-wide focus on supporting student voice
- Best practice and pedagogical approaches to facilitating public speaking in the classroom
- The benefits and drawbacks of debate, including how to use it appropriately and assessing when to employ other techniques
- Creating a supportive learning environment where students may overcome their anxieties about public speaking.

An essential read for parents, teachers, teaching assistants and senior leaders, *Listen* proposes a pedagogical approach to supporting student voice that is backed by current research yet firmly rooted in practical application.

Dr Siobhán Keenan Fitzgerald is a school principal of a Dublin City University (DCU) 'changemaker' school and holds over thirty years teaching experience in Ireland and internationally. She is currently working on curriculum development with the National Council for Curriculum and Assessment (NCCA) in Ireland. Siobhán is also a TEDx and award-winning speaker. She created the 'LET's Stand' public speaking programme and podcast.

LISTEN

How Child and Student Voice Can Change the World

Siobhán Keenan Fitzgerald

LONDON AND NEW YORK

Designed cover image: © Sarah Hoyle

First published 2025
by Routledge
4 Park Square, Milton Park, Abingdon, Oxon OX14 4RN

and by Routledge
605 Third Avenue, New York, NY 10158

Routledge is an imprint of the Taylor & Francis Group, an informa business

© 2025 Siobhán Keenan Fitzgerald

The right of Siobhán Keenan Fitzgerald to be identified as author of this work has been asserted in accordance with sections 77 and 78 of the Copyright, Designs and Patents Act 1988.

All rights reserved. No part of this book may be reprinted or reproduced or utilised in any form or by any electronic, mechanical, or other means, now known or hereafter invented, including photocopying and recording, or in any information storage or retrieval system, without permission in writing from the publishers.

Trademark notice: Product or corporate names may be trademarks or registered trademarks, and are used only for identification and explanation without intent to infringe.

British Library Cataloguing-in-Publication Data
A catalogue record for this book is available from the British Library

ISBN: 978-1-032-75032-3 (hbk)
ISBN: 978-1-032-75033-0 (pbk)
ISBN: 978-1-003-47206-3 (ebk)

DOI: 10.4324/9781003472063

Typeset in Interstate
by Apex CoVantage, LLC

CONTENTS

Introduction	1
1 The Right to Be Heard	**3**
Article 12 of the UNCRC and associated challenges to implementation 3	
The what and why of child voice 7	
Child voice vis-à-vis child protection 9	
The what and why of student voice 9	
Different forms of participation 12	
Listening to young people 12	
Summary reflection on the right to be heard 14	
2 The Importance of Communication Skills, Oral Language, Oracy and Public Speaking	**16**
Communication skills 17	
Oral language 18	
Oracy 19	
Speaking and listening 19	
Public speaking 20	
Communication, speaking and listening skills enhancing children's lives as children 21	
Communication, speaking and listening skills enhancing children's experience of learning in school 23	
Communication, speaking and listening skills enhancing young people's life outcomes and employability 24	
Communication, speaking and listening skills to mitigate disadvantage 25	
Communication, speaking and listening in response to Covid-19 related lockdowns 27	
Terminology: Ambiguity, clarity or a distraction 27	
Summary reflection on the importance of communication skills, oral language, oracy, public speaking, and speaking and listening skills 28	
3 Facilitating an Increased Focus on Child Voice and Student Voice	**31**
How parents can facilitate child voice 32	
Benefits of student voice 34	
How schools can facilitate child and student voice 36	
Models of support for facilitating child and student voice and participation 39	

Examples of student voice in action   40
   Student voice in explicit public speaking skills training   40
   The example of School 21   43
Summary Reflection on facilitating an increased focus on child and
   student voice   44

4 Research on Public Speaking in Primary School   46
A personal journey through public speaking   46
A professional interest in public speaking   47
Further studies in public speaking   48
Context of public speaking study   48
Literature review on public speaking in primary school   49
Action research on public speaking in primary school   50
Self-efficacy and public speaking   51
Vocabulary acquisition and development in public speaking   52
Study participants and methodology   53
Findings   54
   Fear, perceptions and experience of public speaking   54
   Examples of positive self-efficacy   55
   Impact of intervention on vocabulary development   57
   Key recommendations of the study   57
Summary reflection on research on public speaking in primary school   58

5 Why Public Speaking in Primary School   61
More than just a necessary skill-set   61
Aims of primary school education   62
Formal and informal nature of public speaking   63
Public speaking skills on the primary school curriculum   63
Benefits of public speaking skill training in primary school   65
Challenges to public speaking skill training in primary school   67
Gap between policy and practice   70
Primary school years as potentially an opportune time to begin public
   speaking skill training   71
Summary reflection on why public speaking in primary school   73

6 What Public Speaking in Primary School Looks Like   76
Implementing public speaking in primary schools   76
Achieving the oral language learning outcomes of primary language
   curricula through public speaking   77
Current practice in primary schools   78
What can be taught in public speaking   80
Explicit teaching of public speaking skills   83
Assessment of public speaking and oral language skills   83
Embedding public speaking in your school   87
Summary reflection on what public speaking in primary school looks like   88

7 Pedagogical Approaches to Public Speaking Training   91
Dialogic teaching   92
Talk as pedagogy   93
Talk as content   94
Gradual Release of Responsibility Method (GRR)   95

Explicit teaching of public speaking and oral language skills   95
How public speaking skills are developed   96
'LET's Stand' public speaking programme   97
The structure of a speech   97
How general speaking skills are developed   99
Opportunities to practise   99
Cross-curricular opportunities   101
Groupwork   101
Challenges to note and overcome   101
Assessment   103
Summary reflection on pedagogical approaches to public speaking training   103

8   Debate Is Great but WAIT   106
Debating   106
Benefits of debating   107
Drawbacks of debating   109
Debate is not the most effective tool for solving actual problems   111
Experience of debating at school   111
Dialogue rather than debate   113
What we can learn from Toastmasters in terms of communication skills   114
Alternatives to debating   115
   Philosophy for Children (P4C)   115
   More alternatives to debating   115
Debate is great but 'WAIT'   116
Summary reflection on debating in school   117

9   Fear of Public Speaking and Communication Apprehension   119
Fear of public speaking   119
Communication apprehension   120
Public speaking anxiety   120
What does fear of public speaking physically look and feel like   121
Nerves   121
Strategies for managing nerves   121
Longer term impact of fear of public speaking   123
Reasons for fear of public speaking   123
How to manage and overcome the fear of public speaking   124
Feedback in relation to fear of public speaking from my study   126
Summary reflection on fear of public speaking   128

10   Supporting ALL Children to Have Their Voice Heard   132
Shyness and supporting children who are shy   133
   Positives of being shy   134
   Shyness as a cultural trait   134
   Disadvantages and limitations of being shy   135
   Important considerations when training children who are shy in public speaking skills   135
Supporting children from disadvantaged backgrounds   137
Supporting children with special education needs   138
Speech and language difficulties   139
Supporting children with speech and language difficulties   140
Supporting children with other categories of special education needs   141

Supporting children from minority groups and for whom English is not their first language 142
The power of the stories of potential role models 143
Summary reflection on public speaking support for ALL children 143

11 Examples of 'Student Voice' in Practice — 145
The role of the teacher in relation to 'student voice' 145
- Co-creating ground rules 147
- Providing effective feedback 147
- Teacher as public speaker 148
- Teachers' perceptions and expectations 148
- Teachers' confidence 149
- Reflection, practice and training 149
- Additional teacher comments 150

How teachers can promote a culture of more 'student voice' in their classroom 151
How schools can promote a culture of more 'student voice' across the school 155
Attempts to listen to young people's voices at a broader level 156
Summary reflection on student voice in the classroom and across the school 157

12 Welcome to the World of Child and Student Voice — 160
How did we get to this brave new world? 160
Home in this brave new world 162
School in this brave new world 163
- What students learn 164
- Where students learn 166
- How students learn 167

Community in this brave new world 169
What life in this brave new world looks and feels like 170
A day in this brave new world 171
The future in this brave new world 172
The child in this brave new world 172
Summary reflection on this brave new world of child and student voice 173
- Welcome to the world of child and student voice 173

13 Concluding Chapter — 175
Reminder of our obligation as educators and parents 175
Reminder of the benefits of developing children's speaking and communication skills 177
Reminder of how child and student voice can be facilitated in homes, schools and the community and how public speaking and communication skills can be taught 177
Reminder of the ongoing important role of the teacher 178
Reminder of how to overcome the fear of public speaking 178
Reminder of WAITing to debate 179
Reminder of how child and student voice initiatives are for all children 179
Reminder that child and student voice is not something new 179
Concluding thoughts 180

Index 183

INTRODUCTION

The United Nations Convention on the Rights of the Child (UNCRC), Article 12, confers the right on all children to have a say in matters that affect them. How can adults working and living with children actively support the realization of this right?

I grew up in Ireland at a time when the adage "Children should be seen and not heard" was very common. Surely, it doesn't take a rocket scientist to figure out that if you do not have the practice of being heard and listened to as a child, you won't automatically pick up effective communication skills and skills of being an active citizen, participating in democratic processes at age 18. How do we know how anybody feels about a situation unless they say or represent and communicate it in some shape or form? How can every voice be heard and have influence if we are not consciously listening?

What further complicates and discriminates is that some people in society have access to the development of a skill-set that enables and empowers them to more easily express themselves, their needs, their thoughts and ideas, their hopes and dreams. Some are more listened to in their families, schools and communities than others. Communicating the message, loud and clear, that we, the adults, are listening to our young people is a very good place to start, but it's not enough. All children must be encouraged, enabled and empowered to express their true, authentic selves in whatever way they can because **all** children have the right to be heard.

Speaking is power. Communication is power and competent speaking and communication skills are vital for life. The good news is that just like any other skills, speaking, listening and communication skills can be learned. It is a fact of life, that every day people, young and old, face the prospect of speaking in some type of a public forum. Yet, a pervasive fear of public speaking amongst adults worldwide is well documented. It appears that this fear is due, in part, to lack of training, practise, experience, low confidence and for many an initial negative experience of speaking in public in childhood. What if there is something we can do about this? The term 'public speaking' may sound overly formal to some; the simple term itself engendering fear. When I use this term throughout this book, I use it with the Merriam Webster Dictionary definition in mind: "the art of effective communication with an audience". For some, this may not even involve speaking but using whatever means available to communicate and share their message and story with an audience. Training our children in the skills of competent communication is no longer an optional extra that is just 'nice to do'. Because of Article 12 of the UNCRC, it is a moral imperative and a duty. As American poet Maya Angelou said, "now that we know better, we must do better".

For all children's lives as children, for connection and well-being, learning in school and out, life outcomes and employability, public speaking and competent communication skills are skills to mitigate disadvantage and positively impact social mobility and growth. But how does this play out and what does this look like in our classrooms, our schools, our homes and our communities? As a parent, a teacher, a school leader, I am concerned that we are wasting valuable and opportune learning time if we don't explicitly teach skills of competent communication, of self-expression, of talking, of oracy, of public speaking in primary schools. This would give more value and attention to how our young people express themselves through speech and other means. This emphasis could support them to find and express the voice they have a right to. In order for all young people to realize their right to have their voice heard, we need to support and facilitate them to develop the courage, competence and confidence to communicate and speak up to the best of their abilities.

Imagine a world where conflicts might be resolved more maturely and peacefully by articulate active citizens for whom it has become second nature for them to have a say in their world. Too often, we have sat back and let other people do the talking for us, people who claim to represent us but know little about our lives. Every individual has a story and something special and unique to share. I believe that if we do not share, through whatever means available to us, that which is uniquely ours to share, not only do we lose out but the world misses out too. Speaking up and having the experience of having your voice heard has benefits for the individual and the world at large. What might the world look like if everybody shared their story and listened respectfully as others do the same? This may be very difficult for us to imagine as my own generation are all too familiar with being told to "Shhhh, be quiet". However, supporting our children to realize Article 12 of the UNCRC has the potential to positively change their world and the world at large, for the better.

Apart from being a right that our young people have, there are huge life-long benefits for all to gaining facility with self-expression through the process of having a say in matters that affect their lives. It's not just about communication, although that is huge, it's about promoting and enabling social engagement and connection. Nobody else can tell our story. Experiences that are uniquely ours from the cradle to the grave, if we don't talk about them, who will? We all remember the saying 'children should be seen and not heard'. Nothing good ever came of that. Thankfully, we adults, now have a greater awareness of the importance of child voice. So, are we listening? With more awareness, we can play an active, conscious, informed role in empowering child and student voice and self-expression. This could become a game-changer for all of our children in so many ways, but also a world changer for all of us, too, when we stop to lend an ear to the hearts and minds, the voice, of the purest in our population. From choice, negotiations and participation in decision-making within their families and communities, to having a say in their school life, resolving conflicts in school and contributing to policy development at the local, national or international level, we can support our young people to develop the confidence through experience to know at a deep level that their voice matters, and that they make a difference. With a little help from us caring adults, lucky enough to have children in our lives (parents, grandparents, aunts, uncles, teachers, school principals, policy makers, youth workers, social workers), child and student voice can and will change the world.

1 The Right to Be Heard

Twelve-year-old Jehanzeb Khan from Pakistan is sure that "children can change the world if they are given a chance" (Lansdown, 2011, 'Every Child's Right to Be Heard,' Introduction). I, too, am sure of this. Children may be a percentage of our current population but they are 100% the future. All children are citizens of this world. They don't have to be made or perceived as citizens. They simply are citizens by virtue of living and existing in this world. Engaged in a rapid pace of learning and development since birth, they are on a powerful, positive trajectory of growth. All parents know this when they observe the changes and developments in the first few months and years of children's lives. Even as very young babies, before they learn to talk, children can make their needs and preferences known in a variety of different ways. They cry, they smile, they gurgle, the push things away or open up their arms. These communications of need are heard and responded to by the caring adults in the baby's life.

Article 12 of the UNCRC and associated challenges to implementation

The United Nations Convention on the Rights of the Child, adopted in 1989, consists of 54 articles in total pertaining to the integrated rights of children. It is founded on the idea that every child should be respected, protected and recognised as a unique, valuable human being and a holder of specified, inalienable rights. These rights come under four general categories: survival rights, development rights, protection rights and participation rights. Articles 43–54 refer to how adults and governments must work together to ensure that all children can enjoy all of their rights. Article 12 details that children have a right to express their views and have them taken seriously in accordance with their age and maturity, without discrimination on any grounds. Best understood as a fundamental right, it is also a general principle which impacts the realisation of all of the other rights detailed in the Convention. Article 12 literally gives voice to claiming all other rights. It is a sign of new standards of respect that human rights evolve and are taken seriously. The ratification of the UNCRC has led to an increased focus on the reality of 'child voice' and what that might mean and look like in homes, communities and schools as 'student voice'.

Article 5 specifies the family's responsibility to help children learn to exercise their rights, and to ensure that their rights are protected. Article 18 refers to parental responsibilities and government supports and assistance to help parents to raise their children. At all times, what is in the best interests of the child is prioritised and here, children's views and voice is again given due consideration. In cases of a family separation, children have the right to stay in contact with both parents, except where this may cause them harm. Article 28 pertains to every child's right to education, free in primary school with different forms of secondary education available to every child, an education that must respect children's dignity and rights. Article 29 further outlines important goals of education in developing every child's abilities, talents and personality, helping them to achieve their potential. Education must foster the child's respect for human rights, their own and other cultures and the environment as well as respect for their parents.

Article 12 refers more specifically to involvement in decisions and actions that have an impact on the child's life imposing an obligation on the State to introduce active measures to enable the child to be heard and to have their views taken seriously. Under Article 12, children have the right to find out about various matters and share what they think with others, in a variety of ways, for example by talking, writing, drawing, role playing or in any other way suitable to them unless it offends or harms other people. In fulfilment of Article 12, intentionally creating a safe, supportive environment of respect for children to express their views, contributes towards building children's capacities to exercise their right to freedom of expression detailed in Article 13. Therefore Article 12 also strengthens the realization of Article 13. Having a voice helps us to express, claim and stand up for all the rights that are ours. With a strong voice, confidence and experience in using it and having it heard, children will more easily be able to learn and develop as active citizens by expressing, questioning, challenging and discussing from their unique stand point, building self-esteem and confidence in a real, meaningful way.

Article 12 applies to the right of all children to have their voice heard as individuals and collectively. However, Lansdown (2011) acknowledges that since the adoption of the UNCRC in 1989, Article 12 has proven one of the most challenging articles to implement. It is important to bear in mind that "the right to speak is the right to be listened to; in practice there is a gap between speaking and being listened to" (UN, 1989). Lansdown points to the need to build environments in which children are recognized as active citizens, contributing to decisions that affect their own lives, their communities and wider society. Research on the implementation of the Convention on the Rights of the Child (CRC), undertaken for the Northern Ireland Commissioner for Children and Young People to inform his priorities for office found that one of the factors which appeared to hinder the full realisation of the right outlined in Article 12 was the fact that the precise nature of Article 12 was not fully understood by duty-bearers, those with a duty to children.

Other reasons reported from across the world, for the difficulty in implementation of Article 12 are: the assumption that children lack the competence, knowledge and judgement to have a meaningful say; that the adults working and living with children always know what is in a child's best interest; that children simply need to be taken care of; the fear that children may behave badly, make ridiculous and excessive demands if given too much power or control; that 'voice' may lead to lack of respect for parents or those in authority; an assumption that this is too heavy a burden to place on children's young shoulders; that children need to be socialized and that somehow, active participation in and contribution to matters that affect them may expose children to harm; and an unchallenged assumption that smaller and younger somehow equates to weaker and more needy. Long-standing practices, cultures, attitudes and resistance to change pose other barriers. Much of this points to a lack of understanding, confidence and trust on the part of the adults which may be more rooted in fear of the unknown than actual evidence or experience.

Article 12 is an appreciation of human dignity, a right, and is not someone else's to give or take. It doesn't merely suggest or recommend but makes it obligatory to recognise children as active citizens, participants and active contributors to decisions within and about their own lives and wider society which ultimately impacts us all. It applies to every aspect of a child's life: home, school, healthcare, local communities, play, leisure, courts, legal matters and policy-making. Across the world, this right is slowly being realised to varying degrees for children but for some children from more marginalised groups, born into and living in conditions that are not of their making, not at all. Its full realization cannot be dependent only on the courage and determination of the children but the determination and support of the informed adults working and living with them. It is the responsibility of each of us, individually and collectively to help all children enjoy their rights.

In 'Every Child's Right to Be Heard' (UNICEF, 2011), there are practical tips and examples of how this right may be realised for children. It contains examples of legislation and policy, evidence from research, guidelines for practitioners and examples of meaningful participation in practice from around the world. This can support and enable governments and policy makers to learn what it means to listen to children, acknowledging their unique views and contributions. Countries can learn from evidence and from other countries how to broaden their understanding of the scope and meaning of Article 12 and introduce necessary measures across its systems to fulfil their responsibility. Schools and organisations working with children and young people are beginning to explore creative ways to provide students with opportunities for active citizenship and participation.

Children are not obliged to express their view but they have the right to. Children don't have to have the final say but they must be given the opportunity to have a say. As citizens, they must have a seat at the decision-making table. So that they may be enabled to express their views freely, they need access to relevant, appropriate information through means and at a level that they can understand. They have the right to be informed of the choices available to them as well as the nature and consequences of any decisions that are being taken. They need time and safe, supportive spaces where they are supported and facilitated to develop and articulate their views clearly and confidently. They need to feel safe to express their views, even if they are different to and challenge those of the adults in their lives, safe in the knowledge that they will be neither criticized nor punished but listened to.

It is important to note that participation and having your voice heard are not meant as a once off event but rather an ongoing process of participation and expression. This is not just a tokenistic representation on one day, in one decision, at one event. It's an ongoing process of dialogue, information-sharing, facilitation and exploration between children and adults based on mutual respect, strengthening their engagement in democratic processes. Their views once invited, facilitated and received are given full consideration, taking into account the child's age and maturity. These views are acted upon where possible and if not, clear reasons are given for this. Children must be informed and updated as to where and how their voice has had influence in their family, community, school and sometimes further afield. In the publication 'A World Fit for Children', which was adopted by the UN General Assembly Special Session on Children in 2002, governments promised "to develop and implement programmes to promote meaningful participation by children, including adolescents, in decision-making processes" (UNICEF, 2008). It's also noted in this publication that "by giving high priority to the rights of children . . . we serve the best interest of all humanity". Governments and policy makers should start from a presumption that all children have the capacity to form a view. The child does not need to prove this.

The good news is that there are many examples of good practice from across the world vis-à-vis 'child voice' and 'student voice'. These examples can inspire further learning and development in this area. One example of how much more children can achieve through a democratic and socially relevant education is evident in the New Schools programme in Colombia (Lansdown, 2011, p. 6). As part of this programme, schools use a flexible curriculum with mixed-age classrooms where the role of the teacher is as a facilitator. Children take responsibility for various projects with the support of committed adults. During the public hearing on the draft bill when Nigeria's Children's Rights Act was being passed, members of their Children's Parliament made a very impactful presentation called 'Voices of Nigerian Children–Children Are an Investment and Not an Expenditure'. When older children make visible what is possible, younger children can be inspired and motivated by role models they can easily identify with. Role models are created closer to home, within communities when older siblings and other children are encouraged, facilitated and supported to lead the way.

The unfounded assumptions and biases mentioned previously, in relation to why Article 12 is not more fully enacted, blatantly dismiss children's rights. Life and the world are evolving and we learn as we grow. Lest we forget, all concepts and ideas were new once before they became embedded in our culture and social systems. Many people who didn't have a voice in history are thankfully finding and using their voices today. This is for the benefit of everyone. Some of the possible reasons for the resistance to implementing Article 12 demonstrate precisely why children need to be supported to realize this right in the first place. The reasons mentioned come from an adult's mind and view of the world which is seriously limited, biased and possibly scarred by its own controlled experience of childhood. There is no evidence to back them up. In contrast, many adults working and living with children frequently see and experience how even very young children are very capable of showing that they have unique opinions and experiences to express. They recognise that this right is actually critical to improving the quality and nature of the childhood children experience.

Lansdown (2011) advises that supporting a child's right to be heard in the early years helps to embed the values of democracy in the child's approach to life which is a far more effective grounding for democracy than a sudden transfer of power at the age of 18. Within discussions on education research and reform, 'student voice' is not a new concept but a topic that is growing in momentum. Rudduck and McIntyre (2007) point out that student voice was a much-discussed phenomenon in the late 1960s and 1970s. This, they report, was driven by the desire to more fully and deeply understand life in classrooms and schools. So, how can we more easily understand child voice and student voice so that we can more skillfully facilitate their realization in practical, impactful ways?

The what and why of child voice

'Child voice' refers to children's right to have a say in matters that affect their lives. It describes children's real, authentic involvement in decision making. Children can express and share their 'voice' most obviously through talk but also through means such as non-verbal communications, drawing, visual art, movement, dance, music, song, stories, poetry, play, photographs and recordings. This list is not exhaustive. 'Child voice' means whole-heartedly respecting children as citizens and providing opportunities for their active, informed and continuous involvement in what happens in their lives. 'Child voice' recognizes that children have their own point of view, a unique lens and perspective on their world which informs a very valuable contribution to decision making. Decisions should not be made **for** children but **with** them, supporting this decision-making process with age and stage appropriate information and feedback. The child should be perceived as an active partner who brings an important, unique perspective to the decision-making table. Children then will grow in confidence and become more motivated to participate in the world around them when they experience that their 'voice', in childhood, has power and influence and is taken seriously by the adults around them. Importantly, while children have the right to have their voice heard, they cannot be pressurized to do so. Their contributions are voluntary. They also have the right to privacy and confidentiality.

When we take the time to observe and listen to children, they show us in many ways just how pure and powerful they are. They are curious, compassionate and caring. Watching children at play, we see them imagine and work through a multitude of scenarios, solving puzzles through pure and playful exploration. Their instinct is to be active participants in their life and learning. Yes, they are influenced by the adults in their lives but if we are wise, we will step back, stop and open ourselves up to be more influenced by them also.

Lebanese-American poet Kahlil Gibran advises us in the book 'The Prophet' (Gibran, 2021), one of the most popular poetry books of all time, that our children are not our children: "You may give them your love but not your thoughts, for they have their own thoughts". Do we adults really understand what a child's life is like? Can we? What factors and experiences impact their views? How and where are they most comfortable and confident expressing these views? What changes would they suggest and can they be a part of? Recently when I was watching back video clips I took of my own children (now teenagers and young adults) in their early years, I was amazed at how wise and 'wonder-full' they were then. I had forgotten. How easily and quickly we can forget. If I can forget so easily the childhoods of the children within my own family, what can I really know of children from backgrounds different to my own? Do we truly acknowledge how unique each child is? Any of us who have siblings know that, even in the same family, we don't think exactly the same thoughts.

Children of all ages have the right to be heard. Babies, toddlers and very small children have unique views and perspectives on the world even when they are as yet, unable to express them verbally. Just because someone isn't talking doesn't mean they don't have something to say. Very young children are acutely sensitive to their surroundings and environment and quickly gain an awareness and understanding of their own identity as well as the people, routines and places in their lives. They are in tune with their senses. The nature of their participation may be slightly different. Even very young children can express individual preferences. Typically, the range of decisions they will be involved in will increase with age and their evolving capacities but there are ways and means of recording all children's contributions. Younger children may need more support expressing themselves, their needs, their preferences or more time by a caring adult spent with them to carefully observe and note their responses and contributions in certain situations. The issues towards which they contribute, largely due to their realm of experience may be mostly concerned with their immediate environment within the family and their local community. This, however, makes their contributions no less important. As they grow older these areas of contribution expand and broaden.

If we take the time to observe children playing, we very often see how much they love to play in roles of authority and leadership, selecting games, communicating strategies and negotiating rules. They are naturally fearless and courageous, and not only that but we can learn a lot from how compassionate and empathetic they can be towards one another. They can approach things very differently to us adults and are already making decisions and taking responsibilities from a very early age. Historically, a culture of listening to children was not widespread. For too long, some children have been voiceless and invisible within society and often powerless within their families and communities, 'seen and not heard', if seen at all. However, some tribes and people across the world have a culture of listening to and being guided by the voices of children, some religions too. In some cases, there is something spiritual, honest and pure attributed to children's voice. It would seem that ancient wisdom and traditions have much to teach us in this regard but again, we must listen.

Child voice is important because it is the most authentic, reliable way to hear the child's perspective and gain an insight into what is happening and important in their world. It has the potential to more fully engage the child showing value for their contribution, their thoughts, feelings and ideas. With a deeper understanding and awareness of the child's context, lived experience, dislikes, likes and interests, all working with children can more easily build on these strong foundations, enabling all children to grow, develop and make steady progress from where they are at. They can be given the opportunity to bring something of their uniqueness and their thoughts to the world around them. Child voice models in a very real way the values of democracy where every voice has value. It acknowledges children as equal citizens encouraging them to be more agentic in their lives.

The more children express themselves, the more confidently they will express themselves, in childhood and into the future, giving them opportunities of active citizenship now so that they can be active citizens with the associated rights and responsibilities as they grow and develop. It is important for parents, teachers and all who have the privilege of living and working with children and young people to listen deeply to them. Additional measures may be required to ensure that children from 'seldom-heard', marginalised groups or children experiencing or at risk of social exclusion are afforded equal and equitable opportunities to be heard.

Child voice vis-à-vis child protection

In addition to the benefits of participation already mentioned, participation and having their voice heard protects children. Therefore, it plays a vital role in terms of child protection. Abuse and bullying thrive on silence. Silence protects the abuser rather than those being abused. When children are encouraged, enabled and empowered to voice and communicate what is happening to them and have the experience of being listened to, it is much easier for any violation of rights to be exposed and in this way, children are protected and empowered. They can inform adults who can help them of what is happening with information that often only they can provide and receive the help and protection they need and are entitled to. Serious offences and violence against children can be dealt with more effectively when children themselves can expose the perpetrators. Knowing who will listen to them, they can speak out and communicate about situations that make them feel vulnerable or at risk.

The what and why of student voice

Across the world, education and schooling form such a huge part of children's lives. Certainly one of those matters that affects them, it makes sense that students should, as the primary and direct stakeholders of education, have a say in it. Student voice is a way of thinking that strives to reposition students in educational research and reform so that they may have an influence on their own education. It's about what happens day-to-day in schools, classrooms and learning environments. It's about the lived experiences and contributions of children in their educational settings. It encapsulates the experience of being listened to on a daily basis, of having choice where possible, of having needs met, of being appreciated for the unique individual that each student is. Taylor and Robinson explain that "as a field of educational endeavour student voice has been largely seen as oriented to action, participation and change" (2009, p. 163).

Student voice is the individual and collective perspective of students in the context of schools and education, an action-oriented practice with a strong commitment to ideas of student empowerment, liberation and collaboration. In a metaphorical sense, student voice refers to the representation of students' unique perspectives and in a pragmatic way, it refers to how students' voices are heard and taken seriously. Just to be clear, the concept is twofold: participation and representation. It refers to students' actual expression of values, opinions, beliefs and perspectives in the school and education context and also teaching and learning methodologies that are based on and incorporate student choices, interests and passions. Student voice relates to empowering student agency and giving students a say in their own education.

Taylor and Robinson (2009) noted that student voice had received little theorization in the British context even though the Office for Standards in Education, Children's Services and Skills (Ofsted) (2005) specified that its inspection regime expects schools to report on the degree to which they seek and act upon the views of students. Looking at the British context, Taylor and Robinson (2009) explain that power, positions of power and balance of power within the classroom, are significant factors in shaping both the practical assumptions made about what is possible in participation and the philosophical underpinnings of student voice work (p. 161). In their own theorisation of student voice, Robinson and Taylor (2007) identify four core values which they consider underpin much student voice practice: communication as dialogue, conversation that flows from teacher to students but also from students to teacher and to other students; participation and democratic inclusivity; the recognition that power relations are unequal and problematic; and the possibility for change and transformation (p. 162).

There are five different lines of argument that are generally followed in terms of offering a justification for student voice. These are: normative, developmental, political, relevance and educational arguments. The basis of the normative argument is that children are not citizens-in-waiting. They are citizens with rights in the here and now, entitled to participate in decision-making about their education, from the perspective of children's rights (UN, 1989). However, while it might appear logical for students to have a say in their education, I think it would be a significant stretch, at present, to suggest that it might be the 'norm'. Perhaps, someday.

The developmental argument proposes that students are developmentally ready to participate as they frequently show that they are more than capable of assuming more responsibility in activities and decisions outside of school. Lawy and Biesta (2006) argue that, as citizens, children are entitled to opportunities to practice citizenship and so develop citizenship knowledge, skills and attitudes and that schools should offer opportunities to develop citizenship that are appropriate to their age and stage of development. The essence of the political argument is that students are not a homogeneous group, but the student body is made up of many voices. We need to be careful not to assume the singularity of voice, when of course, there are multiple voices in every classroom and indeed, every community and every home. The political argument stresses the importance of including seldom-heard voices, the voices of marginalized groups, perspectives that are often excluded from discussions and decision-making processes. Reaching marginalized groups is very important in terms of developing more inclusive, well-rounded, balanced solutions. It often requires additional resources and effort. Teachers noted how difficult it is to reach students who most needed to be heard from (McIntyre et al., 2005).

The relevance argument refers to the importance of student input into, for example, curriculum design, what is taught in school and how it is taught, in order to make curriculum and education more relevant to the students. It is thought that student input has the potential to add to the quality of the curriculum and increase its relevance. Dewey (1938) had proposed that learning starts with the experiences of the learner and builds on that towards a more systematic growth of knowledge and insights. The educational argument sees student voice as an opportunity for citizenship education. Student voice has the potential to promote democratic attitudes through education. A study by Eurydice (2012) involving thirty-one countries in Europe found that citizenship is featured to some degree in all national curricula, either as a subject, cross curricular theme or in how schools function as places where students actively learn citizenship from experience.

There is considerable overlap between citizenship skills and skills commonly referred to as 21st-century skills including: critical thinking, creativity, communication, collaboration, and personal and social responsibility. Although referred to as 'skills', these include knowledge, skills, attitudes and values. Citizenship education also includes a knowledge of basic democratic concepts, a respect for democratic values and diversity and the ability and willingness to participate constructively in the public domain, including in decision-making through voting (Eurydice, 2012).

While having a student council in schools, most often, is a very positive step towards promoting 'student voice', students, teachers and schools need to be aware of the responsibility involved to try to represent the broad range of individual voices within the student body. In a study by Davey et al. (2010), students who were not as involved as others described the school student council as "tokenistic" and a waste of time with well-behaved, popular children disproportionately represented on it. Participation and democratic inclusivity require that all students have the opportunity to be actively involved in decisions within the classroom and school.

Student voice is important because it is widely recognized that children and young people have a unique body of knowledge about their lives, needs and concerns, together with ideas and views deriving from direct experience (Quinn & Owens, 2014). Given the immense amount of change that has happened globally over the last three decades, it is understandable that young people today have had a very different experience of life than the generation that was young before them. Some of these changes include advances in digital technology, how we access and share information and greater movement and mixing of people and cultures from across the world. Our young people are growing up in a world very different to the one we grew up in. Therefore, the views and insights of our youth warrant careful attention, consideration and response.

There is an expression that says: "We don't know what we don't know". It is impossible for any adult to know what is going on in the heart, mind, life of a young person much and all as we, teachers and parents, would like to think we do. Another expression advises, "we don't see things as they are, we see them as we are". When we look at the younger generation, we see them through eyes clouded by our own experiences and biases. What's more, it is likely that most teachers had a reasonably good experience of school. Why else would we choose to spend the rest of our adult working lives there? However, having enjoyed and succeeded in school ourselves, we are hardly representative of the majority of young people which makes the need to hear directly from them even more important. Prensky (2005) cautions that if we do not stop and listen to the children we serve and make major changes on the basis of the suggestions they offer, we will be left in the 21st century with school buildings to administer but with students who are physically or mentally somewhere else. Students' input and contributions are necessary to adapt their education to their needs.

The potential benefits of student voice have been well-established in research and literature. However, listening to students is not enough. Young people need to know they have been heard, their input and opinions considered, acknowledged and where appropriate, acted upon. When these opinions, once considered, cannot be acted upon at that time, explanation should be provided. Upholding students' right to have a say in matters that affect them contributes to confidence and positive relationship building with the adults involved in this collaborative, consultative process. Student voice initiatives should benefit all students. If all students are not considered in student voice initiatives, it risks being tokenistic and even more damaging, as it could be perceived as and may even become manipulative. Remember, one student or child's voice or one select group of children contributing to student voice does not accurately reflect student voice.

As I stated before, students are supposed to be the beneficiaries of the education they receive at school, therefore they should have a say in shaping it to best reflect their needs, their strengths, their interests and their concerns. Students are the foundation and the very reason for our schools. It makes no sense that their voices would not be heard. A strong culture of empowering student voice encourages students to open up, to get comfortable with sharing their views, thoughts and feelings, to share who they are. It is important because it empowers, engages and motivates students and educators know how important engagement is for learning. It shows and models respect in a very real way for the individuality and uniqueness of each student.

Different forms of participation

There are different forms of participation: consultative participation, collaborative participation and child-led participation. For governments and other groups working with and caring for children, children's perceptions should be sought in order to build understanding and knowledge about their lives and experience. In this way, children participate on a consultative basis. This kind of participation is adult initiated and adult led. Collaborative participation refers to when children are directly involved in designing and undertaking policy development, peer education, research, etc. This provides an opportunity for shared decision-making with adults. Child-led participation occurs when children initiate activities and are facilitated to advocate for themselves on issues of concern that they have identified. Adults act in the role of facilitator, information and resource provider with the children leading and controlling the process.

Basic ethical standards that need to be observed in child participation as outlined by Save the Children's Practice Standards in Children's Participation (2005) are the following: transparency and information sharing about and throughout the process; clear explanation and understanding that participation is voluntary; respect; participation should be relevant to the particular project at hand; and child-friendly in terms of the environments and working methods. The participation should also be inclusive of all children from all backgrounds, actively inviting and supporting the participation of diverse voices, supported by training for adults, safe and sensitive to risk and finally, it should be accountable.

Listening to young people

Listening is powerful and probably one of the greatest gifts we can give to another human being. It is not a passive exercise but rather active, requiring us to be present and tune in to the interaction with more of our senses than just our hearing. It is not only listening with our ears but necessitates learning different ways of listening to hear the various forms of communication by children and young people of all ages. When we listen, we listen in a spirit of trust, love and curiosity (TLC). Think about a time when you felt truly listened to. Conversely, think about the feelings you had when you didn't feel listened to or when something important you felt you had to contribute was neither invited nor welcomed. Listening to children and young people is about respecting them, showing that they have value and modelling for them the importance of respecting and listening to others. When we think about it, not listening is the source of many relationship problems today.

Listening is a crucial component of communication which appears to be missing in many adult negotiations. Carl Rogers (1995) explains that man's inability to communicate is a result of his failure to listen effectively. Sadly, we witness too regularly the ineptitude of many in positions of power to listen, in failed efforts to resolve conflicts across the world. This has serious and tragic consequences. Deep and active listening skills are necessary for promoting understanding, resolving conflicts and finding solutions. It's a vital skill for life with immense impact, a skill that will benefit the child in their family, school and community and benefits communities, families and the world at large. To more effectively facilitate child participation as per Article 12, adults need keen skills of listening to collaborate with children, engaging them in accordance with their evolving capacities. Hallet et al. (2003) report that adults often impose their solutions rather than listening and helping children come to their own conclusions. Let's take a moment to reflect on if or where this happens in our own practices, in our homes, schools and communities.

There is so much we can learn from children when we listen. We are very aware that children have superior competency in some areas to many adults, for example, in terms of how they use and embrace technology, the speed at which they can learn a new language, how they use their imaginations, how open they are to new experiences, how they express creativity, empathy, love, compassion, how they forgive, dream and how they play. It's also important to note the importance of the opportunities to develop the necessary skills that will empower children to develop confidence and self-efficacy and represent themselves to the best of their abilities. Without the opportunity to develop and practise these skills, there may be a risk of reinforcing a self-limiting belief, with some young people internalizing a message such as "if others think and don't believe that I can do it, maybe they're right". For example, I don't and can't play rugby. When I was younger I wanted to but I was told that I was too small and girls don't play rugby. I believed it and didn't even try (excuse the pun). I believed the adults around me, without question. Nowadays, many girls play rugby and play it very well.

As articulate, active citizens, contributing both to decisions that affect their own lives as well as their communities and wider society, children's opinions and experiences, once listened to and acted on can positively contribute to decisions affecting the realisation of other children's rights and well-being. The process and the result of this expression are both important as it benefits the giver and the receiver of the messages in powerful ways. The practice of regularly having your voice heard and witnessing other children having their voice heard too has a positive impact on personal development, greater capacity for active citizenship and democratic engagement and on the decision-making process for everyone. Rajani (2000) points out that participation leads to greater levels of competence which then enhances the quality of participation. Participation begets a cycle of further participation as children develop certain citizenship and 21st-century skills that education in schools in many countries is aiming for. Children's talents flourish and competencies and skills grow through active participation.

Summary reflection on the right to be heard

Concerted efforts are required to understand the reality of all children's lives, connecting and working directly with children to ensure that all efforts with and on behalf of children are informed by the concerns and priorities of children themselves. Instead of sitting down and being quiet, we want children to feel safe and supported to stand up and speak out. Encouraging, enabling and empowering children from the earliest ages to engage in critical enquiry, to acquire the confidence and capacity to express their views and have their voices heard will challenge any abuse of rights for everyone and contribute to wider societal positive change.

The 'Déclaration des Droits de l'Homme et du Citoyen' of 26 August 1789 specifies the "free communication of ideas and opinions" as "one of the most precious rights of man" (Habermas, 1989, p. 71). The rights enshrined in the United Nations Convention on the Rights of the Child (1989) carry with them a responsibility for those who work with children to support and prepare them to claim and avail of these rights. Children should be seen **and** heard. We must listen to them, for they are keenly aware of what emotions are welling up inside of them. They have an innate wisdom. It is only when we teach them to be quiet, to not express themselves, that they risk losing this intuitive wisdom. We ought to and must listen to what they have to say and give them plenty of experiences of having their voices heard.

Only children can speak out and represent issues that affect children, just as men cannot speak out on women's issues and one race, generation or profession cannot adequately or accurately represent another's. It wouldn't make sense and nobody would take these seriously. Similarly, adults cannot have full responsibility for deciding what young people's issues and needs are. Children have a unique body of knowledge and insights into their lives, needs, concerns and interests that even the adults closest to them may not be aware of. These derive from their direct experience. Decisions that take this into consideration and that are fully informed by children's own perspectives will be more effective, relevant and more sustainable.

Lansdown advises that "supporting a child's right to be heard in the early years is integral to nurturing citizenship over the long term" (2011, p. 9). In terms of student voice, as a teacher, I tend to look at it simply; these are our children's schooldays, this is their education, so it stands to reason that they should have a say and have that say heard. The teacher is not redundant in the realisation of student voice. Very much a partnership between the adult and student, the teacher in the school context, is facilitating the student in order to empower them to find and use their authentic voice. Students have long been trying to express their opinions and have their voices heard. What possibly makes it different in recent years is a greater willingness and awareness amongst educators, parents and other adults as to the importance of facilitating and listening to student and child voice.

Facilitating child and student voice is not just a 'nice to have' or a 'nice to do' concept to consider. It is embedded in legislation. The UNCRC requires that governments ensure that children's rights are respected. It is legally binding in Ireland and other countries that have ratified it, committing to policy development that reflects the rights of children and young people. Regarding the topic of 'student voice', it is required that opportunities are provided for all children and teenagers to be heard on education matters so that their views are not just listened to, but given due consideration in decision-making. Lansdown (2011) notes that it is a measure of human dignity that children are able to be involved in decisions that affect them, consistent with their levels of competence in accordance with this important fundamental right enshrined in Article 12 of the UNCRC. For those endeavouring to cultivate a culture of facilitating and celebrating child and student voice in the home, community and school, possibly the best starting point may simply be, in a spirit of trust, love and curiosity (TLC), **to listen.**

Reference List

Davey, C., Lea, J., Shaw, C., & Burke, T. (2010). *Children's Participation in Decision-Making*. Participation Works for CRAE (Children's Rights Alliance England) and NCB (National Children's Bureau).

Dewey, J. (1938). *Experience and Education* (Vol. No. 10). New York: The Macmillan company.

Eurydice. (2012). European Commission/EACEA/Eurydice. *Developing Key Competences at School in Europe: Challenges and Opportunities for Policy*. Eurydice Report. Luxembourg: Publications Office of the European Union.

Gibran, K. (2021). *The Prophet*. First Avenue Editions.

Habermas, J. (1989). *The Structural Transformation of the Public Sphere*. Blackwell Publishers Ltd.

Hallett, C., Murray C., & Punch, S. (2003). Young People and Welfare: Negotiating Pathways. In *Hearing the Voices of Children: Social Policy for a New Century,* Routledge Falmer, London.

Lansdown, G. (2011). *Every Child's Right to Be Heard,* a resource guide on the UN Committee on the Rights of the Child, general comment no.12, Gerison Lansdown. Save the Children and UNICEF.

Lawy, R., & Biesta, G. (2006). Citizenship-as-Practice: The Educational Implications of an Inclusive and Relational Understanding Of Citizenship. *British Journal of Educational Studies*, 54(1), 34-50.

McIntyre, D., Pedder. D., & Rudduck, J. (2005). Pupil Voice: Comfortable and Uncomfortable Learnings for Teachers. *Research Papers in Education*, 20, 149-168.

Ofsted (2005). The Annual Report of Her Majesty's Chief Inspector of Schools 2003/2004, (London, The Stationery Office).

Prensky, M. (2005). Learning in the Digital Age. Listen to the Natives. *Educational Leadership*, 4, 8-13.

Quinn, S., & Owen, S. (2014). Freedom to Grow: Children's Perspectives of Student Voice. *Childhood Education* Vol 90:3, 192-220.

Rajani, R. (2000). *Discussion Paper for Partners on Promoting Strategic Adolescent Participation*. UNICEF, New York, 2000

Robinson, C., & Taylor, C. (2007). Theorizing Student Voice: Values and Perspectives. *Improving Schools*, 10(1), 5-17.

Rogers, C. R. (1995). *On Becoming a Person: A Therapist's View of Psychotherapy*. Houghton Mifflin Harcourt.

Rudduck, J., & McIntyre, D. (2007). *Improving Learning Through Consulting Pupils*. Routledge.

Save the Children's Practice Standards in Children's Participation, (2005). International Save the Children Alliance, London, UK.

Taylor, C., & Robinson, C. (2009). Student Voice: Theorising Power and Participation. *Pedagogy, Culture & Society*, 17(2), 161-175.

UNICEF. (2008). A World Fit for Children. The United Nations Children's Fund.

UNICEF. (2011). *Every Child's Right to Be Heard*, A Resource Guide on the UN Committee on the Rights of the Child General Comment No 12. Save the Children UK.

United Nations. (1989). United Nations Convention on the Rights of the Child.

2 The Importance of Communication Skills, Oral Language, Oracy and Public Speaking

"The things we say and how we say them can inform, influence, inspire and motivate others and express our empathy, understanding and creativity" (Millard & Menzies, 2016, Foreword). Therefore, oral language, oracy, communication skills, listening and speaking and public speaking are clearly, very important skills for life and for active participation in the world we live in. We can get caught up on what terminology we use to define and describe these areas but the most important thing is actively learning and practising the skills. Essentially, these are all skills that enable and empower us to learn, to have our voices, individual and collective, heard and to listen to and build on the voices and views of others.

The Cambridge Primary Review highlights how the link between thinking and language provides an imperative for developing every child's capacity to express and develop ideas through talk. The National Council for Curriculum and Assessment (NCCA, 2019) in Ireland explains how oral language empowers children to develop their thinking, expression, reflection, critique and empathy and supports the development of self-efficacy, identity and full participation in society. Much education literature and research (Alexander, 2008, 2012; Cregan, 2010, 2012; Mercer & Mannion, 2018; Millard & Menzies, 2016) reflects the importance of intentionally training children to develop their listening, speaking and communication skills. Cregan (2010) described oral language as the building block of literacy as it represents many children's first encounter with literacy. It is also recognized as the single most important element in realising an integrated language curriculum. Communicating a very clear message gained from many years of research experience on the topic of oral language for children, Áine Cregan stated that "to foster oral language skills among all our children is not merely an option, it is an imperative" (Cregan, 2019, p. 39).

Different terminology is used to describe similar aspects of this curriculum area. Definitions and terminology matter to the extent that they can clearly describe what the term encompasses. Disputes or debates over which terminology to use can, in my opinion and experience, lead to distraction and wasting valuable learning time that could better be used to address the actual tasks at hand. In this chapter, I will endeavour to give a brief description of some of the common terminology used in relation to developing speaking, listening and communication skills and detail their importance, so that we can then get on with the very important business of supporting our young people to develop these skills and grow in confidence and competence as they do so.

Communication skills

Communication skills enable and empower us to express ourselves, our needs, our ideas, our wants and our dreams. Competent communication skills allow us to do this well sharing something of ourselves with others. Take a look around you and notice, how are people in your environment communicating their needs, thoughts and feelings? From the very young to the very old: we smile, we cry, we speak, we whisper, we shout, we gesture, we write, we draw, we compose, we sing, we play music, we act, we text, we touch, we hug, we post on social media, all to communicate our message. Communication skills are daily skills and some might say, survival skills, we use to connect with others in a variety of contexts.

Communication skills include verbal communication, non-verbal communication, written communication and active listening. Verbal communication involves speaking and expressing ideas, thoughts and emotions through words and language when face-to-face with others (individuals or groups) or via telephone calls or voice messages. Non-verbal communication includes body language, facial expressions and gestures. It complements verbal communication, allowing individuals to convey emotions and intentions, establish rapport and enhance the message's impact. Gestures can be used on their own in the case of sign language to communicate with others. Technology in the form of phones and other devices can also provide alternative means of communication. Communication directly impacts all facets of life, including all that is involved in the creation, export, import and processing of information and messages. In our world today, technology plays a huge role in communication. It's worth considering its immense positive potential and how or if it can compare with face-to-face human communication and connection.

Written communication entails crafting messages through written words, whether in emails, reports or texts. Do you remember sending written notes to your friends during class at school? Nowadays, multiple written messages are communicated to us through newspapers, posters, flyers, letters and online via email and social media. But has communication happened if we haven't received the message? If we haven't read the email, the text, the memo, the blog? If we haven't observed the gesture? If we haven't listened. George Bernard Shaw famously said, "The single biggest problem with communication is the illusion that it has taken place". Active listening is the foundation of effective communication, requiring focus, empathy and the ability to comprehend and respond to others' messages accurately. It fosters trust, collaboration and deeper connections.

With multiple methods available, we can choose how best to communicate our messages not just to those around us but to many, across the world. Effective communication skills are essential for personal and professional success and well-being. They improve relationships, enhance teamwork and reduce misunderstandings. They foster meaningful connections and help resolve conflicts. All types of communication play a crucial role in ensuring that individuals can express themselves, understand others and build meaningful connections in an increasingly interconnected world. Richmond and McCroskey (1993) explain that their definition of communication includes three different types of communication: accidental, expressive and rhetorical. Accidental, when a person unintentionally stimulates meaning in another's mind. Expressive, expressing emotions, intentions and motivation at a particular point in time. Rhetorical takes place when one person is specifically, strategically and intentionally attempting to stimulate a particular meaning in the mind of the receiver using both verbal and non-verbal cues.

The Bercow Report in the UK in 2008 specified that communication is a skill which has to be "taught, honed and nurtured" (The Communication Trust, 2015, p. 9). Knowing about communication is not enough. The bottom line is doing and understanding it. Communicative competence requires not only the ability to perform adequately certain communication behaviours, it also requires understanding those behaviours and making choices of appropriate behaviours based on the context, the message and the parties involved. Communication skills are skills that can be taught, learned and practised to maximise one's communication competence and confidence. It is generally regarded that there are three main components of communication: the speaker, the listener and the message although the Shannon-Weaver (1949) communication model suggested eight components: sender, encoding, message, channels, receiver, decoding, feedback and noise. The **sender** of the message may apply various tools, techniques and thought processes to **encode** the message and then decide on the most appropriate **channel** through which to send the **message**, e.g., in writing, speech or otherwise. The **receiver** then decodes the message based on their own interpretation and skills, providing **feedback** through their response with **noise** referring to the impact that message may have.

McCroskey describes 'communication competence' as "the modest ability to talk and write so that others can understand" (McCroskey, 1984, p. 261). Brink and Costigan (2015) identify three predominant types of oral communication: presenting, listening and conversing, including both non-linguistic and linguistic forms. Proficient communication skills empower children to convey meaning, express needs, preferences, ideas in a variety of social contexts and in doing so, connect with others in meaningful ways.

Oral language

The National Early Literacy Panel (NELP, 2008) described oral language as the ability to produce and comprehend spoken language. At the most basic level, oral language means communicating with other people (Hong & Ajex, 1995) involving a process of using thinking, knowledge and skills in order to speak and listen effectively. 'Oral Language' is the term most frequently used in the Irish education context. Cregan (2019) explains how we use oral language for a purpose which may be to greet, describe, question, inform, explain, report, express and justify an opinion or to narrate. Munro (2009) developed a useful model for investigating oral language. His model, ICPALER, is an acronym for Ideas, Conventions, Purpose, Ability to Learn and Expressive and Receptive language. Oral language is given a key role throughout the primary school curriculum with the important aim of developing competence and confidence also serving as the main medium through which new learning takes place. Listening is recognized as an essential part of oral language. LeLoup and Pontero (2007) explain listening as a pervasive communicative event and make the point that we listen significantly more than we read, write or speak. Therefore, it is worth ensuring that we are listening effectively and conscientiously work to develop these skills accordingly.

Oracy

Mercer and Mannion (2018) advise that the term 'oracy' represents the best way for educational researchers and practitioners to refer with greater consistency and clarity to "children's capacity to use speech to express their thoughts and communicate with others, in education and in life" (p. 9). It is "that teachable set of competencies to do with spoken language" (Millard & Menzies, 2016, p. 11). The Collins dictionary defines it as "the capacity to express oneself in and understand speech". Donaldson (2015) writes of the centrality of oracy to both thinking and learning. He explains that oracy is not just about public speaking, debate or dramatic role-playing; it also includes skills involved in collaborative problem solving, guiding or teaching another person, listening sensitively to another's experiences, interviewing and being interviewed to share information. Oracy is to speaking as numeracy is to Maths, that is, it defines the area of study including the knowledge, skills, dispositions, attitudes and behaviours students require to use speaking in a broad range of contexts. Wilkinson (1965) described oracy as a curriculum concern, one in which spoken language is treated not just as a means to an end, but as a 'fit object of educational knowledge' in and of itself. He also drew attention to oracy as a pedagogical concern, where spoken language is recognised and treated as 'a condition of learning in all subjects'. Some teachers interviewed by Millard and Menzies (2016) said that they do not regularly use the term 'oracy' and some felt that the term, itself, is somewhat off-putting (p. 19). However, other teachers thought that the term 'oracy' helps to pin down and clearly define an otherwise abstract set of ideas.

The Oracy Skills Framework created by Cambridge University (2014) clearly outlines four domains for oracy: physical, linguistic, cognitive and social and emotional. The physical domain refers to the physical voice and body language. Linguistic refers to language variety, vocabulary, structure and rhetorical techniques used. The cognitive domain includes the content of our speech, what we choose to say and how we question, clarify, summarize and reason. It reflects an awareness on the part of the speaker of the social context as well as an awareness of the audience/listeners. Finally, the social and emotional domain refers to the connection between speakers and listeners, including listening, responding, and on a personal level, speaking with increased levels of confidence as we work and interact with others.

Speaking and listening

Speaking and listening are inextricably linked. Even though we may speak to ourselves from time to time and self-talk has been proven to have certain benefits, in general when we speak, it is the listener who is important and when we listen, the attention and greater importance lies with the speaker and the message. Active listening, mentioned briefly in the section on communication skills, a critical part of communication interactions involves listening not just with our ears but really tuning in to the speaker, to what's said, how it's said and sometimes even considering what's not said. Active listening engages as many of our senses as possible, to receive, understand and remember the message.

Public speaking

Salim and Joy (2016) suggest that public speaking is commonly understood as the formal, face-to-face talking of a single person to a group of listeners. Jaffe (2015) explains that public speaking "occurs when one person prepares and delivers a talk for a group that listens, generally without interrupting the speaker's flow of ideas" (p. 2). My experience of public speaking is that it is much broader than these definitions and defining it too narrowly is not a good idea. When I use the term 'public speaking', I take it to mean speaking clearly in any public situation to audiences of all sizes, from one to many more, for a specific purpose. It refers to the ability to express needs, thoughts, ideas and learning clearly and coherently to an audience. Not just the act or process of making speeches in public, it is defined in the Merriam Webster dictionary as "the art of effective communication with an audience". Typically, people think of it as formal communication, but that's not always so. Public events and occasions are those that are open to all and often involve formal incidences of individuals engaging in public speaking. Private occasions such as weddings and family gatherings also involve incidences of individuals presenting perhaps slightly less- formal speeches in public. Pouteaux and Berg (2013) report on how public speaking is perceived in the American context: "In our culture, fluency and talkativeness are seen as indicators of intelligence, competence, friendliness, and other positive attributes". They elaborate that public speaking is a major component of day-to-day communication, and as Bourdieu (1991) explained, the ability to speak well is seen as a form of cultural and social capital.

There's more to public speaking than formal presentations although this may be where many people's minds first go to when they hear the term. Possibly the most dreaded form of communication, public speaking (or for those who don't speak but still present their messages to a public audience, 'public presentation') is an important skill to have and to hone and everyone can master it, to some degree. Public speaking skills matter on many levels for young people. Teachers have reported that these skills matter because they can increase students' confidence and independence and empower them to share their learning as well as their individual stories. Although there are several definitions of public speaking competence, the construct is often considered to comprise three underlying dimensions: knowledge, motivation, and skills (Morreale et al., 2007). It is suggested that whether or not a person is able to give a public speech or presentation competently does not depend on one single dimension, but rather on a combination of the three (Backlund & Morreale, 2015).

The term 'public speaking' originated in the 16th century and is attributed to John Bridges, Bishop of Oxford. The term 'public speaking' itself was not used widely until the 18th century. Prior to that, public speaking was studied and practised under the term, 'rhetoric'. Public speaking is still a significant part of rhetoric, the field of persuasion. The aim of rhetoric and public speaking may be to do any one or a combination of the following: to inform, educate, persuade, entertain or motivate specific audiences in specific situations. Aristotle studied and researched the subject of rhetoric for much of his life, and sometime in the mid- 350s B.C. proposed three modes of persuasion that are still applicable today: (1) ethos, the credibility and trustworthiness of a speaker, (2) pathos, the emotions of the audience, and (3) logos, logical arguments. Bailey (2019) suggests that public speaking is a very broad subject area and "has a history as long as community itself, a history tied tightly to political and linguistic developments". The conversational style of public speaking used by some speakers today was not considered as 'public speaking' until the early 20th century.

From the explanations I've given of the various terminologies used to define the area of communication and presenting, we can see that there is much overlap between the various terms used in education circles in relation to the acts of communicating, speaking and listening. Bringing this terminology discussion back to the topic of 'child voice', I will consider now, the importance of communication, oral language, speaking and listening and public speaking skills for children's lives as children, for learning at school, for life outcomes and employability and as a skill to mitigate disadvantage.

Communicating, speaking and listening skills enhancing children's lives as children

By the time a child speaks their first word, they already understand a lot more of the words their parents and adults in their lives speak to them and what they hear in the world around them. Since birth, and some might say even before birth, they are listening to everything they hear as they soak in their environment through all of their senses. Babies absorb language and messages about the world from the moment they are born and communicate their needs, likes and dislikes through various other means before they learn to use language. They can demonstrate their understanding by responding to simple commands such as 'wave good-bye to granny' and 'roll the ball to mama'. Parents and carers play a very important role in modelling language for children, responding to their gestures and providing a language rich environment.

Use of gestures is an important part of language and communication skill development. By carefully observing, listening to and participating in conversations, parents can help children to make that important connection between their gestures and language. Speaking to them slowly and clearly and keeping it simple while providing a space for them to speak to you, others and themselves in whatever way they choose benefits their development of communication skills. When a toddler shakes their head, for example, the adult can use the word 'no' and perhaps, 'I see you don't like it'. When a toddler gestures towards an object of their interest, the adult can put a word or a sentence on that also. For example, 'Do you want the toy bus?' Waiting for 'yes' or 'no' which the toddler may say or gesture, you might then extend the conversation by saying, 'Do you want the blue bus or the red bus?' 'I know a song about wheels'. The many benefits of singing songs, jingles, nursery rhymes and reading colourful picture books to and with young children cannot be over-emphasized in terms of language development and relationship building.

Babies and toddlers need to be involved directly in the communication act. They want to interact with you face-to-face, responding to your smile, your loving eye gaze. Approaching these interactions in a playful way further deepens the learning and the relationship connection. It is said that children, and smaller children especially, are great imitators, they are constantly learning by imitating and copying what they see around them. You will notice them act out and extend these imitations in their play. Actively listening to and communicating with them at this stage helps them to imitate and develop those skills which you are modelling. Your interaction, attention and time with them is communicating to them that all-important message that they are seen, they are heard and they are important.

At home, in the community and at school, engaging in different speaking genres with different audiences involves developing an awareness of polite forms and more informal forms, as well as social awareness of different audiences. Through using language in different contexts, children develop an awareness of the situation and the purpose or intent of the communication (Cregan, 2019). Cregan (2019) also writes about the necessary extra-linguistic knowledge which enhances and deepens communication including pitch, intonation, emphasis, pace, pause, volume of voice and the ability to interpret and use body language, hand gestures, eye contact, facial expression and proximity.

Language plays a vital role in children's lives. An important relationship exists between language and thought. Language also contributes to children's acceptance by peers, self-regulation, imagining, academic success and sociability (van der Veen et al., 2017) as well as facilitating a deeper understanding of their own identity. Language "enables children to engage emotionally, socially, cognitively, imaginatively and aesthetically in relationships and cultural experiences" (NCCA, 2019, p .6). Well-developed language skills enable children to express needs, better understand and regulate their feelings, interact and get along with other people, learn about and construct meaning of the world around them, create and share stories, and communicate ideas and information. Children communicate when they play and interact with peers and the relevant adults in their lives. Language and communication help children to build strong relationships and friendships, and through dialogue, questioning and discussion, they can explore and deepen their sense of belonging.

A focus on oral language development in schools enhances students' ability to communicate with greater clarity and effectiveness (Cronin, 1990; Alexander, 2008) particularly those who find self-expression through writing difficult (Maxwell et al., 2015, p. 24). Teaching students how to use spoken language more effectively also enables them to develop their empathetic capabilities and social confidence (Mercer & Mannion, 2018; Mercer, 2016). Cregan (2010) researched the topic of oral language in DEIS schools (schools catering for students from disadvantaged backgrounds) in the Irish primary school context and described the impact of poor facility with required language skills in the classroom on students as reported by teachers: reduced achievement of individual potential for these students, considerable communication difficulties, low self-esteem, lack of confidence and poor behaviour (p. 6). These students find it difficult to communicate with their peers which leads to problems socially. This, understandably, has a negative effect on certain experiences and interactions in childhood. There is a strong connection between mental health challenges and oral language skills and a correlation between children with untreated speech, language and communication needs and mental illness (Royal College of Speech and Language Therapists, 2012).

Children's social and emotional well-being has seldom been of more critical concern than now, post Covid-19 pandemic-related lockdowns and school closures. Even for children lucky enough to live in stable, relatively calm home environments, the full impact of the isolation and anxiety caused by these lockdowns, is still unknown. Opportunities for conversations in a safe, supportive environment were limited. They will have missed out on hundreds of hours of intentional and targeted speech development. Isolation, grief, anxiety, worry and fear of the unknown are very difficult for any of us to process and deal with and even more difficult for children who control far less in their environment than most adults. It has placed young people at higher risk of developing mental health problems. Some teachers have found that the speaking and communication skills of some students have been adversely affected by national lockdowns. While all children's skills were impacted by the Covid-19 disruption, this impact appears to be felt more by children from lower socio-economic backgrounds and those living in poverty. The report of the All-Party Parliamentary Group on Oracy confirmed that Covid-19 widened the language gap for some students. Consequently, in the UK, a cross-party group of MPs called for oracy skills to be prioritised as part of Covid-19 recovery.

Communication, speaking and listening skills enhancing children's experience of learning in school

The paper 'Oral Language in Early Childhood and Primary Education (3–8 years old)' (Shiel et al., 2012) confirms the centrality of language to the Primary School Curriculum in schools. Skill in oral language is a developmental pre-cursor to reading acquisition. Oral and written forms interrelate and spoken language provides children with the building blocks they need to master reading and writing. Cregan (2010) stresses the link between oral language and the ability to access effectively all that the curriculum and the institution of the school have to offer. Facility in oral language enables children to be more willing to ask questions, participate in discussions and seek help from the teacher. It empowers children to communicate what they know, shaping content so others can receive and understand it, enabling a constant interaction with the world of knowledge (Alexander, 2018).

Mercer and Mannion (2018) explain that students will become more able at learning, reasoning, problem solving and developing new knowledge in a range of different contexts by becoming skilled in using spoken language to acquire, share, present and develop ideas and information. Where schools place a strong emphasis on explicit and structured speaking and listening approaches, they see results improve. Mercer and Mannion (2018) have found that, by supporting students to develop their oracy skills through making public speeches, reasoning skills are also developed, skills that are important for further academic study and life in the world beyond formal education (Xie & Dong, 2017). The Oracy All Party Parliamentary Group (OAPPG, 2021) described talk as "the currency of politics" and "the currency of learning" facilitating "how we develop and grow our ideas, understanding, thoughts and feelings and share them with others" (p. 4).

Critical thinking, widely recognised as a 21st-century skill is also developed through preparing a speech, presentation or argument, choosing supporting materials to convince an audience, assessing the reasonableness of the connections between the supporting materials and message and delivering the presentation effectively. The eight categories of critical thinking skills identified by Rankin et al. (2015) are employed when developing and delivering an oral presentation. These include: focusing, gathering information, remembering, organising, analysing, generating, integrating and evaluating. Critical thinking is also practised and developed by the audience, i.e., the rest of the students listening and attending to a presentation in the classroom context.

Communication, speaking and listening skills enhancing young people's life outcomes and employability

There is no doubt as to the value of communication skills in the workplace. Success in many careers and occupations depends upon effective oral presentation skills. Proficient oral communication is one of the most important competencies employers look for in their employees. Communication skills are used between bosses and employees, between employees themselves and between employees and clients/customers. Workforce Connections, a project funded by the United States Office of International Development (USAID, 2015), identified communication skills (including oral communication) as one of its five critical 'soft skills' young people need competency in to succeed in the workplace (Lippman et al., 2015). It is thought that these skills will be in even higher demand in the 21st century workplace. They will be important in the work that people do but also in how they work. Littleton and Mercer (2013) point out that, in addition to using language to interact, we also use it to "interthink", the "everyday process whereby people collectively and creatively use talk to solve problems and make joint sense of the world" (Littleton & Mercer, 2013, p. 115). With the potential to bring teamwork to a whole new level, this collaborative approach to using language to build on one another's ideas is another potential benefit of explicit oral language development and a feature of 21st-century skills.

With specific reference to public speaking, being an engaging and fluent public speaker is one of the keys to successful public relations (Spohr, 2009). Salim and Joy (2016) make the point that even if you do not need to make regular presentations in front of a group, there are plenty of situations where good public speaking skills can help advance your career and create opportunities. For example, you might have to speak up at a meeting in-person or online, explain a matter concisely to a customer or group of customers, talk about your organization at a conference, pitch a product or idea, deliver a presentation as part of your work, present an award, make a speech after accepting an award, or teach a class or group. Public speaking skills will also enable and empower those applying for a job at the interview stage, to get the job in the first place.

Competent public speaking skills are important in other areas of life, for example: speaking at a friend's wedding or a family or social occasion, sitting on a local or community committee, giving a eulogy for a loved one, or standing up for yourself or others. The list of occasions on which you may be called on to speak in public is endless and the opportunities are limitless. We take note and are impacted when people speak with authority, authenticity and gravitas (Salim & Joy, 2016). Studying public speaking skills can also help young people become aware of the power and influence of language and communication in a very concrete way, causing reflection on how our lives are impacted every day by other people's use of rhetoric.

Mercer and Mannion (2018) explain that "people's life chances can be predicted so powerfully by their exposure to and immersion in oral communication as children" (p. 12). Of great concern is that the negative impacts of poor oral language ability can persist into the long term for children. Stothard et al. (1998) reporting a longitudinal follow-up of seventy-one adolescents with a preschool history of speech and language impairment, found that 70% of children with oral language difficulties at age 5 and a half still demonstrated oral language problems at 15 years of age, and of these 93% also had literacy difficulties. The Communication Trust (2015) explains that children who struggle with language at age 5 are six times less likely to reach the expected standard in English at age 11. This evidence surely points to a need for additional and explicit work in the area of oral language development in schools to ensure that disadvantages that can be mitigated do not continue into adulthood.

Communication, speaking and listening skills to mitigate disadvantage

The Oracy All Party Parliamentary Group noted that "addressing social disadvantage through increasing students' confidence in speaking" helps students to "become leaders of their own learning and develop the interpersonal skills they will need for further training and employment" (OAPPG, 2021, p. 27). The Department of Education in Ireland noted in 2005, that Irish primary school teachers consistently reported that children in disadvantaged contexts come to school with "a significant oral language deficit" and that "the necessary oral skills and competencies that are a prerequisite for the development of literacy skills" (DES, 2005, p. 25) had not been developed by the students which, if not addressed, placed them in real danger of education disadvantage and social exclusion. Cregan (2010) suggests that the ability of a child to express themselves clearly, competently and confidently can be the solution to many problems such as behaviour, academic difficulty and social inclusion.

The English-Speaking Union, a UK charity that supports young people to develop and build the speaking and listening skills they need to thrive in a changing world, stresses the importance of teaching children how to use spoken language not just because of how it contributes to developing thinking skills but also because of its high social value and how it can support children to participate more successfully in society (ESU, 2016). Every child from every background should be given the support and the opportunity to develop these skills in order to have a fair chance of social mobility and growth. The Social Mobility and Child Poverty Commission found in a qualitative evaluation of non-educational barriers to elite professions that elite firms define 'talent' according to a number of factors including strong communication and debating skills, confidence and 'polish' (Ashley et al., 2015). Those who are equipped with these skills are at a clear advantage.

Evidence suggests that the impact of poor oral language skills is extremely serious and long-lasting for children from disadvantaged backgrounds (Alexander, 2012; Cregan, 2010). In general, students from economically deprived backgrounds are less likely to have had a rich talk experience in their home environment (Mercer & Mannion, 2018). About one million children in the UK have long-term, persistent difficulties (The Communication Trust, 2015a, p. 5). In addition, the Communication Trust also reported that in areas of social deprivation, more than 50% of children start school with delayed language. Although, these reports may paint a dismal picture, there is hope and certainly much that educators and those working with children can do. It starts with an awareness and understanding of the fundamental importance of these skills for all children. Cregan (2010) explains that research shows that a focus on oral language can hold considerable power in bridging the gap, improving access to the curriculum and improving these students' readiness to avail of opportunities within school and beyond. However, Cregan (2010) also reported that children who most need classroom-based, oral language development intervention were the least likely to get it making it considerably more difficult for them "to achieve their potential through the school system than is the case for their more privileged, mainstream counterparts" (p. 23). Cregan investigated extensively the use of a specific oral language register known as 'literate', 'standard' or 'academic' language (Pellegrini, 2002) which is fundamental to becoming literate in school (Cregan, 2010). The value ascribed to certain patterns of language variation is closely aligned with the social status of people. The "accepted norm for the oral variety of language is accorded prestige, higher value, power and authority" (Wolfram et al., 1999, p. 12). For those children whose language use is different, unconscious but biased negative judgements are made (Michaels & Cazden, 1986). All teachers, as reflective practitioners, may need to be aware of this in terms of encouraging and supporting all of their students from diverse socio-economic and cultural backgrounds to speak up in their classrooms.

Fairclough (2001) claimed that "language has become perhaps the primary medium of social control and power" (p. 2). Bourdieu (1991) cautioned that "one must not forget that the relations of communication 'par excellence' are also relations of symbolic power" (p. 37). Bourdieu argues that the standard variety of the official national language becomes the dominant language which is used as an instrument of power and functions as 'cultural capital'. According to Bourdieu this "linguistic capital" is unequally distributed among people from different social classes. The less linguistic capital a speaker possesses, the greater his/her disadvantage (Cregan, 2010, p. 14). When we factor into this, children in our schools for whom English is not a first language, the situation gets even more complicated and challenging.

Classroom oracy has "the power to both imprison and liberate the lives of young learners" (Evans & Jones, 2007, p. 558), to provide or restrict curriculum access for groups of students. "The most privileged in society are given the power of words and language to enable them to succeed in life" (ESU 2016, p. 96), while others may be left behind. To give every child from every background a fair chance, explicit instruction in the skills of communication/oral language/oracy/speaking and listening/public speaking can make a significant difference. Niedermeyer and Oliver (1972) suggested that one reason why many children have difficulty expressing themselves verbally in a way that is clear, relaxed and fluent is that they do not have enough opportunities to practise public speaking skills. They advised that if children are to express themselves well orally, they may need a considerable amount of systematic, structured instruction and practise.

In 2010, Alexander suggested that we inherited from the Victorian founders of public education, a view of literacy which focuses mainly on reading and writing but not speaking because their aim for education was to fit children for their "preordained station in life". He speculates that a concern may have been that the potential of talk might subvert that aim. In spite of its importance, there is still a gap between research, policy and practice in the area of oral language/communication skills/public speaking in schools. Also, there is still a considerable gap between what employers require from employees and what is being prioritized in schools (Brink & Costigan, 2015). In many national curricula across the world, these skills are still subsumed under the term, literacy and the degree to which they are covered may depend on the vagaries and priorities of the school and its teachers.

Communication, speaking and listening in response to Covid-19 related lockdowns

The Oracy All Party Parliamentary Group (OAPPG, 2021) report in the UK, 'Speak for Change', confirmed that in a world rocked by the Covid 19 pandemic, developing speaking and listening skills, skills of clear communication and public speaking skills may play a vital role in supporting citizens to engage actively and thoughtfully in the democratic process, to enable people to talk about how they feel in a way that encourages discussion, empathy and understanding. In evidence to the OAPPG (2021), one Year 6 student (aged 10-11) reported, "Oracy is really crucial following lockdown and isolation". Another shared that "without these crucial oracy skills, settling back into school would have been a real difficulty. Our oracy culture has enabled us to speak, be heard and be valued" (OAPPG, 2021, p. 32).

Terminology: Ambiguity, clarity or a distraction

The terminology we use when referring to this area of the curriculum is important to some degree. We frequently hear terms such as communications skills, oral language, speaking and listening, oracy and public speaking and sometimes they are used interchangeably. Though there may be slight differences in what each term refers to, research and policy have consistently pointed to their importance in primary school. Millard and Menzies (2016) advise that ensuring teachers have a common name and language for oracy would improve awareness and increase the chances of it being given more equal status with literacy and numeracy on the curriculum. While there may be value in deciding on common terminology to refer to this area, playing with semantics and terminology may be wasting or delaying our children's valuable learning time and yet, if we are not clear on what the terminology means, it risks ambiguity and confusion. Alexander (2012) and Mercer and Mannion (2018) have a preference for the use of the term 'oracy' to represent the best way for educational researchers and practitioners to refer to "children's capacity to use speech to express their thoughts and communicate with others, in education and in life" (Alexander, 2012, p. 10) across a range of formal and informal settings. Oracy is not a term that has been used with any degree of frequency or consistency in the education field in Ireland and educators in other countries may be more familiar with other terms.

Of the teachers I surveyed as part of my study, 65% stated that they thought 'public speaking' was a good term to use. Alternative terms suggested by the other 35% included: 'speaking skills', 'presentation', 'communication', 'debating', 'oral presentations', 'oral language', 'art of speaking' and 'solo speaking'. Terminology is a challenge because there is a range of different terms currently used in school settings to refer to this skill-set. Even where the desired outcome of a lesson is that students stand in front of the class to make a presentation or a speech, the term 'public speaking' is rarely if ever used. Is it possible then that some students don't know that it is, in fact, public speaking that they are doing when they are doing it? I had to search intensely and intentionally to pinpoint public speaking on the curriculum. It's almost hidden because it is not explicitly named. And if it is not explicitly named, can or how can it be explicitly taught?

Part of the issue here might also be achieving clarity on what the term 'public speaking' itself means. It can mean different things to different people. The definition I used throughout my doctoral studies and continue to use today, is that preferred by 93% of the teachers who responded to my research survey: "the art of effective communication with an audience" (Merriam-Webster, 2005). Might the use of other terms be advantageous in so far as they may help students disassociate from the fears widely associated with public speaking? However, once students have acquired a certain degree of competency in these skills, it may be necessary and empowering to inform them that these are in fact also public speaking skills as 'public speaking' is the term that is used more widely in the world beyond formal education.

Summary reflection on the importance of communication skills, oral language, oracy, public speaking, and speaking and listening skills

While it's a valid point that using a common term may ensure consistency and common understanding of the curriculum area being referred to, what's more important than the terminology is ensuring that all students have fair access to the development of this skill-set. Whether we call it 'oracy', 'oral language', 'communication skills', 'public speaking' or 'speaking and listening', the field of study is similar and leads to clearer and more competent expression, with many of the same skills coming under these titles. It is what the school does to support the development of children's capacity to use speech to confidently and clearly express their thoughts, experiences, learning, preferences and communicate with others, in education and in life, empowering them to more wholly realize their right to have their voice heard under Article 12 of the UNCRC. Therefore, as illustrated in this chapter, it is of huge, significant importance to all children and students on many levels. I think it's best that we intentionally do not allow the debate and discussion over appropriate terminology overshadow or distract from the job at hand, the acquisition and teaching of the skills. If young people don't learn how to speak and listen effectively in a range of contexts, life and learning opportunities may be severely limited for them. That is our shame, not their fault.

Reference List

Alexander, R. (2008). *Towards Dialogic Teaching: Rethinking Classroom Talk*, Fourth Edition. York: Dialogos UK.

Alexander, R. (2012, February 20). Improving Oracy and Classroom Talk in English Schools Achievements and Challenges. Presentation given at the DfE seminar on Oracy, the National Curriculum and Educational Standards.

Alexander, R. (2018). Developing Dialogic Teaching: Genesis, Process, Trial. *Research Papers Education*, 33(5), 561–598.

Ashley, L., Duberley, J., Sommerlad, H., & Scholarios, D. (2015). *A Qualitative Evaluation of Non-Educational Barriers to the Elite Professions*. London: Social Mobility and Child Poverty Commission (6, 11).

Backlund, P. M., & Morreale, S. P. (2015). Communication Competence: Historical Synopsis, Definitions, Applications, and Looking to the Future. *Communication Competence*, 11–38.

Bailey, E. (2019). A Historical View of the Pedagogy of Public Speaking. *Voice and Speech Review*, 13(1), 31–42. Routledge.

Bercow, J. (2008). Bercow Review of Speech, Language and Communication Needs: Call for Evidence.

Bourdieu, P. (1991). Language and Symbolic Power. In John B. Thompson (ed.). Cambridge: Polity Press.
Brink, K., & Costigan, R. (2015). Oral Communication Skills: Are the Priorities of the Workplace and AACSB- Accredited Business Programs Aligned? *Academy of Management Learning and Education*, 14(2), 205-221.
Cambridge University. (2014). *Oracy Skills Framework*. Assessing Oracy.
Cregan, A. (2010). From Policy to Practice. The Oral Language Challenge for Teachers.
Cregan, A. (2012). Empowering Teachers to Promote Oral Language in Culturally Diverse Classrooms in Ireland. *Journal of Multilingual Education Research,* 3 (Article 5).
Cregan, A. (2019) Promoting Oral Language Development in the Primary School. NCCA and Primary Developments.
Cronin, M. (1990) Debating to Learn Across the Curriculum: Implementation and Assessment. Paper presented at the Southern States Communication Association Convention, Birmingham, Alabama (11).
DES, (2005). The Department of Education and Science. Literacy and Numeracy in Disadvantaged Schools: Challenges for Teachers and Learners, An Evaluation by the Inspectorate of the Department of Education and Science. Government Publications, Dublin.
Donaldson, G. (2015). *Successful Futures. Independent Review of Curriculum and Assessment Arrangements in Wales.* Cardiff: Welsh Government.
ESU. (2016). *Speaking Frankly: The Case for Oracy in the Curriculum*. London, English Speaking Union.
Evans, R., & Jones, D. (2007) Perspectives on Oracy—Towards a Theory of Practice. *Early Child Development and Care*, 177, 557-567.
Fairclough, N. (2001). *Language and Power* (second edition). Pearson Education Ltd. London: Longman.
Hong, Z., & Ajex, N. K. (1995) Oral Language Development across the Curriculum, K-12.
Jaffe, C. (2015). Public Speaking: Concepts and Skills for a Diverse Society. Cengage Learning, 1 Jan 2015 - Performing Arts.
LeLoup, J. W., &, Pontero, R. (2007). *Listening: You've Got to Be Carefully Taught*. Language Learning & Technology.
Lippman, L. H., Ryberg, R., Carney, R., & Moore, K. A. (2015). Key 'Soft Skills' That Foster Youth Workforce Success: Towards a Consensus Across Fields, *Child Trends Publication*, 24(5).
Littleton, K., & Mercer, N. (2013) *Interthinking: Putting Talk to Work*. Routledge, London.
Maxwell, B., Burnett, C., Reidy, J., Willis, B., & Demack, S. (2015) *Oracy Curriculum, Culture and Assessment Toolkit: Evaluation Report and Executive Summary.* London: Education Endowment Foundation.
McCroskey, J. C. (1984) Communication Competence: The Elusive Construct. In Robert N. Bostrom, (ed.). *Competence in Communication: A Multidisciplinary Approach,* p. 259. Beverly Hills, CA: Sage.
Mercer, N. (2016) Oracy and Thinking Skills. In *Speaking Frankly: The Case for Oracy in the Curriculum*. London, English-Speaking Union.
Mercer & Mannion. (2018). Oracy across the Welsh Curriculum. A Research-Based Review: Key Principles and Recommendations for Teachers. EAS, Education Achievement Service for South East Wales.
Merriam Webster. (2005). The Merriam-Webster Dictionary, Merriam-Webster Incorporated, Library of Congress Cataloging in Publication Data.
Michaels, S., & Cazden, C. (1986). Teacher/child Collaboration as Oral Preparation for Literacy. In Schiefflin, B. B. & Gilmore, P. (eds), T*he Acquisition of Literacy: Ethnographic Perspectives,* 132-154. Norwood, NJ: Ablex.
Millard, W., & Menzies, L. (2016). *Oracy: The State of Speaking in Our Schools,* London: Voice 21.
Morreale, S. P., Moore, M. R., Surges-Tatum, D., & Webster, L. (2007). *"The Competent Speaker" Speech Evaluation Form* (2nd ed.). Washington, DC: National Communication Association.
Munro, J. K. (2009). *Oral Language Learning: The Primary Years*. Course notes (460735), The University of Melbourne.
NCCA (2019) Primary Language Curriculum.
NELP (2008) National Early Literacy Panel, Developing Early Literacy: A Scientific Synthesis of Early Literacy Development and Implications for Intervention.
Niedermeyer, C., & Oliver, L. (1972). The Development of Young Children's Dramatic and Public Speaking Skills. *The Elementary School Journal*, 73(2), 95-100. The University of Chicago Press.
OAPPG. (2021). The Oracy All Party Parliamentary Group 'Speak for Change' Inquiry Report.
Pellegrini, A. D. (2002). Some Theoretical and Methodological Considerations in Studying Literacy in Social Context. In Neuman, S. B. and Dickinson, D. K. (eds.) **Handbook of Early Literacy Research,** 54-65. London: The Guilford Press.

Pouteaux, K. and Berg, E. (2013). Literature Review on Public Speaking: *Public Speaking as a Form of Literacy*.

Rankin et al. (2015). Practical Assessment, Research, and Evaluation. *Defining and Measuring Academic Success*, 20(5).

Richmond, V. P., & McCroskey, J. C. (1993). Diverse Perspectives on Communication – Communication Overview and Framework.

Royal College of Speech and Language Therapists. (2012). Speech, Language and Communication Needs in the Criminal Justice System and Best Practice Responses to These.

Salim, S. S., & Joy, E. I. (2016). Public Speaking Skills. In: *Training Manual on Theeranaipunya - Equipping Fisherwomen Youth for Future*. ICAR-Central Marine Fisheries Research Institute, Kochi, 129-132.

Shannon, C. E., & Weaver, W. (1949). *The Mathematical Theory of Communication*, Urbana: University of Illinois Press.

Shiel, G., Cregan, Á., McGough, & Archer, P. (2012). "Oral Language in Early Childhood and Primary Education (3-8 years)", *NCCA Research Report* No. 14.

Spohr, C. (2009). Public Speaking Skills Are Key to Successful Public Relations. *AAILL Spectrum*, 14, 8-9.

Stothard, S., Snowling, M., Bishop, D., Chipchase, B., & Kaplan, C. (1998). Language Impaired Preschoolers: A Follow-Up into Adolescence. *Journal of Speech, Language and Hearing Research*, 41, 407-418.

The Communication Trust. (2015). *Universally Speaking: The Ages and Stages of Children's Communication Development from Birth to 5 Years*. London: The Communication Trust.

USAID. (2015). Lindsay, J. & Babb, S. Workforce Connections. Measuring Employment Outcomes for Workforce Development.

van der Veen, C., van der Wilt, F., van Kruistum, C., van Oers, B., & Michaels, S. (2017). Model2Talk: An Intervention to Promote Productive Classroom Talk. *The Reading Teacher*, 70(6), 689-700.

Wilkinson, A. (1965). *Spoken English*. Birmingham, University of Birmingham Press.

Wolfram, W., Adger, C. T., & Christian, D. (1999). *Dialects in Schools and Communities*, New Jersey: Lawrence Erlbaum Associates.

Xie, Z., & Dong, Y. (2017). *Contributions of Bilingualism and Public Speaking Training to Cognitive Control Differences among Young Adults*. Bilingualism: Language and Cognition, 20(1), 55-68.

3 Facilitating an Increased Focus on Child Voice and Student Voice

How can we facilitate an increased focus on child voice and student voice? In our homes, communities, schools? I may be biased but it seems to me that perhaps the most obvious way to hear child and student voice is to hear children's and students' actual voices, to tune in, listen to and hear what they are saying and communicating to us in a variety of ways every day. Children need to see, experience and know that their voice has value and is important from a young age. It is likely that the caring adults in their immediate environment are the first ones they will look towards for this validation so parents, guardians, grandparents, carers, child-care professionals, teachers and all who have the privilege of working and living with children have an important role to play in this.

Starting at home, parents respect their child's voice when they acknowledge, accept and celebrate the uniqueness of who their little one is and take their opinions and interests seriously on matters within the home. This gifts the child the opportunity to communicate, through whatever means they can, who they are and what they are experiencing without fear of judgment doing wonders for a child's self-confidence, sense of identity and future participation in matters that affect their lives. The most magical and powerful ingredient of all for a child is the experience of being seen, listened to and having their views taken seriously especially in matters that affect their life, starting with the immediate environment in the home and then branching out into the wider community.

Children can have a voice in their community when we talk with them in age-appropriate ways about their local community and get involved with them in local, community-based initiatives. On walks or car drives, in the local playground or shops, they can begin to think about their local environment and share their related likes, dislikes, interests, concerns. They may not always share these in words but in their actions and choices. Moving from the home and community to the school and the concept of 'student voice', the concepts of dialogue, 'communication', 'consultation', 'debate' as well as the more general understandings put forward by Rudduck (2006, p. 137) referring to talking with students "about things that matter in school", have a central place in writing about and realising student voice practice (Fielding, 2004b).

Certain conditions are essential for facilitating and promoting student voice. Creating or better still, co-creating with students a safe, supportive environment in the classroom in which all students can feel comfortable expressing themselves is a very important place to start. Rules will need to be clarified and put in place with regard to mutual respect and turn taking. Students need support and encouragement to learn how to use their voice, whether it is to advocate for themselves, express their opinions, or stand up for others.

How parents can facilitate child voice

Strengthening skills, confidence and capacity for democratic participation during childhood will certainly bring profound lifelong benefits for the child and indeed benefits to all. Parents may find facilitating child voice more challenging if they, themselves have not had their rights respected or have felt powerless in exercising their rights. However, realisation a child's rights can ultimately help their families too. Serving to protect the informed, empowered rights of every individual within the family, it thereby makes the family stronger. In a UNICEF review of the impact of child participation in South Asia in 2004, many parents and families reported positive outcomes, such as improved family relationships, greater respect for parents, enhanced confidence and skills, new opportunities for the children and increased contributions to the local community (UNICEF, 2004).

In the early 1990s, I lived in Japan. Once a week, on a Friday night, I had the privilege of doing a homestay with a Japanese family, the Aoyagi family. I saw first-hand a very strong example of empowering children and listening to them. Every Friday evening, I would teach a 'fun' English class to the Aoyagi children and other children from the neighbourhood, teaching English mainly through song, rhyme, drama, movement and play. Prior to our class, I would sit down with the Aoyagi family for dinner. We took our time eating and part of the ritual was for everyone at the table to take turns sharing the best and most challenging part of their week. Their children were aged 3, 6 and 8 at that time. It was obvious from how easily they could express themselves that this was a regular practice. On Saturday morning, when we got up, everybody spent about an hour tidying. Everyone, from the youngest to the eldest had their jobs to do. We then sat down together for breakfast. Again, everybody took it in turn to share what they were looking forward to most about the week ahead.

When all is working well within the family, embedding routines and giving children space and time to express their preferences, experiences and concerns reap many benefits. However, in times of family struggle or conflict, for example, separation or divorce, children have the right to have a say too, a say over where and with whom they live and the levels of contact with parents. Parents may need to be supported with examples of child participation and will benefit from seeing how schools and other groups empower this. The following steps may be helpful for parents in ensuring child voice is encouraged, listened to and heard within the home:

- Create a safe supportive environment in the home where children can be and express their true authentic selves.
- Acknowledge and understand that each child is unique with individual perspectives and that their voice is important, that nobody else knows, as well as your child, what's going on in their life.
- Take the time to observe, play with and listen to your child. This time is precious, will never come again and will be repaid manifold in the benefits to the child's development and in what you as parent or guardian will learn about your child, directly from them.

- Talk to your child in an age-appropriate way, showing interest in and curiosity about what they are interested in.
- Children can struggle with putting their feelings into words so it's necessary to pay close attention to their actions and behaviours. It's said that all behaviour is communication. Often a child who is perceived as being 'bold' is struggling to communicate something important. Strive to understand the message in their actions.
- Play with each child and give them ample opportunities to play. This will provide invaluable insights into their world and is guaranteed to be a lot of fun.
- Establish routines which enhance a sense of safety, but allow for flexibility within these routines for each child's preferences.
- Give your child choices at every opportunity. For example, What would you like to wear? What music would you like to listen to? What movie would you like to watch? It can be a very open choice or a choice between two or three options, e.g., What would you like with your potatoes, carrots or peas?
- Children are notorious for asking questions. Always encourage your children to ask questions and keep asking questions as they grow. It's a valuable skill to take with them through life. Every question does not need to be answered. Sometimes the question itself is more important.
- Perhaps we could ask more questions of them and allow them time and space to answer and a choice of different ways to feedback their responses. Questions such as: What would you like to do today? Which do you prefer? What makes you happy? What makes you sad? What do you think? Can and how can I help you? Can and how can I play your game? These questions together with the space and time to respond and receive a listening ear convey a clear respect for the child's voice, individuality, interests, customs and rights.
- Encourage your child to speak up for themselves and others and be sure to positively acknowledge it when they do.
- Help them to prepare for difficult situations they may face, such as bullying and peer pressure situations. Talk through what they can do to protect themselves and role play what they can say and do in such scenarios. This empowers them to defend themselves in a socially acceptable way, to ask for help where needed and develop assertiveness skills.
- Encourage and facilitate your child's active participation within the family. Ensure that all children (siblings) have the opportunity to contribute to decisions such as, for example: the next family holiday, whether or not to get a family pet, tidying up rotas, rules for bedtimes or rules for use of electronic devices.
- Provide opportunities for your child to engage in teamwork. Children can very naturally engage in teamwork when playing team sports. These sports can spark interesting discussions about what it means to be a team player, how every position on the team is important and how important it is to step up to take the lead from time to time.
- Listen to your children and to demonstrate that you're listening to your children, you might:
  - Turn off and put away all other distractions
  - Take note of the times when your child is most likely to talk to you, e.g.; in the car, at dinner, when they come home from school or at bedtime. Make sure that you are

available at this time. A child might rarely say, 'I want to talk' but they may convey the same message when they say, 'come play with me'.
- You might want to designate a particular space for specific listening time to your child, e.g., a comfy couch, a floor space on a nice soft rug, a place in the house where you know your child feels particularly relaxed and comfortable.
- Make eye contact with the child.
- Face the child and use your body language to demonstrate that you are listening.
- Listen with your ears, eyes, heart and open mind. Observe your child's body language, facial expressions and gestures to more deeply understand what your child is trying to say.
- Extend communication with prompts such as, 'What happened next?', 'Tell me more'.
- Try not to jump in too often to finish your child's sentences or solve your perception of their dilemmas for them. Just listen.
- Be silent as much as possible. It's not possible to talk and listen at the same time. Remember 'silent' and 'listen' are spelt with exactly the same letters.
- Remind yourself of your purpose here, i.e., to facilitate your child to have their voice heard.

Some of this may sound simple but like many things in life, they're easier said than done. All of this requires the parent/guardian/teacher/carer/practitioner to step back into a facilitator's role, but don't be fooled into thinking that this is a more passive and easier role. It's a role that requires a different set of skills. It's a role that requires action of a different kind and results in babies, toddlers, children feeling safer, more valued, important and empowered to be the best they can be. Listening also enriches that all-important relationship between parent/carer/teacher and child.

Through participating in family matters early in life, children get the message that they matter, what they say and do matters and that they can contribute to positive change in their environment in meaningful ways. When children have the experience of being encouraged and enabled to open up and communicate with you about the 'little' things in everyday life, they are much more likely to approach you to share and discuss some of their bigger ideas and concerns as they arise. How many of us in our 30s, 40s, 50s and older still don't know what we like, dislike, are interested in or even want in life? Did you ever wonder how different this might be if we were more listened to as children, at home and at school?

Through regular opportunities to participate, children gain a deeper sense of belonging and solidarity. They believe in themselves, gain a respect and care for and understanding of everyone's rights. They learn tolerance, respect and very importantly how to effectively engage in dialogue and negotiate with others when engaged in decision making, aware through experience that others have a right to be heard too. They are empowered and further motivated to engage in other democratic processes when they experience that their contribution can and does make a difference.

Benefits of student voice

There are many benefits to facilitating, enabling and empowering student voice, benefits for the students of course, benefits for the teacher and classroom and benefits for the whole school. Obvious benefits for students are visible in how it empowers and engages students. Listening to and acting on students' perspectives, preferences and interests helps students feel more involved in their own learning. Their sense of self-worth increases as does their sense of purpose in school. It can help to ignite passions and increase students' persistence and tenacity when it comes to more challenging tasks. Students' level of effort, persistence and self-efficacy are positively impacted, all of which affect achievement (Toshalis & Nakkula, 2012). Research shows that students who believe that they have a voice in their school are seven times more likely to be academically motivated than students who don't (Quaglia, 2016).

Students become more competent and confident in making responsible decisions, advocating for themselves, and deciding their own course of action when they get to practise using their voice and agency. They feel respected and valued when their voice is listened to and heard. More student engagement leads to increased confidence, enhanced self-efficacy and ultimately better school performance. They are less afraid of failure when they know that they can talk through and about the experience with classmates and/or staff. They become more resilient and better prepared to collaborate with peers. Students can move on through their education path and out into the world assured in the knowledge through experience that their voice matters. In this way, they are better prepared to become active citizens and embrace all that active citizenship entails in their lives. There are also many benefits reaped through practising discussions and exploratory talk where ideas are thought out in the course of their expression. Students also benefit from listening to and building on one another's ideas. I have heard it said, and noticed in my own practice, that children remember most what they hear in their own voice, next what they hear their peers saying and thirdly, what their teacher says. This is certainly worth reflecting on.

In terms of life outcomes and gains beyond school, Mercer and Mannion (2018) report that research shows how training in oracy skill development is positively linked with overcoming social disadvantage (p. 4). Headteacher Sarah Wild (ESU, 2016, p. 36) states "it's about advocacy, so that they don't feel marginalised". Equipped with skills of public speaking and competent communication, students from marginalised communities may be empowered to speak out as advocates on behalf of themselves, their families and their communities. Of significant social concern is the fact that many public representatives who claim to represent people from marginalised or disadvantaged backgrounds are not from within those social circles or communities. Therefore, the degree to which they can accurately reflect their lives and their needs is questionable. Empowering 'student voice' and all students' voices from an early stage can lead to enhanced social mobility, equity and growth for all.

This growing movement within education benefits not only students, but also teachers. Teachers also benefit because they learn a lot about their students directly from the students when student voice is prioritised in classrooms. Some of what they find out could not have been found out through other means. Traditionally, teachers ask questions in class to which they almost invariably know the answers. Asking questions of the students to which they don't know the answers opens up the path to learning something new. It also models for the students that nobody knows everything, we are all continuously learning and that dialogue and discussion are important. Information teachers get from listening to students enables them to better tailor their lessons to the needs, interests and strengths of their class.

If students are more actively engaged, there is less chance of disruptive behaviour and even where behaviour issues arise, the students can, once again, be involved in finding solutions. A classroom of empowered learners who are actively engaged in learning can further empower one another. Students who are supported to use their voice and choice become proactive learners, are more inclined to take initiative to explore new concepts and become more deeply engaged in learning. Doesn't that sound like a win-win scenario for teachers and students?

The aim of student voice is to increase students' representation and participation in processes and practices from which they have historically been excluded (Robinson & Taylor, 2007, p. 163). Lansdown (2011) suggests that the realisation of Article 12 within education requires action in a number of areas: involvement of children in individual decisions affecting their education, the introduction of child-centred learning, the establishment of democratic structures within school and opportunities for children to inform the development and implementation of education legislation and policies (p. 44). Again, it is important to stress that child and student voice is a right, not a privilege, and in addition to leading to many tangible benefits in the short term, according to the literature (McIntyre et al., 2005), the development of voice is also linked to future outcomes.

How schools can facilitate child and student voice

Many schools already do great work in facilitating 'student voice', providing many opportunities and spaces on an ongoing basis for its young people to have their voice heard in their education and their school life. When we think of it practically, why wouldn't this be the case when students make up the greater percentage of the demography in the school environment and after all, it is their education. At school, many students are empowered to get involved in advocacy work, peer education, political dialogue, community development, and democratic participation and many also have access to public speaking, communication and debating skills training and practise. They are involved in co-creating effective learning environments because students have a unique window of perception into how and where they learn best. Through participation, a virtuous circle is created. The more they are enabled and empowered to participate and exercise their agency over their own lives, the more effective their contributions and the greater the impact on their development.

Article 29 of the UNCRC outlines every child's right to an education. To adhere to Article 29's values of education enabling and empowering children to use and develop their talents and abilities, schools need to be child-friendly and child-centred in the fullest sense of the terms. Article 29 specifies that a child's education should help the development of their mind, body and talents as well as building a strong respect for the world around them. "The participation of children in school life . . . should be promoted as part of the process of learning and experiencing the realization of rights" (CRC, 2001). Children are not obliged to participate but empowered so that they are ready to choose to participate when necessary. All children can be supported to participate and express themselves in ways that are meaningful and most comfortable for them. Possible ways may include: through drama, speech, photographs, pictures, writing, drawings, art, music, discussions, interviews and group work.

Public speaking and communication skill development and plenty of opportunities to practise sends a very strong, clear message of a school's intention and the value it places on student voice and empowerment. Importantly, public speaking, communication and debating skills are not innate and do not develop incidentally as children mature, they need to be given explicit attention and instruction. Andrews (1994) suggests that democracy can function only if young people learn to argue effectively. If students are to serve on school committees and student councils, they need to be given time to consult with other students and prepare for meetings so that they can be ready to express themselves and represent their peers' views to the best of their ability.

Education plays a hugely important role in terms of optimising children's development and encouraging, enabling and empowering each child to achieve their individual and collective potential. Respecting the inherent dignity of the child, skills are built in an intentional way and opportunities created for children to collaborate and participate in a more participatory and democratic school environment. The practice of 'Restorative Practice', for example, throughout the school provides an opportunity for involving students in positive behaviour development and management in a structured, supported way. General Comment No. 1 of 'The Aims of Education' (CRC, 2001) details that:

> the participation of children in school life, the creation of school communities and student councils, peer education and peer counselling, and the involvement of children in school disciplinary proceedings should be promoted as part of the process of learning and experiencing the realization of rights.

The realisation of Article 12 within schools can be made possible in many ways. The following are some simple strategies that make a big difference:

- Creating safe, supportive, child-friendly, child-centred, child-led learning environments where exploratory and inquiry-based learning are prioritised.
- Actively and visibly encouraging and empowering participation.
- Involving children/students in decisions affecting their education.
- Constantly inviting children's/students' input until this becomes embedded in the culture of the school.
- Ensuring that efforts are made to allow for equal opportunities for participation by all children, including children with SEN, EAL children and those from marginalised communities.
- Ensuring that all children have the opportunity to express choice in their play and recreation.
- Conscientiously building a culture of listening, embedding practices of listening to and valuing all voices.
- Sharing the control and management of the class with students.
- Explicitly teaching public speaking, communication and leadership skills.
- Ensuring 'circle-time' discussions are part of daily, weekly time-tables.
- Using a variety of interactive learning methodologies and participatory pedagogies.
- Trusting children and giving them responsibilities of increasing complexity.
- Involving children as peer educators and mentors for younger children.

- Establishing democratic structures within the school, e.g., facilitating involvement of all students on committees, student councils/student advisory panels and also as student representatives on school boards.
- Involving students as peer mediators in conflict situations, equipped with the tools to help resolve conflicts, practising problem-solving and negotiation skills.
- Actively seeking their advice and input on the design or adaptations to the design of the school and playground.
- Encouraging children to question, to think critically and express their opinions.
- Establishing a fail-safe environment, promoting the message that it's okay and even beneficial to make mistakes as we can learn more in experiences of perceived 'failure' than we do from perceived 'successes'.
- Inviting students' feedback and evaluation regularly on the curriculum, teaching methods, and what's working/not working for them.
- Availing of opportunities for children to become involved in having their voices heard outside the school, including their local community.
- Embedding the values and principles of peace, democracy, inclusion, equality of opportunity for all children, acceptance and celebration of diversity.
- Clarifying the role of the teacher in facilitating participatory learning rather than simply transmitting knowledge.
- Adapting the curriculum to children's local environment, community and context, making it more relevant to children's lived reality while also touching on universal concepts and global realities.
- Working with and seeking advice from local and national groups that work with children, e.g., the office of the Ombudsman for children, youth groups, health organizations, etc.
- Partnering with parents and on occasions, creating opportunities to partner with parents and their children together.
- Being open to exploring new ways of involving children in decision-making.
- Considering holding Parent-Teacher-Student meetings instead of or in addition to Parent-Teacher meetings.

Student voice does not mean that teachers won't have a role to play. Teachers will remain responsible for the planning, development and facilitation of the participation process, determining the scope of influence students can have, ensuring that, as far as possible, all voices are heard and curricular requirements are met. It is important for us to be honest in our reflection and analysis. The list above is certainly not designed to scare anyone but rather to support and give some guidance as to how we can begin and continue to develop practices that will fulfil our commitment and duty to implementing Article 12 of the UNCRC. This is not what we, teachers, experienced ourselves as children and furthermore, very few of us have received training in promoting and facilitating student voice. In reality, the right to be heard and taken seriously remains elusive for most children across the world. Do parents know about Article 12 of the UNCRC? Are all adults working with children aware of this right and how they might better facilitate it?

Models of support for facilitating child and student voice and participation

Dr Harry Shier's 'Pathways to Participation' model of child participation (Shier, 2001) supports, guides and scaffolds those working and living with children to explore different levels of child and youth participation. It outlines a developmental progression for authentic child participation. Comprising an ordered sequence of 15 questions, this model can support individuals, teams and organisations to take necessary meaningful steps to bring their practice of facilitating child voice and participation to the next level. A very useful tool for self-reflection and planning, simple questions are provided at each level to help the user locate themselves along the path and identify possible next steps to increase the level of participation. The five levels are: 1. Children are listened to, 2. Children are supported in expressing their views, 3. Children's views are taken into account, 4. Children are involved in decision-making processes and 5. Children share power and responsibility for decision-making. Between Level 3 and Level 4 is the minimum point we must achieve to endorse the UN Convention on the Rights of the Child (UN, 1989).

The Lundy (2007) model of child participation, a model for rights-compliant children's participation, which has been widely welcomed in research, policy and practice, is based on four key concepts: Space, Voice, Audience and Influence. This model has been used and adopted by national and international organisations, agencies and governments across the world to inform their understanding of children's participation. It is a very useful and supportive guide and helps practitioners to effectively and meaningfully implement a child's right to participate in matters that affect their lives. Lundy (2007) makes the point that "voice alone is not enough". All four key concepts mentioned above must be provided for. 'Space' refers to the opportunity children are given to express their opinion. 'Voice' pertains to facilitating children to express their views. 'Audience' requires that the child's view is listened to and 'Influence' intends that the opinion or view expressed must be acted upon, as and where appropriate. Children need to know they have been heard, who has heard them and what difference their contributions have made.

Taking a closer look at each of Lundy's four concepts, the following guiding questions under each of the headings may be helpful. Space: Has a safe space been provided where children can express themselves freely? Have measures been put in place to ensure that all children can take part? Voice: Have the children been given enough clear information at their level to express a view? Have they been given a choice of options as to how they can express themselves? Audience: Are the children clear on who will be listening to their views? Does the audience have the power to act on the views being expressed? Influence: Are there procedures in place to ensure that the children's views will be considered by those in a position to effect change? How will the children be provided with feedback regarding how their views were considered?

Hart's Ladder of Participation (1992) also supports and encourages those working with children to reflect on the nature and purpose of children's participation. This model, featuring eight ladder rungs, identifies eight levels of children's participation as: 1. Manipulation, 2. Decoration, 3. Tokenism (each of these three bottom rungs of the ladder are clearly described as non-participatory), 4. Assigned but informed, 5. Consulted and informed, 6. Adult-initiated, shared decisions with children, 7. Child-initiated and directed and 8. Child-initiated, shared decisions with adults. Rungs 4-8 involve varying degrees of participation. Hart (1992) notes that the confidence and competence to be involved in democratic participation at a community level must be gradually acquired through practise. More opportunities for children to participate, to speak for themselves will lead to empowerment and further participation in matters that affect them now and into the future.

Alexander (2011) points to the importance of empowering local, national and global citizenship. To help children become active citizens, Alexander points out that we need to advance their understanding of human rights, democratic engagement, diversity, conflict resolution and social justice (Alexander, 2011 p. 24). For children to be inspired to become active citizens, they must feel, see and experience that their voice matters and is valued. There is something to be learned and important support and insights gleaned from each of the three models: Shier's Pathway to Participation, Lundy's Model of Child Participation and Hart's Ladder of Participation. A combination of all three models may more thoroughly inform an individual and organization's approach to facilitating and supporting child and student voice and participation.

Examples of student voice in action

What are some examples of 'student voice' in action and what measures can teachers and schools take to increase the level of 'student voice' in their classrooms and schools? Various different activities are easily identifiable as student voice. These include: involvement in planning, teaching, decision-making, research, advocacy and evaluation. Student voice is encouraged through providing students with choice at the various stages of their learning and throughout their school day. From allowing and encouraging students to contribute to the classroom layout, planning of the classroom timetable to creating structures that allow students to choose their own topics and/or methods of study. Student voice enactment requires the teacher to see themselves less in a position of power at the top of the class and more as a coach, facilitator or partner supporting, guiding and encouraging students in their education.

Student voice in explicit public speaking skills training

As part of the implementation of a structured approach to explicit public speaking skills training which formed part of my research, we intentionally and carefully spent time creating the safe, supportive environment in the classroom in which all children could feel comfortable to speak. Students who were observed to be 'shy', reluctant to speak, had additional needs or who expressed a wish to speak to a smaller group were facilitated to do so. Over the course of the intervention, the following is some of what the students shared and what the teachers observed of students. Some strengths identified by the teachers were that:

- Most students were eager to speak once the ground rules had been co-created but were not as enthusiastic about spending time preparing their presentations. Teachers reporting this suggested that this may be connected to their lack of confidence in their writing

ability. Students were reassured when it was pointed out that spellings did not matter at this stage as it was not a 'writing lesson'. Many were also relieved when they were told that they could give their feedback orally rather than in writing.
- Most of the older students (aged 10-12) preferred to write out their speech entirely before they presented it, with two students preferring to use bullet points. The younger students (aged 5-6) used their choice of mind-maps, the fingers on their hands for structure or images we called 'picture prompts' to support memory and help prompt themselves in the delivery of their presentation, while students in the middle classes (aged 7-9) used a combination of all of the above.
- Scaffolding students' input and supporting them to prepare their presentations by using strategies and supportive tools such as mind-maps and tables with key words, phrases and bullet points that students had contributed to, were found to be very helpful.
- Most students were enjoying and participating in giving feedback to peers although the feedback was not always specific to the particular skills that were being focused on for that project.
- Students were using their own language when evaluating peers and were able to be quite specific with this, for example: *"I liked your facial expression, the way you smiled when you came on at first"*.
- Teachers noted that the students were very witty, which seems to imply that the students were relaxed and felt comfortable trying to use humour.
- Using some 'In-Class Support' time, when another teacher was in the classroom for public speaking skill training, made it more possible to give every child a chance to speak and receive feedback in the group situations.
- Students were carefully listened to and explicitly told that their views would be shared with myself, the main researcher. Their feedback would be considered and appropriate adaptations would be made to the intervention based on their input.

It would appear that students and teachers enjoyed the process and that student voice was certainly a feature of the public speaking approach. From the self-efficacy checklists, teachers were learning more about how students rated themselves in terms of self-efficacy, what they thought they were and weren't already good at and how able they rated themselves at carrying out certain tasks. Throughout the intervention, teachers could observe what methods of preparation for and presentation of speeches worked well for individual and groups of students. Students were revealing sides to their personalities that teachers had not previously been aware of, for example, their wittiness. Their presentations also revealed some interests that teachers said they had not previously been aware of. Teachers reported that students were more capable of planning their own presentations and providing feedback to peers when a clear structure and support were provided.

It was agreed that student feedback would be regularly invited orally during the intervention and again at the end. Some of what students shared included: *"My favourite was talking about my family"* (age 5), *"I have lots more stories"* (age 5), *"I wouldn't like to speak in front of strangers"* (age 6), *"I liked talking about my toys best"* (age 6), *" I liked describing how to bake a cake"* (age 7), *"I really liked when everybody gave me positive feedback"* (age 8), *"I liked making my friends laugh"* (age 9), *"I don't like to speak in front of lots of people"* (age 10), *"It's *better than writing, more fun"* (age 11), *"I really enjoyed listening to the other presentations"* (age 11), *"I was nervous at first but then I grounded myself"* (age 12).

It was agreed with teachers not to mention nerves or public speaking related fear to the students until or unless they mentioned these themselves. We also had previously taught and practised with our students the practice of grounding ourselves to help us deal with nervousness before performances of any kind. Students in the junior classes (age 5–6) did not mention fear or nerves. A few students in the middle classes (age 7–9) were supported to deal with nerves. In the senior classes (age 10–12), the teacher reported that students seemed more conscious of what their peers thought. They were supported to deal with nerves by providing them with a choice of techniques to use: deep breaths, repeating affirmations to themselves, labelling 'nerves' as 'excitement' rather than 'nerves', grounding exercises and encouragement to focus on the message of the presentation and the value that it could bring to the audience.

Concern was expressed by four teacher survey respondents with regard to the *"shy"* or *"naturally quiet child"*. One suggested that *"some kids are more confident naturally"*, that children *"should have a choice. It (public speaking) should not be made compulsory"*. Teachers were also concerned about how to differentiate for English Additional Language (EAL) students and Speech and Language difficulties. While it may be beneficial for students to have an awareness of their own dialect and accent and how this needs to be considered in connection with the audience being spoken to, a challenge perceived by some teachers was to not let this limit the students at the early stages of speaking in public. Cregan's work (2010) points to the need to positively acknowledge the language and dialects that students come to school with especially when it is not the same as the 'literate' language of school.

The practicality of hearing every child speak, *"getting the quieter, more nervous pupils to participate"*, balancing speaking and listening opportunities fairly between the *"outspoken"* and the *"shy"* child and managing the noise level in the classroom were also mentioned as challenges. These are important considerations when looking at how speaking skills can be taught most effectively in the classroom context to facilitate inclusion and learning for all children. Teachers who participated in my research reported that the co-created ground rules for listening, speaking and evaluating helped considerably here, by providing a sense of safety, a structure and clear expectations. Having a set time limit of one or two minutes for each presentation was also helpful as students who were inclined to speak more were challenged to structure the main points of their message so that they could present it in the given time-frame and students with less to say were challenged to add to their content, to aim for the time limit. Feeding back one or two words or phrases to a speaker during the 'evaluation' phase of the lesson was also noted as a less pressurised and purposeful way for 'shy' children to begin to develop as speakers.

There were many learnings and takeaways with regard to 'student voice' from my research. When young people are involved in research or their feedback is sought by way of surveys or interviews, we learned that it is important for the researchers and participating adults to be mindful of both the impact of the 'adult gaze' and the Hawthorne Effect (Wickström & Bendix, 2000). 'Adult gaze' refers to where an adult may reflect their view onto the child, thereby negatively influencing the authenticity of the child's responses. The Hawthorne Effect is where students or children may be trying to please their teacher or an adult close to them, replying with what they think the adult would want them to say. Constant reflexivity and checking for any potential adult bias go a long way towards mitigating these possibilities and hearing the child's authentic voice.

Many of the teachers currently in the education system, most likely, did not receive training in 'student voice'. Therefore, in addition to specific training, a shift in mindset may be required to view students as partners in and the main stakeholders and beneficiaries of education. Taylor and Robinson (2009) note that the responsibility to 'empower' students in 'student voice' work, placed with teachers, would involve 'some change in the balance of classroom power' (p. 166). McIntyre et al. (2005) are optimistic that students can become 'the catalysts for school-wide change' by confidently contributing their opinions and ideas and experiencing those contributions being valued.

The example of School 21

As part of my studies on oracy and public speaking, I also looked at the example of School 21, a 'changemaker' school in London. School 21 provides an insight into what an explicit emphasis on oracy development in a school can achieve. Located in Stratford, East London, School 21 opened in 2012. It is an all-through state comprehensive school, catering for students from age 4-18 across the primary school-secondary school divide. School 21 recognizes and takes very seriously the importance of developing students' speaking skills to support students in learning and in life "to find their voice physically and metaphorically" (ESU, 2016, p. 12). Speech is placed at the heart of every lesson and underpins all aspects of the school's curriculum, culture and community. From the start, School 21 intentionally gave speaking an equal status to reading and writing and designed into its DNA the pedagogies and approaches the founders felt would make "the biggest impact on students' success" (ESU, 2016, p. 11). Ofsted's (2014) report on School 21 noted that the "strong focus on oracy, the ability to talk fluently and accurately and express ideas, develops pupils' confidence, self-esteem and communication skills" and "makes a significant contribution to the high standards that all pupils achieve".

Millard and Menzies (2016) explain how School 21 works with all of its secondary level students as part of its 'Ignite programme' (p. 51) which involves students working towards and delivering 5-minute presentations without notes. Some important foundational work for this would also have been covered at primary level. "The focus for each year group is different, and cumulatively builds pupils' skills as public speakers" (p. 51). Year 7s deliver speeches on topics they are passionate about, Year 8s on topics they have special expertise in and Year 9s on an issue of political significance. Amy Gaunt, Head of Oracy Primary, notes that this has a profound, positive effect on students' confidence. School 21's discrete curriculum for oracy is built around the following four oracy strands: physical, linguistic, cognitive and social and emotional.

For School 21, better oracy is not just an educational ambition but a moral cause. Founders and staff believe that better oracy is one of the great engines of social mobility, giving everyone the chance to participate in the great conversations of society and especially, to participate in conversations that affect them. School 21 is an example of what can be achieved when speaking and oracy skills are explicitly taught to all students. I attended the 1st 'Great Oracy Exhibition' in School 21 on 22 March 2018. This event consisted of student showcases, teacher masterclasses and panel discussions, all meaningful demonstrations of oracy in action. An extremely inspiring event, the oral competence and confidence of students and teachers alike was highly impressive.

Summary reflection on facilitating an increased focus on child voice and student voice

All adults, living and working with children have a duty to facilitate 'child voice' and educators have a duty to facilitate 'student voice'. There are responsibilities that go with this duty and many benefits to be reaped by all through the process. We can be guided by the questions of Shiers' (2001) Pathways to Participation, Lundy's model (Lundy, 2007) ensuring space, voice, audience and influence and Hart's (1992) Ladder of Participation. Facilitating 'child voice' and 'student voice' from an early age, through vocal participation and representation, provides an effective grounding for democracy far better than assuming a sudden transfer of power to our young people at age 18. Furthermore, it helps students and teachers more fully and deeply understand and enjoy life and learning in classrooms and schools.

For real, sustainable change, children's voices must be heard at national, international as well as local level in family matters, the local community, child protection measures, education policy, teaching methods, school curricula, use of technology and other resources providing invaluable information on how, where and when children and students learn best. Students need to be invited into the discussion on what is relevant to learn so that learning can be connected to their lived lives. Governments need to encourage and support the development of independent children's organisations, student organisations and advisory groups as well as relevant CPD for adults working with children. Governments that have ratified the UNCRC, have a duty to provide information and support to parents as well as ongoing pre-service and in-service training for all professionals working with and for children on the UNCRC. Not merely a privilege, a 'nice to have' or an example of good practice, child and student voice is an imperative, an entitlement, a right. "It's not the gift of adults. It's the right of the child" (Lundy, 2007).

Reference List

Alexander, R. (ed) (2011). *Children, Their World, Their Education: Final Report and Recommendations of the Cambridge Primary Review*, 305-307. Abingdon, Routledge.
Andrews, R. (1994). Democracy and the Teaching of Argument. *The English Journal*, 83, 62-69.
CRC. (2001). Convention on the Rights of the Child Distr. GENERAL CRC/GC/2001/1 17 April 2001, General Comment No. 1, 'The Aims of Education', CRC/GC/2001/1.
Cregan, A. (2010). From Policy to Practice: The Oral Language Challenge for Teachers.
ESU. (2016). *Speaking Frankly: The Case for Oracy in the Curriculum*. London, English Speaking Union.
Fielding, M. (2004b). 'New Wave' Student Voice and the Renewal of Civic Society. *London Review of Education*, 2, 197-217.
Hart, R. A. (1992). Children's Participation: From Tokenism to Citizenship (No. inness 92/6).
Lansdown, G. (2011). *Every Child's Right to Be Heard, a resource guide on the UN Committee on the Rights of the Child General Comment*, no.12, Gerison Lansdown. Save the Children UK on behalf of Save the Children and UNICEF.
Lundy, L. (2007). 'Voice' Is Not Enough: Conceptualising Article 12 of the United Nations Convention on the Rights of the Child. *British Educational Research Journal*, 33(6).

McIntyre, D., Pedder. D., & Rudduck, J. (2005). Pupil Voice: Comfortable and Uncomfortable Learnings for Teachers. *Research Papers in Education*, 20, 149-68.

Mercer & Mannion. (2018). *Oracy across the Welsh Curriculum. A Research-Based Review: Key Principles and Recommendations for Teachers*. EAS, Education Achievement Service for South East Wales.

Millard, W., & Menzies, L. (2016). *Oracy: The State of Speaking in Our Schools*, London: Voice 21.

Quaglia, R. (2016). *School Voice Report 2016*, Quaglia Institute for School Voice and Aspirations, https://quagliainstitute.org/dmsView/School_Voice_Report_2016

Robinson, C., & Taylor, C. (2007). Theorizing Student Voice: Values and Perspectives. *Improving Schools*, 10(1), 5-17.

Rudduck, J. (2006). The Past, the Papers and the Project. *Educational Review*, 58, 131-43.

Shier, H. (2001). Pathways to Participation: Openings, Opportunities and Obligations. *Children & Society*, 15(2), 107-117.

Taylor, C., & Robinson, C. (2009). Student Voice: Theorising Power and Participation. *Pedagogy, Culture & Society*, 17(2), 161-175.

Toshalis, E., & Nakkula, M. J. (2012). Motivation, Engagement and Student Voice. *Students at the Center*.

UNICEF. (2004). Regional Office South Asia, Wheel of Change, Children and Young People's Participation in South Asia, Kathmandu.

Wickström, G., & Bendix, T. (2000). The "Hawthorne Effect" – What Did the Original Hawthorne Studies Actually Show? *Scandinavian Journal of Work, Environment & Health*, 26(4), 363-367.

4 Research on Public Speaking in Primary School

The topic of public speaking has long been an interest of mine. My interest in the topics of having one's voice heard and public speaking is both personal and professional. Public speaking is a widely reported top fear of many adults across the world (Pearson et al., 2007) even though it is a feature of life that most people will encounter at one stage or another (Salim & Joy, 2016). I began to wonder where, when or if public speaking skills are taught in the education system and what, in particular, its relevance might be to primary school education and the promotion of child and student voice. As a primary school principal, a teacher, a member of Toastmasters International, a parent, and someone who has suffered, throughout my life, with erythrophobia, a pathological fear of blushing, which impacted my own experience of speaking in public, my interest in this topic is deep.

I was a very shy, quiet child, the middle child of seven siblings. Growing up, I learned communication and even leadership skills quite naturally through interacting with my brothers and sister. We played outside every day in large groups with the other children from our street. Through play, we were constantly involved in communicating, planning, plotting, persuading and negotiating. We'd tell jokes and stories. We'd ask endless amounts of questions and exaggerate news just to get a reaction. I quickly realized that speaking was important for life, for survival, for having my needs met and even just for having fun with my friends. Speaking up at school was neither easy nor natural. Not only was it not encouraged, in my experience, knowing that I was bound to blush every time I opened my mouth was often paralyzing. This made even the simple, regular act of answering a question in front of the class so much more daunting. The fact that I didn't put my hand up in class didn't mean I didn't know the answer. However, simultaneously, as a child, I always had a strong sense of justice and thought it only right and fair that I, like everyone else should have my voice and opinions heard.

A personal journey through public speaking

In primary school, the closest experience to public speaking I had was reciting poetry in front of the class and reading at Mass from time to time. I was given no specific training for this and learned mainly from observing others. I dreaded when I had to speak impromptu in front of the class, for example, when answering a teacher's question. My mother would encourage me to recite and perform poetry at home especially when neighbours and relatives would visit. While my siblings were encouraged to sing, I was praised for my recitations. Some may have seen this as an indirect acknowledgement of my poor singing voice. I chose to see it as a recognition of my proficient poetry recitation skills. I'd stand in front of the fridge, which for us children, was our stage, to perform. I think at some level, I revelled in the attention I got from my mother and 'the audience' for my recitation of poetry and consequently, with each new recitation, I'd put more and more effort in, playing around with my voice, hand gestures, facial expressions and body language. I didn't know at the time that these were all skills of public speaking and I was beginning to experience, in a real, meaningful way, that my voice, somehow, had impact and power.

In secondary school I was encouraged to join the class debating team. The reason for this, I now believe, was because I was reasonably good academically and two of my older siblings had been on debating teams. Not all students in the class were given this opportunity. In fact, only five out of approximately eighty students from each year group were chosen to develop their debating skills. I know for sure that the public speaking training and opportunities I received through debating in secondary school and at university, greatly impacted my readiness and willingness to avail of the many opportunities I've had to speak in public beyond formal education. As a shy person, I did not find public speaking easy at first, but I always found it to be very empowering as a form of expression. Across the trajectory of my life so far, I've experienced both the fear and the feeling of fulfilment and achievement of public speaking.

In 2004, I joined Toastmasters to continue to work on my communication, presentation and leadership skills. Toastmasters is a non-profit, global, educational organisation that aims to help people worldwide to develop communication, public speaking and leadership skills. Through Toastmasters, I began to see and experience the challenges of public speaking for myself and also for fellow Toastmasters who may have been highly qualified and highly competent in other areas of their life. I would say that I am still a shy adult, that is a part of my personality. However, I know that I have something unique to say and contribute. I've begun to enjoy speaking in public and although I always feel nervous before a presentation, I am confident that I can do it. Why? Because I've studied the skills and I've done it before, again and again and again. Simply put, I've learned the skills and I've practised them. I've learned to greet my nerves as a sign that I care, to label them as excitement rather than nerves and consequently, I somehow manage to get the butterflies that gather in my stomach to fly in formation.

A professional interest in public speaking

As a teacher I began to explore and investigate how a public speaking approach to oral language development might support the achievement of the learning outcomes of the Primary Language Curriculum (NCCA, 2019) in Ireland, while simultaneously providing training for my students in what I considered to be an important life skill. Furthermore, given that the majority of the students I was teaching came from a minority ethnic background, i.e., the travelling community, I wondered if these skills could build on their already rich oral traditions and possibly add more value to them. In 2015, at a Toastmaster meeting, as I watched a pharmacist visibly struggle to present her ice-breaker to our audience, a question occurred to me. Why is this happening? How can someone so academically qualified thanks to the education system find the act of introducing herself to an audience, so difficult? Had she gone through the whole education system without having received any training in these skills? How might I mitigate this kind of experience for my students? As Teaching Principal at the time of a 'DEIS' Primary School, catering mainly for students from designated disadvantaged, lower socio-economic backgrounds, I also began to wonder what impact, if any, training all of our students in these skills might have in terms of social equity and better outcomes for our students throughout school and beyond.

My passion now is to empower all young people as best I can to proudly and proficiently stand up, speak up, communicate for themselves and have their voices heard, confident in the knowledge that they have something valuable and unique to contribute, that they matter and their voice matters. That's the legacy I would like to leave for my children and students. A legacy that feeds into holistic well-being: social, emotional, mental and spiritual. Furthermore, it's a legacy, I believe, that may facilitate the realization of Article 12 of the UNCRC.

Further studies in public speaking

I began my PhD studies when I realized that 'Public Speaking in Primary School' was a topic I wanted to find out more about. I had many questions. I quickly found that there is little systematic enquiry internationally by researchers into the topic of public speaking in primary schools. Interestingly, as I began to search for literature on public speaking, it became clear that there is a considerable amount of literature available on the topics of fear of public speaking, public speaking anxiety (PSA) and "communication apprehension" (CA), a "broadly based anxiety related to oral communication" (McCroskey, 1970). There is much research on public speaking in third level education and some in secondary schools but an apparent paucity of research internationally on public speaking in primary schools. I was sure that this topic was worth investigating in case there may be an opportunity we're missing or not, in primary schools. Aware of how deeply and intensely I had to search for references to public speaking in primary school, I was also caused to consider how difficult it may be for interested teachers to find support and guidance in relation to teaching this area of the curriculum.

So, what is the place of public speaking in primary schools? My doctoral thesis, reporting on mixed methods research, investigated the policy, practice, perceptions of parents and teachers and the potential for public speaking training to empower learning in primary school. From pre-empting the development of the pervasive, potentially life-long fear of this commonly used life skill to maximizing the potential to empower all young people with proficient public speaking skills for life, my study aimed to investigate the place and potential of public speaking in primary school. Some have told me that my aspirations in relation to wanting to equip all primary school children with the skills of public speaking and competent communication are over-ambitious but as Michelangelo said, "the greatest danger for most of us is not that our aim is too high and we miss it, but that it's too low and we reach it".

Context of public speaking study

My doctoral thesis is underpinned by a review of a vast body of literature on the somewhat related areas of oral language, oracy, communication skills, public speaking, communication apprehension and public speaking apprehension. At the time of embarking on this study, the National Council for Curriculum and Assessment (NCCA, 2019) had just released the Primary Language Curriculum in Ireland, and shortly after completion of my thesis, the Primary Curriculum Framework (PCF) (NCCA, 2023) for all primary and special schools in Ireland was published which places a certain emphasis on skill and competency development. In 2021, the Oracy All Party Parliamentary Group (OAPPG, 2021) in the UK released its report, 'Speak for Change' on a two-year inquiry on the importance of oracy in education for young people with a special reference to the additional potential to positively impact students' communication skills and well-being in the aftermath of Covid-19 related lockdowns. Currently, the concept of 'student voice' is more regularly being discussed in education circles across the world, in part due to the responsibility for all working with young people to promote and facilitate the realization of Article 12 of the UNCRC (UN, 1989).

Literature review on public speaking in primary school

Themes that emerged in literature I reviewed on public speaking in primary school included: terminology; the importance of oral language and public speaking; fear of public speaking; related practice and assessment in primary schools; teaching methodologies; the role of the teacher; teacher training; challenges to implementing oral language in schools; and the gap between policy and practice in relation to this area. The term 'public speaking' itself is a term that seems to engender fear for many and is not immediately identified as an activity that children engage in. Children, in schools around the world, however, constantly stand up in front of groups of peers of varying sizes and audiences of younger and older students, in classrooms and school settings, to present on their work and their learning. Yet, the degree to which they are prepared for this activity, if at all, is unclear.

It appears to matter to policy makers, curriculum advisers, teachers and students what we choose to label this area on the curriculum. What started out as a search for literature on public speaking in primary school quickly became a deep dive into the related and interconnected areas of Oral Language, Oracy, Speaking and Communication skills as well as a reflection on why the term 'public speaking', though commonly used in life outside of formal education is rarely, if ever, used within school. Definitions of public speaking vary slightly as do people's understanding and experience of the topic but all refer to communication with an audience. One of the difficulties, as outlined by Pouteaux and Berg (2013) is that students are often not introduced to public speaking methods until after they have already inherited or acquired the fear and decided that standing in front of a group of people is too intimidating, as if it is something that we can avoid for the rest of our lives. Consequently, many students progress onto university or the workforce unable to communicate ideas to a large group (Shafer, 2010). However, as literature states that anxiety connected with public communication increases about age 10 (Combes et al., 2008), I began to wonder if it might make a difference if we introduced children to the experience of public speaking before this age. It quickly became clear that public speaking, defined as "the art of effective communication with an audience" (Merriam-Webster, 2005) is on the curriculum though not named as 'public speaking'.

In addition to reviewing relevant literature on this topic, I also collected additional information and feedback through teacher interviews. I gathered the perspectives, perceptions and experiences of teachers and parents through surveys and carried out an action research project in our school identifying what factors and methodologies helped or hindered the process of public speaking skill training. While one respondent to my survey reported that the majority of teachers "*see it as something for the academic and confident children*", others saw it as an approach through which confidence could be developed. Many teachers I spoke to quickly connected public speaking with confidence and spoke about concerns around adequate vocabulary in terms of oral language. This feedback from teachers contributed to the formation of a research question around how explicit public speaking training might impact students' self-efficacy and vocabulary development.

I carefully considered whether to use the term 'public speaking' or not from the outset. A few teachers in the teacher surveys had indicated that it was off-putting. However, many adults who report a crippling fear of public speaking attribute this fear in part to having received no training at school. They reported that they did do some speaking in front of groups, albeit without specific training, but never did 'public speaking'. I would suggest that the term 'public speaking' has had formal connotations for a long time for many people, which has made it very difficult to connect with and relate to the practice of speaking in front of groups or the whole class at school. I would also suggest that almost all speaking we do is public speaking or at the very least, skills we learn through public speaking training are skills that will benefit every oral and communication interaction we have with others. If we talk freely and openly about a 'fear of public speaking', then perhaps we need to name the antidote to the fear: 'training in public speaking skills'. These skills need to be accurately named so that teachers and students can feel more empowered, knowing when, where, why and how they are covering them. For this reason, my study refers clearly to the impact of **explicit public speaking training** in primary school.

Action research on public speaking in primary school

I chose action research as I concur with Reason and Bradbury's description of action research as "a family of practices of living inquiry that aims, in a great variety of ways, to link practice and ideas in the service of human flourishing" (Reason & Bradbury, 2008, p. 1). Mercer and Mannion (2018) recommend that schools should "encourage and enable teachers to conduct small-scale research inquiries to determine which practices and strategies 'work' for them, in their context" (p. 6) and for their particular students. In our school context, I saw that through action research, we were engaged in developing something in practice to support practice. Action research involves change and growth and this aligned with the values and context of our school. The cyclical process of intervention implementation, monitoring, review, reflection and adapting small changes, is very similar to the school self-evaluation process that currently takes place in all schools in Ireland and across the world. The ultimate goal of teacher-based action research is to use findings to make changes or choices in teachers' own classrooms. This benefits the teacher involved in the research, their students and also other teachers who can learn from the practical example of what works in another teacher's classroom.

Self-efficacy and public speaking

Confidence, something that everyone wants more of, for themselves and their loved ones, can be a very elusive concept. We all want to be more sure of ourselves and our abilities. Though we refer to someone as being a 'confident' or 'not confident' person, confidence is not a personality trait or type, we are not born with it. What's more, we may be inclined to confuse extrovert tendencies with confidence. Confidence is a skill that everyone of us can develop and a disposition that all of us can nurture and grow through mastery experiences. Or, on deeper reflection, is it something that we are born with? What if it is? What if the store of confidence we are born with is constantly chipped away at as we grow, when we regularly get the message that we are not enough, not good enough perhaps at different skills we haven't had a fair chance to practise and perfect.

Self-efficacy, "the belief in one's ability to influence events that effect one's life and control over the way these events are experienced" (Bandura, 1977) is the more academic term for 'confidence in our abilities'. Albert Bandura's Social Learning Theory posits that people learn from one another, through modelling, observation and imitation. According to his theory, we learn not only by doing but by watching what others do and how they do it. Bandura's theory of self-efficacy continues to shape thinking in the field of positive psychology. Self-efficacy for children is extremely important because when it is developed, it can positively affect many facets of human experience. Of particular interest perhaps to educators, Bandura (2008) explains how self-efficacy can be influenced and developed and how anyone, regardless of their past or current environment, has the ability to strengthen their self-efficacy. Students' belief in their ability to learn and perform well in school—their self-efficacy—can predict their level of academic performance above and beyond their measured level of ability and prior performance (Dweck et al., 2015) influencing also their academic tenacity and how long they will persevere on certain tasks.

There are concrete ways that educators can support students to build self-efficacy. Bandura's self-efficacy theory outlines four ways self-efficacy can be developed and strengthened: Mastery experiences, Social Modelling, Social Persuasion and States of Physiology (Bandura, 2008). Mastery experiences refers to working towards mastery in certain skills and experiencing the results of self-efficacy first hand. Essential to mastery is acknowledging the satisfaction of goals that are achieved as well as experiencing failure and treating every failure as a learning opportunity so that we can build resilience. Social Modelling or vicarious experiences occurs when we choose and learn from role models who demonstrate self-efficacy in their lives, often inspiring through achieving their goals despite considerable adversity. Role models can come from our own social surroundings but Bandura notes that thanks to modern technology, we now have access to the lives of many inspiring role models from across the world. Seeing people we perceive as similar to ourselves succeed by their sustained effort has the potential to raise our beliefs that we too can succeed.

Social or verbal persuasion is about having others directly influence one's self-efficacy by providing opportunities and feedback for mastery experiences in a safe and purposeful manner. Influential people in our lives such as parents, teachers, coaches can strengthen our beliefs and lead us to believe that we can cope successfully with what has overwhelmed us in the past (Bandura, 1977). States of Physiology refers to how all of our emotions, moods and physical state act as magnets to influence our self-efficacy. By recognising that it is normal and okay to experience such states in life, while working to "relieve anxiety, build physical strength and stamina, and change negative misinterpretations of physical and affective states" (Bandura, 2008), self-efficacy can be interpreted in a more salient way. Psychologist James Maddux (2012) suggested a fifth route to self-efficacy through "imaginal experiences", the art of visualising yourself behaving effectively or successfully in a given situation.

Understanding and applying Bandura's theory of self-efficacy is particularly relevant to the topic of public speaking, a potentially empowering activity, as we know about the pervasive fear of public speaking. By conjuring up fear-provoking thoughts about their ineptitude, individuals can rouse themselves to elevated levels of anxiety that far exceed the fear experienced during the actual threatening situation (Bandura, 1977, p. 199). The opposite is also true. Bandura further explains that self-efficacy can be used to uplift society, highlighting Gandhi's self-sacrifice as an example of his "unwavering self-efficacy for social change under powerful opposition" Bandura (2008). Without a strong, resilient sense of self-efficacy, people can be easily overwhelmed by adversities. If people believe that they are not able to achieve a certain task, they are less likely to try and may give up easily in the face of challenge. Bandura proposes that it is in the face of difficult circumstances that self-efficacy becomes most necessary.

Vocabulary acquisition and development in public speaking

Another necessary component of literacy and oracy is vocabulary acquisition, understanding, development and use. Therefore, I wanted to take a closer look at it and how this might be impacted by an explicit focus on public speaking skill development. In oral language activities, children have the opportunity to hear new vocabulary in various contexts and practise using it which builds children's vocabulary knowledge. Learning outcomes 5 and 6 of the Oral Language strand of Ireland's Primary Language Curriculum for primary schools refer to the understanding, acquisition and use of vocabulary (NCCA, 2019).

Vocabulary is learned gradually over many encounters with a new word (Stahl, 2005). First Steps (2013) recommends that teachers and care givers use "sophisticated" words when conversing with children to expand their vocabularies and create opportunities for students to use new vocabulary (p. 139). Also recommended is involving students in discussions that require giving and justifying opinions, developing topic knowledge by immersing students in investigations and experiments, and providing opportunities for students to pursue and discuss topics that interest them. Harris et al. (2009) suggest that we can learn from the crib that vocabulary acquisition takes place in the course of natural conversation as children indicate their interests either vocally or through gesture. Vocabulary comes alive for the child when parents and caregivers build on children's focus of attention by offering information that the child is craving.

Miller and Gildea (1987) draw attention to the sheer magnitude of the child's achievement in terms of vocabulary acquisition as for many years after starting to talk a child learns new words at a rate of more than ten per day. By age 3, the child will have mastered the basic structure of their native language and be well on their way to communicative competence. However, Hart and Risley (1995) report that children from disadvantaged homes hear roughly

25% of the words of their more advantaged peers. Of particular note in terms of oral language and public speaking is the fact that children learn the words that they hear most. Children learn not only language that is directed to them, but profit also from overheard speech (Akhtar, 2005). Children are more likely to succeed at learning to speak when they are encouraged to develop their own oral language skills through many opportunities to practise using words to express their own ideas (NELP, 2008).

Children learn vocabulary everywhere and in a more formal way at school. According to studies by Miller and Gildea (1987), the rate of learning vocabulary runs far ahead of teaching with a reported 5,000 words learned in a year compared with 200 taught. This reminds us that school children are learning much more than they are explicitly taught. Biemiller (2010) stresses that we will not begin to close the gaps between advantaged and disadvantaged children until we also succeed in ensuring adequate vocabulary development and use for all students. Biemiller notes that when children and adolescents improve their vocabulary, their academic and social confidence and competence also improve.

Teachers who participated in my research agreed to choose three specific new words as key vocabulary for each of the public speaking projects they would cover with their class. This would help us attempt to assess the acquisition of this vocabulary at the end of the intervention. We agreed on three questions to ask for assessment purposes, the first two of the student, and the third, of the class teacher: What does the word mean? Can you put it into a sentence? And of the teacher: Did you notice/observe the student using the word in another context, either orally or in writing?

Study participants and methodology

One hundred and fourteen primary school teachers teaching at various class levels in a variety of primary school contexts in Ireland, 136 parents and 30 primary school children participated in my study. The school in which action research was carried out is a small, rural DEIS (catering for students from designated disadvantaged backgrounds) school. The school is one of nineteen (at time of the study) primary schools in the Dublin City University (DCU) Changemaker Schools Network (DCU, 2020). As such, the school is committed to empowering all of its students to be active changemakers.

The public speaking programme ('LET's Stand', 2018) implemented with all children in three classrooms from Junior Infants (aged 4 or 5) to 6th Class (aged 12 or 13) is a programme I designed in 2016 and continue to develop. Having searched for a structured approach to teaching public speaking skills to children, I couldn't find one. That's when I began to design one myself incorporating learnings from relevant literature (Pearson & Gallagher, 1983; First Steps, 2013). In the design of the programme, I combined my knowledge of the Toastmasters education programme for adults, which builds in an incremental way public speaking and communication skills, with my experience of working with children since 1991, and knowledge of the learning outcomes of the oral language strands of the Primary Language Curriculum (NCCA, 2019) in Ireland.

The main features of the programme are that it provides a structure for explicitly teaching and developing skills of listening to, evaluating and presenting public speaking presentations under specified skills of public speaking which include: eye contact, body language, hand gestures, facial expressions, presentation structure, 'lovely language' (including new, relevant vocabulary), use of props, voice, pause and story. The programme aims to develop skills in the areas of listening, evaluating and speaking through explicit instruction in the skills, structured opportunities to practise and feedback. Although explicit time is spent teaching each of the areas, to make it workable in a busy classroom context, each area is simultaneously being worked on and developed by different students and at different rates. For example, while one child is presenting, the other children are supported to be actively involved in listening and preparing to evaluate and feedback on their classmate's presentation. To this end it is very important that time is spent in the initial stages, setting up and creating a safe, supportive environment with clear, co-created, mutually respectful rules for listening, evaluating and speaking.

The chosen skills of public speaking were taught, two per lesson. Examples of phrases and vocabulary for how to evaluate these skills were provided, explored and practised with the students. Topics for the presentations were chosen from the curriculum with input from the students. Students were encouraged to adapt topics to their own interests. The teaching methodology of the gradual release of responsibility (Pearson & Gallagher, 1983) was followed, with all students being given the opportunity to stand in front of peers to deliver their presentations with many more opportunities being provided to listen to and evaluate their peers as they did the same. The average time for each presentation was 1-2 minutes. It was planned to spend 1 hour 30 minutes a week with an explicit focus on the intervention. This was time-tabled within the time allocation for Oral Language. Giving more opportunities to students to speak could be meaningfully integrated with other areas of the curriculum depending on the topics being spoken about.

This research was not about evaluating the actual public speaking programme itself, but an analysis of an explicit, structured approach to public speaking skills training. The use of the programme was to support the teachers, providing them with a structured framework through which to explicitly teach skills of public speaking. Using the programme also ensured some degree of consistency in how the skills were being taught. When teachers suggested minor changes or adaptations based on their own observations, experiences and related reflections, this was encouraged and supported and shared amongst all teachers participating in the action research. Student voice was incorporated through the class teacher inviting, listening to and observing students' feedback after each project/speech of the intervention and at the end of the period of the intervention itself.

Findings

Fear, perceptions and experience of public speaking

From a choice of three definitions of 'public speaking' offered in the survey, 93% of teachers surveyed chose the Merriam-Webster definition: "the art of effective communication with an audience". 94% of parents and 98% of teachers surveyed responded that they have been called on to speak in public at some stage throughout their lives, indicating that this is a common experience. Survey respondents were asked to list the first five words that come to mind initially when they hear the term 'public speaking'. The most common were "*debating*", *"nerves"*, *"fear"* and *"audience"*. *"Confidence"* was top of the list. On a scale provided, 50% of respondents perceived public speaking skill training for children to be "very important" and 47% rated it as "important". The majority expressed the view that training should begin for children in the early years of primary school. 59% of teachers indicated that public speaking training should begin for children at age 4 or 5.

Although 70% of teachers replied that they had never received training in public speaking skills themselves, 78% reported that they do teach their students public speaking. 49.5% of teachers thought that these skills were on the curriculum. Just over 25% of teacher respondents stated that it wasn't on the curriculum and the rest were unsure. These percentages would seem to indicate that some teachers have been teaching these skills even though they were not sure if they were on the curriculum or not. It is still unclear if many teachers are explicitly teaching the skills or providing the opportunities for practise or both. What also emerged from the survey is teachers' concern for how to support *"shy"* children.

Significant findings from my study indicate a pervasive fear of public speaking amongst adult respondents including parents from a range of professional backgrounds which some traced back to an initial unprepared-for or negative experience of speaking in front of a group as a child. Others attributed this fear to a lack of opportunity and training in public speaking skills in primary and secondary school. 67% of parents and 70% of teachers had never received training in public speaking skills. 48% of parents and 46% of teachers reported a fear of public speaking, with 17% of parents and 4% of teachers rating their fear as *"terrified"*. No respondent to the teacher or parent survey reported having received training in public speaking skills in primary school and less than 3% in secondary school. Some shared that opportunities they had received for public speaking or debating skills training in secondary school were not available to all students. Others who had received training in public speaking had received it in their adult years. All teachers surveyed and interviewed indicated that they had not received training in how to train students in public speaking skills.

In the school context, the use of many different terms for oral language seems to create ambiguity and confusion as does the balance between explicit instruction, natural development and opportunities for practise (organically arising and planned). Three teachers expressed the assumption that good speakers are naturally gifted. Additional consideration needs to be given to supporting the shy child, the child with special educational needs (SEN), children who are learning English as an additional language (EAL) and the child from a disadvantaged background who may be coming to school with a deficit in the 'literate language' of the school.

Examples of positive self-efficacy

Here are some examples of where positive self-efficacy was observed by teachers during the period of the public speaking intervention. A 10-year-old girl chose to do a speech outside during break time, assembling her own audience unprompted by a teacher. One teacher expressed surprise at some of the students who quickly volunteered to speak. One example here was an 11-year-old boy with high functioning autism. His teacher thought that it may be because of the increased amount of practise he had had speaking in front of his peers that he put himself forward for a main part in the Christmas play that year.

During 'Free Play' in the Juniors' classroom, it was observed that some of the younger children recreated a formal speaking situation in the classroom and stood up behind a lectern to speak during 'free play'. It appeared that in their imaginations, there may have been an audience in front of them. One 5-year-old girl assembled an audience of teddies. As the children spoke during these child-led play activities, they visibly used some of the skills they had been learning through the explicit public speaking training such as hand gestures, facial expressions and props. Another teacher noted that two boys, aged 10, who tended to usually sit back in class and not put themselves forward for much else apart from sport, volunteered to speak in front of their peers.

The opportunity arose during the intervention for one of our students to speak at an International Functional Medicine Conference in a nearby city in front of approximately 350 adults, professionals from the field of health. When I offered this opportunity to our Senior Room students (aged 10-13), fifteen out of eighteen students immediately put their hand up to volunteer. It was decided to run an in-school competition to select the speaker. When competition was mentioned, eight students requested to withdraw from this process, three said they did not want to compete. This appears to be because they did not want to be judged on their presentations. A nervous reaction was evident when competition was introduced with one student who had previously put herself forward for the opportunity saying, *"I can't do that"*. This alerted me to the distinction between judging (as in competitions) and evaluating (as in providing feedback for further progress).

Not all students may want to compete in public speaking competitions but this doesn't necessarily mean that they don't want to avail of an opportunity to speak. The seven remaining volunteers were supported to prepare and practise their presentations on 'Health in My School'. Criteria for judging the speeches was agreed with the students and three students sat with three teachers on the judging panel. In the end, a 10-year-old girl was selected to represent the school. One week later, she delivered her speech to this large audience of unfamiliar adults made up of functional medicine related professionals, with her parents also in attendance. I asked her afterwards had she been nervous. She replied, *"A little but I knew I had done it before. I really liked it"*. This is a significant response as it demonstrates this child's self-efficacy, her belief that she could do it based on previous mastery experiences.

Another interesting observation was noted by the senior room teacher. In response to a critical incident which happened in our school during the year that the action research was being carried out, one student (aged 11), who had been reluctant to speak in front of a whole class of her peers at the beginning of the intervention, volunteered immediately to sing acapella in front of a packed church at her friend's funeral. Her teacher speculated that this may be connected to the practise she had received and confidence she had gained by standing up in front of her peers to speak. It was also noted by an external, independent education psychologist that the school culture of encouraging students to speak in a safe supportive environment may have helped them to express their thoughts and feelings in response to and in the aftermath of the critical incident, which contributed to supporting their well-being at this difficult time. Significant increases in self-efficacy were observed on a whole-school basis with more students volunteering to lead and/or take a speaking role at School Assemblies. Having seen older students model this may also have contributed to younger students' belief in their own ability to do so. It quickly became clear that public speaking is one area where there is significant potential to build self-efficacy.

Impact of intervention on vocabulary development

In terms of vocabulary acquisition and development, while teachers agreed that it was beneficial for students to hear the same words being modelled and examples of the word used in context by the class teacher as well as being used many times in their peers' presentations, it was difficult to say conclusively that it was because of the explicit public speaking intervention alone that students acquired this vocabulary. In a school situation, it's difficult to isolate other contributing factors to vocabulary acquisition. However, teachers agreed that the explicit teaching of public speaking skills followed by opportunities to practise definitely supported the acquisition, use and practise of new vocabulary in meaningful contexts.

The teachers conscientiously tried to create an environment in which the students could be *"braver"* around language, *"have fun with words"* and not shy away from using or attempting to use *"big words"*. They commented that this was something that linked meaningfully to the curriculum while explicitly teaching public speaking skills. All teachers agreed that consistency and plenty of repetition as well as good modelling of vocabulary are key and this can be achieved in an even more purposeful way through public speaking training. Through observation, they reported witnessing students attempt to use specific vocabulary learned and *"bigger"* words in their public speaking presentations that they would not normally have the opportunity to use in everyday conversation.

Key recommendations of the study

Key recommendations that emerged from my study are that we educators:

- Consider naming public speaking explicitly on the curriculum, where these skills are being taught and where they are expected as a learning outcome. This may reduce any ambiguity so that teachers know they are teaching and students know they are learning and practising these skills. It may also help to somewhat mitigate the pervasive fear of public speaking or at least, lessen its impact.
- Try to achieve some consistency and agreement on common terminology for this curricular area and skill-set but be aware that it may take time. In the meantime, the training and practise can progress.
- Clarify where it is on the curriculum. Is it a skill-set or a pedagogical approach or both?
- Remember that apprehension associated with communicating increases at about the age of 10 (McCroskey et al., 1981), therefore, begin public speaking training for children younger than 10. This study demonstrates that many young children are eager and comfortable being the centre of attention.
- Provide pre-service and in-service training for teachers in this area to boost their confidence and competence.
- Consider the needs of shy children, children with SEN and EAL children when differentiating, as teachers naturally and regularly do with other areas of the curriculum, allowing

students to speak to audiences of varying sizes depending on their ability, preference and need.
- Children should not be expected to stand in front of an audience to speak if time has not been spent on equipping them with the necessary skills to do this to the best of their abilities, as evidence from my research shows a link between these unprepared-for experiences as children and a long-lasting, limiting fear of public speaking.
- It is important to bear in mind that while debating is a very useful and beneficial activity, it is only one genre of public speaking and possibly not the best starting point for public speaking training.
- Competitions in this area tend to have limited value. Perhaps 'events' rather than 'competitions' could be held.
- As with the training of other skills, explicit teaching of the skills with regular opportunities for practise is recommended for all students from all backgrounds. It's important *"to allow children to speak in the same way that they speak at home"* (survey respondent), but take the opportunities to make them aware of different dialects and the different language appropriate to different social contexts when speaking in public.
- Teachers indicated some key areas to consider in beginning the process of public speaking skill training. These are: carefully setting up the safe, supportive environment and being aware of and taking advantage of the many opportunities for practise that present organically across the school day and the life of the school. It was acknowledged by teachers participating in the action research that a structured approach would provide a valuable guide, reassurance and support for teachers.

Mercer and Mannion (2018) make the point that even though initiatives to develop children's skills and confidence in participating in public speaking have proliferated in recent years, there has been remarkably little systematic enquiry by researchers into either the effectiveness of the training techniques used, or the effects of that training on outcomes such as improvements in social confidence, articulacy, academic achievement or social mobility (p. 22). While my research provides some evidence in relation to some of this, these outcomes may be best observed over a longer period of time requiring a longitudinal study and investigation.

Summary reflection on research on public speaking in primary school

At a time when there is much talk about hearing student voice as an instrument for change in education circles, and there is an obligation on state bodies to fulfil their commitment to realizing Article 12 of the UNCRC, it has often occurred to me that students' physical voices and oral contributions and communication modes are like the proverbial 'elephant in the room' at some of these discussions. I've heard 'student voice' talked about, at times predominantly, in the slightly more abstract and representational sense. That is why, in part, I thought it worthwhile investigating to what extent we are listening to children's physical voices and empowering all children to develop them.

While speaking skills are on the curriculum for all schools, it's been reported that in the UK, activities associated with public speaking and debating skills are engaged in by a few state schools but rarely if ever explicitly taught (ESU, 2016). Explicit public speaking training has the potential to positively impact primary school students' self-efficacy, broaden students' vocabulary banks and improve communication skills as evidenced from my research. Public speaking skill training can provide all children with what I believe is a gift of timed periods of uninterrupted speech exploration, development and expression, that some children may never get elsewhere.

The principles of equality and inclusion that underpin many education systems are questionable if some students receive training in certain skills that can significantly impact life opportunities and some do not. We know that very bad things have happened to children in the past and have been made worse by silence. This is evidenced in many cases of child abuse reported over the last few decades in Ireland (McAlinden, 2012). People could not and did not speak up at the time. Worse still, perpetrators may have felt somewhat protected by their victim's silence. There are obvious potential gains on many levels to encouraging, enabling and empowering children to speak up and use their voice. Change has to start somewhere. Though relatively small-scale, my mixed-methods study is significant and important as it provides an original and 'first of its kind' contribution on the topic of public speaking in primary school, thereby contributing to enhanced knowledge and understanding for primary school teachers, parents and policy makers.

Reference List

Akhtar, N. (2005). The Robustness of Learning Through Overhearing. *Developmental Science*, 8, 199-209.
Bandura, A. (1977). Self-efficacy: Toward a Unifying Theory of Behavioral Change. *Psychological Review*, 84(2), 191-215.
Bandura, A. (2008). An Agentic Perspective on Positive Psychology. In S. J. Lopez (Ed.), *Praeger Perspectives. Positive Psychology: Exploring the Best in People*, Vol. 1 Discovering Human Strengths, 167-196. Praeger Publishers/Greenwood Publishing Group.
Biemiller, A. (2010). Chapter 3: Teaching Vocabulary in the Primary Grades. In *Vocabulary Instruction*.
Combes, B. H., Walker, M., Harrell, P. E., & Tyler-Wood, T. (2008). PAVES: A Presentation Strategy for Beginning Presenters in Inclusive Environments. *Teaching Exceptional Children*, 41(1), 42-47.
DCU. (2020). Changemaker Schools' Network. https://www.dcuchangemakernetwork.com/
Dweck, C. S., Walton, G. M., & Cohen, G. L. (2015). *Academic Tenacity: Mindsets and Skills that Promote Long-Term Learning*. Paper prepared for the Gates Foundation.
ESU. (2016). *Speaking Frankly: The Case for Oracy in the Curriculum*. London, English Speaking Union.
First Steps. (2013). Speaking and Listening Resource Book FIRST005 | Speaking and Listening Resource Book. Department of Education, WA.
Harris, J., Golinkoff, R. M., & Hirsh-Pasek, K. (2009). Lessons from the Crib for the Classroom: How Children Really Learn Vocabulary. In S. B. Neuman & D. K. Dickinson (Eds.), *Handbook of Early Literacy Research*, New York: Guilford Press.
Hart, B., & Risley, T. R. (1995). *Meaningful Differences in the Everyday Experience of Young American Children*. Baltimore, MD: Paul H Brookes Publishing.
LET's Stand. (2018). http://www.letsstand.ie/
Maddux, J. E. (2012). Self-efficacy: The Power of Believing You Can. In C. R. Snyder, & S. J. Lopez, (Eds.), *Handbook of Positive Psychology* (pp. 227-287). New York: Oxford University Press.
McAlinden, A. (2012). An Inconvenient Truth: Barriers to Truth Recovery in the Aftermath of Institutional Child Abuse in Ireland. Legal Studies: *The Journal of the Society of Legal Scholars*, 13(2), 189-214.
McCroskey, J. C. (1970). Measures of Communication-Bound Anxiety. *Speech Monographs*, 37, 269-277.
McCroskey, J. C, Anderson, J. F., Richmond, V. P., & Wheeless, L. R. (1981). Communication Apprehension of Elementary and Secondary Students and Teachers, *Communication Education*, 30, 122-132.
Mercer & Mannion. (2018). *Oracy across the Welsh Curriculum. A Research-Based Review: Key Principles and Recommendations for Teachers*. EAS, Education Achievement Service for South East Wales.

Merriam Webster. (2005). The Merriam-Webster Dictionary, Merriam-Webster Incorporated, Library of Congress Cataloging in Publication Data.

Miller, G. A., & Gildea, P. M. (1987). *How Children Learn Words*. Scientific American.

NCCA. (2019). Primary Language Curriculum.

NCCA. (2023). Primary Curriculum Framework.

NELP. (2008). National Early Literacy Panel 2008, Developing Early Literacy: A Scientific Synthesis of Early Literacy Development and Implications for Intervention.

OAPPG. (2021). The Oracy All Party Parliamentary Group 'Speak for Change' Inquiry Report.

Pearson, J. C, DeWitt, L., Child, J. T., Kahl, D. H., & Dandamudi, V. (2007). Facing the Fear: An Analysis of Speech-Anxiety Content in Public-Speaking Textbooks. *Communication Research Reports*, 24, 159-168.

Pearson & Gallagher. (1983). *The Gradual Release of Responsibility in Literacy Research and Practice*. Literacy Research, Practice And Evaluation, Volume 10.

Pouteaux, K., & Berg, E. (2013). Literature Review on Public Speaking: Public Speaking as a form of Literacy.

Reason & Bradbury (2008). *The SAGE Handbook of Action Research: Participative Inquiry and Practice*. Published by SAGE.

Salim, S. S., & Joy, E. I. (2016). Public Speaking Skills. In *Training Manual on Theeranaipunya - Equipping Fisherwomen Youth for Future*. ICAR-Central Marine Fisheries Research Institute, Kochi, 129-132.

Shafer, S. (2010). Building Public Speaking Skills across the Curriculum. *The International Journal of Learning*, 17, 2.

United Nations. (1989). United Nations Convention on the Rights of the Child.

5 Why Public Speaking in Primary School

My interest in the topic of public speaking in primary school was sparked by my direct experience in the primary school classroom over many years: as a school leader, a teacher, a parent and also my own personal experience of public speaking growing up. I experienced first-hand that "talk is arguably the true foundation of learning" mediating "the cognitive and cultural spaces between adult and child" (Alexander, 2008, p. 93). Constantly hearing that communication skills are regarded as one of a vital set of 21st-century skills and acutely aware of how "oral language permeates every facet of the primary school curriculum" (PDST, 2013), as well as considering the many occasions on which public skills are necessary throughout life, I had often wondered if we were missing something or covering everything we could or should during these formative years of children's lives. Was I really helping to prepare my children and students for the 21st century they were living and rushing into? Was I equipping them with relevant skills, I knew would benefit them in their lives as children and in their futures? Speaking to parents whose children had grown, gone on through the education system and into the world, I very often heard them say that what concerned them about schooling was the over emphasis on information their children didn't need, while skills their children clearly needed weren't taught in primary school, when they might have found it easiest to learn them. Public speaking skill was mentioned as one of these skills.

More than just a necessary skill-set

To survive and thrive in today's world, requisite skills and knowledge have changed. We are faced with the need to teach communication skills that most children in previous generations may have acquired quite naturally through extended periods of time playing outside, interacting with more siblings, and negotiating their way more freely through their local surroundings. I know that was my experience of childhood. I had to communicate to survive and get what I needed. It happened naturally and I loved it. We were constantly involved in conversation, explanation, storytelling, collaboration and negotiation, as a natural part of our outdoor and childhood play experiences.

Primary school may be the most ideal environment in which to begin public speaking skills. The youngest children appear to really enjoy being the centre of attention and love talking. So much so that they may often risk being told to 'stop talking' in the classroom setting to ensure that everyone, including the teacher, gets a fair chance to be heard. School naturally provides many opportunities for social interactions and with an already present audience, has the potential to create a safe, supportive environment in which the skills, once learned, can be frequently practised with feedback provided in a positive, purposeful way. With a broad and balanced curriculum, public speaking is a skill that can be used to present thoughts, ideas, and new learning from various areas across the curriculum. Already, "each and every day youngsters—as well as adults—must face the prospect of talking in a public forum of some type. The question is whether one will be adequately prepared for the rigors of this fact of life" (Anderson, 1997, p. 5).

There is considerable evidence from researchers, educational practitioners and politicians to argue for the value of training students in the skills of public presentation and debate (ESU, 2016). "Speech and oracy are too often treated by schools as being the preserve of the most able" (Millard & Menzies, 2016, p. 98). It is imperative that children learn to effectively communicate with a wide variety of audiences in different situations. Anderson (1997) suggests that learning to speak in public is every bit as important as learning to read, learning to write, and learning to compute. Public speaking is a valuable skill that can benefit students in many ways, and starting early can provide a strong foundation for students' future academic and professional success. Students who can confidently and effectively speak in front of others are better equipped to connect with others, ask questions, give presentations, participate in debates, deliver speeches and put themselves forward for certain opportunities. As students move through formal education and into their careers, these skills will become increasingly more important and perhaps less easy to learn as an associated fear and anxiety may have started to develop.

Aims of primary school education

The aims of primary school education in Ireland have long been to enable the child

> to live a full life as a child and to realise his or her potential as a unique individual, to enable the child to develop as a social being through living and co-operating with others, to contribute to the good of society and to prepare the child for a continuum of learning.
>
> (Curaclam na Bunscoile, 1971)

The National Council for Curriculum and Assessment (NCCA) further elaborates that "the Irish primary education system aims to provide a holistic education to enable children to live their lives to the full and to realise their potential as unique individuals" (NCCA, 2017). Most recently, the NCCA Primary Curriculum Framework (NCCA, 2023) recognizes that "education plays a pivotal role in contributing to a democratic, equitable, and just Irish society" (p. 4). The Framework acknowledges the experience of children "in primary schools and special schools as a time of 'being' and 'becoming'—both celebrating children's current childhood experiences, and looking to their futures and what might be" (NCCA, 2023, p. 4). A stated part of the communication priority is "Child's Voice", enabling children to find their voices and providing and creating opportunities for children to share thoughts and feelings in a respectful, caring manner (p. 16), as well as the need to "give children opportunities to develop a sense of power and agency". When we truly reflect on these aims, we will see that proficient speaking and communication skills must surely have a role to play in enabling and empowering children to equitably benefit from these aims.

Donaldson (2015), writing about the Welsh school curriculum, explains that curriculum must equip all young people with the knowledge, skills and dispositions for future challenges, developing as "ethical, informed citizens of their own country and the world and healthy, confident individuals, ready to lead fulfilling lives as valued members of society" (p. 29). School time, he advises, must be used judiciously and productively to help each child "grow as a capable, healthy, well-rounded individual who can thrive in the face of unknown future challenges" (p. 5). Inherent in this is being able to communicate effectively, explain ideas, concepts, emotions, evaluate and use evidence in forming views, engage with contemporary issues based on knowledge and values, listen, and understand and exercise human and democratic responsibilities and rights.

Formal and informal nature of public speaking

Hewitt and Inghilleri (1993) comment on the concern that children may be asked to "present as little adults" (p. 319). This need not be the case. Alexander (2003) explained how the National Curriculum in the UK promoted a conception of orality aligned with the 19th- and early 20th-century tradition that emphasises "the aesthetics of oral performance" through "the recitation and the performance of dramatic or poetic texts" (p. 59). Hewitt and Inghilleri (1993) also reference "the discursive tradition emphasising logic of argument and clarity of expression" (p. 319). However, all public speaking is not and does not have to be this formal. The relatively informal style of TED Talks of recent years, online speeches featuring 'ideas worth spreading', some of which are performed by children and young people from across the world, has in many ways, contradicted the historically formal nature of speeches which has made speech writing and presentation more achievable, understandable and attainable for all.

Public speaking skills on the primary school curriculum

There appears to be a paucity of literature on public speaking instruction for primary school students. The difficulty in finding literature specific to public speaking in primary school confirmed to me the need for further research. Scholars in fields such as communication studies, psychology, rhetoric and speech science have researched public speaking competence (Backlund & Morreale, 2015). The idea of teaching public speaking skills itself is not new. Historically, in the 4th century BC, Aristotle set out procedures for understanding and teaching rhetoric in 'The Art of Rhetoric'. What may be a relatively newer concept or idea is access to this skill set training for all and at a younger age through the public-school system.

What is the current context in relation to public speaking in primary school? Cregan (2010) asserts that a focus on oral language development is manifest in policy documents of education systems worldwide (p. 5). Cregan (2010) further recommends that oral language should "feature significantly and consistently at all class levels throughout the primary school and most importantly in those school settings which serve children from non-middle-class backgrounds" (p. 19). Anderson (1997) referred to the virtually forgotten "4th R" of primary school education in the US, 'recitation', as perhaps the most overlooked, understated, underrated component of the primary school curriculum of the day. The Oracy All-Party Parliamentary Group (OAPPG) Inquiry Report 'Speak for Change' also confirmed that the fundamental importance of oracy skills continues to be widely underestimated as the Bercow '10 Years On' Report reminds us of their importance: "Speech, language and communication skills are crucial to every person: for brain development in the early years and our attachment to others, for expressing ourselves and understanding others, for thinking and learning, for social interaction and emotional wellbeing" (OAPPG, 2021) in school and beyond. Boyce et al. (2007) also noted that although speaking is an integral part of language, it tends to be a neglected part of the elementary school curriculum in the US.

Alexander (2012), looking at the international context, explains that while talk may be enlisted to support reading and writing, it is less commonly pursued as an educational goal in its own right. He noted then that it was rare to find, outside the teaching of Drama, entirely oral lessons. The 2005 Ofsted report, referring to schools in the UK, states that "too little attention has been given to teaching the full National Curriculum programme of study for speaking and listening and the range of contexts provided for speaking and listening remains too limited". Alexander (2012) wrote to the Secretary of State in the UK to alert him to the implications for oracy in the national curriculum, referring to evidence from over twenty major international studies which confirm that high quality classroom talk raises standards in core subjects.

Recalling that the definition of public speaking I use is "the art of effective communication with an audience" from the Merriam-Webster dictionary, it is clear that "the art of effective communication with an audience" is on primary school curricula in many countries. The skills of public speaking appear to come under the primary school curriculum areas and terms: oral language, oracy, communication skills and speaking and listening though rarely if ever named as 'public speaking skills'. The curriculum in Northern Ireland specifies that students "should be enabled to express thoughts, ideas, feelings and imagination with confidence as in a range of dramatic contexts using verbal and non-verbal language" (CCEA, 2007). It requires that students can show an awareness of audience, include the use of multimedia presentations, talk with people in a variety of formal and informal situations, use appropriate quality of speech and voice, speak audibly varying register according to the purpose and audience, recognise and discuss features of spoken language, including formal and informal language and practise presentational and self-marketing skills (CCEA, 2007). Focusing on the language conventions needed for clear and coherent communication, the Ontario English Curriculum (Ontario, 2007b, p. 4) outlines how children will learn to express world views and realize and communicate artistic vision. It states the need to provide opportunities for students to engage in various "thought-provoking oral activities" which will involve "presenting and defending ideas or debating issues, and offering informal critiques of work produced by their peers" (p. 15).

Closely aligned to skills of public speaking, the content objectives of the 1999 English Curriculum in Ireland for Infants (4-6-year-olds) state that infants should be enabled to talk about past and present, choose appropriate words, experiment with descriptive words to add elaborate detail, develop self-confidence and express their own views, opinions and preferences. It specified that 5th and 6th class students (11-13-year-olds) should be enabled to discuss issues of major concern, listen to a presentation on a particular topic, argue points of view, justify and defend, and try to persuade others to support a particular point of view (NCCA, 1999, p. 53).

In my study, almost half (49.5%) of teachers replied "yes" that public speaking is on the primary school curriculum, 26% said it's not and 24.5% indicated that they didn't know. Much ambiguity seems to exist regarding where exactly it sits in the curriculum. Like oral language, is it a curricular or pedagogical concern or both? Some thought it had relevance across the curriculum with presentation and effective communication skills being beneficial and necessary in group work and presentation work in all curriculum areas. One teacher explained: *"All areas of the curriculum require recall and recount of information, as well as explanation of work, therefore public speaking is easily integrated into all areas."* One teacher pointed out that *"most of the primary school day is a group setting of children interacting and speaking within small groups. How much more confident would they be if equipped with this skill set."*

A few teachers expressed the perception that public speaking is something that is done outside the classroom. Some teachers and parents reported that in their experience, these skills have been taught in many primary schools as an extra-curricular activity or as part of fee-paying Speech and Drama Club lessons and/or self-selecting or selective Debating Clubs. According to Millard and Menzies (2016), there is a genuine risk that "speech and oracy are too often treated by schools as being the preserve of the most able" (p. 98). Shafer (2010) explains that even though the development of public speaking skills "maintains both a cultural and historical presence for mankind" as well as being highly recognized across educational sectors and the industrial marketplace, "in many cases, educators fail to arm (all) students with the essential skills to perform even the most rudimentary public speaking engagement" (Shafer, 2010, Abstract).

The point is that in primary school classrooms across the world, students are required to stand up in front of their peers, answer questions, present their work and feedback on what they have learned. The degree to which they are prepared for this act of standing up and speaking out is unclear. Shafer (2010) expressed the concern that students as young as five years old are often required to speak in public without adequate training. Shafer notes that consequently, in some cases, students learn to connect public speaking experiences with fear and anxiety and this can negatively impact their ability to speak in public later in their lives. As my research found, if students are not supported and facilitated to prepare before these presentations, the risk of a negative long-term impact on the speaker's confidence and the individual's experience of speaking in public is too great. If students are, in fact, being prepared but it's not being called 'public speaking', it's worth reflecting on why the term 'public speaking' is not being used. The problem then could be that students may be covering the skills and teachers teaching them but don't know it and therefore, don't feel empowered! Bringing that conscious and purposeful intention to this activity is important.

Benefits of public speaking skill training in primary school

Many benefits have been observed in relation to public speaking skill training in primary school. By providing opportunities for all children to practise public speaking, teachers can help students develop the confidence, self-efficacy and communication skills necessary to effectively share their opinions and ideas in ways in which others will listen. Some obvious benefits of public speaking training are improved confidence and more competent communication and social skills. Confidence is developed naturally and meaningfully as students learn actively how to effectively express their thoughts and ideas in front of the class. When they gain a certain level of mastery over this, they will also become more comfortable and confident in various other social situations. Furthermore, being able to communicate competently can enhance relationships with peers, parents and teachers (e.g., Hunt et al., 2014).

With direct, explicit instruction combined with multiple opportunities to practise and observe their peers' presentations also, students learn how to articulate their ideas in a concise, coherent and clear manner. Listening skills benefit also. Students learn how to actively listen to others and respond appropriately. It also fosters empathy when students have the opportunity to actively listen to and try to understand the opinions, ideas and stories of others. Having the experience of putting clear intention into their own communication, students are better prepared to understand other's communication efforts and intentions. Through impromptu public speaking activities, they can also practise thinking on their feet and responding to various questions and challenges.

Teaching public speaking skills encourages active participation from students, giving them a voice in the classroom and allowing them a space to express their opinions and ideas. When students have the experience of presenting on a topic, "they understand it deeply and can explain how it relates to themselves as well as to their community" (Baker, 2008). By teaching public speaking skills, primary school teachers can help their students be better prepared to become active citizens, who are engaged in their communities and able to participate in decision-making processes. Children will be enabled and empowered to more articulately advocate for themselves, their families and their communities expressing their thoughts and opinions and having those opinions taken into account in matters that affect them.

Public speaking develops critical thinking skills as it requires students to think critically, question and analyse information, organize and present their thoughts in a clear, coherent and compelling way. Developing critical thinking skills will further empower students to make informed decisions in other areas of their lives. Conflict resolution and behaviour management also benefit when children are more confident and articulate in expressing their views. Whereas unclear communication can exacerbate conflict, clear communication has more potential to bring about resolution. Children are very capable of resolving many conflicts for themselves. Killen and Nucci (1995) found that nursery school children in Japan were well able to resolve most disputes that arose amongst them. It was noted that they skilfully used bargaining and compromise and also often used moral justifications.

Mastering public speeches is acknowledged as a core competence for well-educated students (van Ginkel et al., 2015). Shouldn't all students have access to training in this skill-set? Public speaking has already been integrated into the educational standards of several countries such as Germany (Halbhuber, 2005) and the United States (Common Core State Standards Initiative, 2010). Even primary school children need to give informative public speeches, but Hunt et al. (2014) suggest, and my research confirms, that the promotion of public speaking skills of this age group has long been neglected in research and practice.

Challenges to public speaking skill training in primary school

To effectively engage in public speaking skill instruction, it is important to be mindful of the challenges/barriers that may exist. Fear of public speaking immediately comes to mind. However, it is very important not to assume that all children will have this fear and for teachers to be aware of when and where their own fears are impacting their decisions. My experience has been that many children, especially younger children, are less likely to have this fear. To the contrary, they seem to love the attention and opportunity it brings. Interestingly, it has been said that 'fear of public speaking' is somewhat of a misnomer as it refers less to a fear of actual speaking and more to a fear of being 'the centre of attention'. However, being mindful and aware of the possibility of fear and its debilitating, limiting potential will help teachers put measures in place to address and mitigate it, if need be. Differentiation can play a role here in helping students overcome their fears. Every student's speaking journey will look different, and all students can be facilitated to progress through it at their own rate and stage of readiness with plenty of gentle support, encouragement and positive feedback.

When I asked teachers in my study about the challenges to public speaking training in primary school, the most frequently mentioned by teachers were: *"time"*, *"over-loaded curriculum"*, *"lack of teacher training"* and *"teacher confidence"*. One teacher said, *"most of us were not taught public speaking ourselves"*. It is very rare for teachers to teach something that they were never taught themselves. Suggested also was that *"fostering a love of public speaking can be challenging"* and *"some schools just don't recognise its importance"*. Increased noise level in the class during the group-work and presentation preparation and practise stages was also mentioned as a possible barrier although some teachers in my study said that this wasn't excessive and was similar to any group-work activities. Some teachers questioned the notion of quiet classrooms as optimal learning environments and if quiet classrooms really reflect that all children are learning and engaged. It was mentioned that as the teacher and the students became more familiar with the structure of the explicit public speaking lessons, it became easier to manage the noise level in the class. Students knew when quiet and attention was expected and necessary and when it was time to talk in groups or individually.

Language may also be a potential challenge. All teachers will have some students who are not yet fluent in the language of instruction of the school and therefore, may have difficulty with public speaking activities in that language. If the requirement is that students prepare speeches and presentations in the 'literate' language of the school, teachers may need to provide additional support and accommodations to help all students participate and succeed at a level at which they are making individual progress. However, diverse languages also pose an opportunity. Why not encourage students to present in their own language? This has many additional benefits. The child has a unique opportunity to use their own language proudly and purposefully for a period of time, they may engage their parents in helping them prepare their presentation, they feel through experience that their language, culture and by extension, they themselves are valued. It's also an opportunity for the teacher and the rest of the class to hear another language spoken and to use their understanding of everything they will have learned about non-verbal communication (i.e., body language, eye contact, hand gestures, etc.) to challenge themselves to understand as much of the presentation as possible. Perhaps, a few students in the class who speak the same language could, collaboratively, work on the presentation together.

Some teachers may see different needs and abilities amongst the students as a challenge. Public speaking is an activity to which students can apply their different learning styles and abilities. Students will have different preferences for how they like to prepare their speeches. Some might prefer to write them verbatim, some prefer bullet points, some may record them on a device and some may find sketching their main points on a mind-map most helpful. Public speaking can provide an opportunity to celebrate diversity reinforcing the message that we all have something unique to say and contribute. Even if every child in the class is given the same title for their speech or topic to speak about, when they prepare a speech, they will all come up with something wonderfully different and original.

The ESU (2016, p. 12) list several barriers to oracy teaching including: the lack of currency in the qualifications system, the challenges of assessing oracy and the pressures for schools to deliver other outcomes (Millard & Menzies, 2016) and meet external accountability targets. Other challenges include: teachers' views of the difficulties in managing behaviour in talk-based lessons, anxiety about handing control over to students which talk-based activities can entail (ESU, 2016, p. 56), teacher concern that some children are too shy or disruptive to respond to oracy teaching in a constructive way, insufficient knowledge on the part of the teacher to confidently model and discuss language with students (Millard & Menzies, 2016) and teachers' own confidence in modelling good oracy skills. Millard and Menzies (2016) report a worrying tendency for students' low confidence and ability in oracy to result in teachers avoiding oracy-based activities. Mercer and Mannion (2018) suggest as another possible barrier the fact that talk is ephemeral and difficult to account for in a culture of high accountability. Millard and Menzies (2016) reported that almost one in five teachers state that the frequency with which they initiate talk-based activities is sometimes limited by the fact that their school prioritises students producing written work (p. 61). Teachers interviewed by Millard and Menzies (2016) felt that embedding oracy is about mindset.

Mercer and Wegerif (1999) found that teachers very rarely offer their students explicit guidance in the area of oral contributions and presentations and researchers (Barnes & Todd 1995; Edwards & Mercer, 1987; Mercer & Mannion, 2018) have found that students commonly lack any clear, shared understandings of the purposes of many of the oracy activities they are engaged in and the criteria by which they are judged by teachers, and so are often confused, unfocused and unproductive in their use of language orally. Cregan (2010) found that teacher planning for oral language may not be as explicit and clear as is needed to enhance children's oral language skills effectively (p. 90). Where most teachers expressed confidence about modelling the spoken language they expect their students to use during lessons, Millard and Menzies (2016) consider that 'modelling' can mean different things to different teachers and may conceal a variety of classroom practices.

An analysis of relevant literature and research would suggest that if students are to be trained in oral language skills, "there is a huge need to upskill primary teachers in this area" (Cregan, 2010). Findings in the literature suggest that significant teacher knowledge is required for effective teaching of oral language in school. Seventy percent of teachers responding to my survey indicated that they had never received training in public speaking skills themselves, and 47% indicated that they would feel confident in their ability to train students in these skills. Cregan (2010) found that when teachers were empowered with knowledge about language, the practice of oral language development improved (p. 179). Furthermore, teachers in Cregan's study who had received support in oral language training shared that they were often surprised and even amazed at what children could actually do with language when scaffolded and facilitated in the process and given feedback when they spoke.

Assessment of oral language and public speaking skills is also a possible challenge and concern as, according to Millard and Menzies (2016, p. 5), few schools evaluate the quality of students' verbal contributions in lessons, or communicate with parents about the quality of these contributions. In schools, the impact of standardised testing may also have encouraged less conversational activity. The perception that because a child can speak a language, they can speak it well is also a barrier. "Becoming a native speaker is a rapid and highly efficient process, but becoming a proficient speaker takes a long time" (Berman, 2004, p. 10). Another challenge identified is attaching literacy-based outcomes to oral activities which alters the very nature and the qualitative experience of the oral event (Hibbins, 2016).

Lack of time in the school day and perceived curriculum overload are real barriers to any activity or programme that may be perceived as extra-curricular. Public speaking activities can be time-consuming and may require significant planning, preparation and practise, especially in the initial stages. Addressing the issue of time and curriculum overload, the ESU recommends that the first step in embedding oracy into the classroom is accepting that it already happens, students talk a lot, and teachers can leverage this (ESU, 2016, p. 13). It may be helpful to point out that many of the skills taught and practised under 'oracy' are also skills of public speaking and teachers themselves use many skills of public speaking very effectively in their classrooms every day, as noted by teachers interviewed in my study. What if public speaking is not extra-curricular? What if, in fact, it has the potential to cover, reinforce and integrate with a lot of current curriculum content? Once the skills are explicitly taught, it can be used as a cross-curricular methodology. It's worth remembering also that while public speaking skill training can be challenging, especially in the initial stages, it can also be fun, enjoyable and extremely beneficial on many levels.

You will have noticed, that for some of the challenges mentioned above, there is a solution and not only that, but a potential learning opportunity too. Some solutions found to support teachers to move beyond these challenges include: a supportive school ethos that values and endorses talking in lessons, gathering different forms of evidence for assessment and progression purposes, from a variety of assessment methods including video footage, photographs and diary logs, setting or co-creating ground rules for talk with students and explaining clearly why talk-based activities are important (Millard & Menzies, 2016). Before we require any of our students to engage in a public speaking activity, **I want to highlight and underline the vital importance of spending time on the groundwork,** on creating a safe, supportive environment in the classroom and supporting all children in their preparation to speak.

Anderson (1997) emphasizes that the acquisition of public speaking skills cannot be left to chance. He stresses that it is crucial that we approach this topic in an organized, coherent and non-haphazard way. Millard and Menzies (2016, p. 6) comment that what is needed is a shift in mindset so that teachers and schools truly believe that oracy forms an integral part of teaching and learning. A very important point is that, as stated previously in this chapter, in primary school classrooms across the world, we are already requiring our students to speak in public in our classrooms. It is the degree to which they are prepared for these occasions and opportunities that is unclear. Anderson (1997) insists that children must ultimately learn to be prepared to "volunteer" for periodic public speaking challenges as well as to feel comfortable when asked to recite in a non-volunteer capacity (i.e., when the teacher randomly calls on a student who did not have their hand up). All children will ultimately benefit and prosper if they are able to handle the anxiety of speaking in public and progress their public speaking skills and competency.

This might come as a shock to some adults who have experienced a debilitating fear of public speaking throughout their lives but teaching public speaking skills to primary school children can actually be a fun, playful, and engaging way to help them develop important communication, oral language and critical thinking abilities. I know because I've done it and not only that, I've observed other teachers do it too. Children's individual, authentic personalities begin to emerge as they get more comfortable and confident presenting. Knowing that some children get the opportunity, support and encouragement to develop and practise their public speaking skills and others don't obviously places those who don't at a disadvantage both in terms of learning to speak confidently and authoritatively in public and also, in terms of equal access to and sharing of positions of power in their future. Children who are particularly shy or inhibited may be at an even greater disadvantage. As Millard and Menzies (2016) point out, there is a worrying tendency for students' low confidence and ability in oracy to result in teachers avoiding oracy-based activities. By learning to express themselves to a wide variety of audiences, in different situations, children become empowered to express their opinions and better prepared to claim their rights as set out in the UNCRC. Furthermore, when you see public speaking in action in the classroom, you realize there's even more at play in the social dynamics and interplay. Students are listening to each other, learning tools and techniques of persuasion, self-awareness, making associations, connections, questioning, demonstrating empathy and self-regulating. Public speaking is about way more than speaking.

Gap between policy and practice

In spite of the acknowledged importance of oral language, available evidence (Alexander, 2012; Cregan, 2010; Mercer & Mannion, 2018) suggests a considerable gap between policy and practice. Cregan (2010) notes that translating the policy which advocates the development of children's oral language skills into effective practice in the classroom has long been challenging and problematic, especially in schools serving disadvantaged contexts in Ireland (p. 5). Alexander (2003) stated that "primary education has long claimed to give high priority to fostering talk for learning, communication and social development" as one in reality where the dynamic and content of oral language "belie the rhetoric of pedagogic and curricular reform" (p. 23) describing oracy as "at best a poor relation" of literacy (p. 24).

Research into the nature of classroom interactions consistently shows that teachers tend to dominate talk situations, and that as a result talk does not support as many opportunities to stretch and challenge students as it could (Smith et al., 2004). Classroom talk very often takes the form of 'IRF', or 'initiation, response and feedback', in which the teacher asks a closed question, receives a short answer, and offers brief praise in return (Howe, 2013). Alexander points out the lack of talk which challenges students to think for themselves, the dominance of closed questions, ubiquitous and unspecific praise rather than constructive feedback to inform future learning, and the rarity of autonomous student-led discussion and problem solving (Alexander, 2003). In spite of their agreement on the importance of oral language development in the school context, Cregan (2008) found that no formal, dedicated, targeted, focused oral language lessons were taught by teachers in the designated disadvantaged schools that she studied at that time. Alexander (2012) also points out that in England, it is rare to find (outside the teaching of drama) wholly oral lessons. Millard and Menzies (2016) found that in terms of whole-school practices, schools do not consistently provide meaningful opportunities for students to develop oracy outside the classroom apart from inviting students to speak or present as part of assemblies. Only a small proportion of schools studied by Millard and Menzies (2016) engage in practices such as reviewing the quality of teachers' and students' verbal contributions during lesson observations, or communicating with parents about their children's spoken communication in school. Alexander (2011) was clear that the gap between the curriculum as prescribed and enacted can be considerable.

Alexander (2012) asserts that in the UK, it is not policy that has been guiding talk reform but rather it's been led and championed by researchers and teachers with a particular interest in this area and some local authorities and charities, such as Voice 21. Alexander (2012) proposed that talk reform in the UK had become an "intensely political matter" (p. 7) backing up his claim with a commentary on how from 1998, the previous government's National Literacy Strategy focused attention on literacy at the expense of oracy, so much so that when in 2003 the Literacy and Numeracy Strategies were merged as the Primary National Strategy, talk was not mentioned at all in the new strategy's manifesto document, 'Excellence and Enjoyment' (DfES, 2003). The Oracy All Party Parliamentary Group (OAPPG), set up in 2019, investigated the value and current provision of oracy in schools. This group went on to collect and collate the views of teachers and students with regard to the impact of lockdown on children's oral language development stressing the even greater importance of oracy, post-Covid-19-related lockdowns, to support all young people.

In addition to the gap between policy and practice in terms of oral language in primary schools, it has been proposed by Brink and Costigan (2015) that there is a considerable gap between what employers require from their employees and what is being prioritised in schools. In the world beyond school, the reach and impact of public speaking has expanded exponentially thanks to digital technology. Because of technology and various social media platforms, public speakers now have the opportunity to reach, connect with and influence even more people. While public speaking and rhetoric are all around us, as noted by Martin Robinson (ESU, 2016, p. 101), its global reach has never been more possible.

Primary school years as potentially an opportune time to begin public speaking skill training

A substantial amount of research would point to the early years and primary school being the most opportune and important time for oral language training (Shiel et al., 2012) as the quality of children's language experience in the early years can powerfully predict their subsequent educational achievement (Alford, 2016; Hart & Risley, 1995; Shiel et al., 2012). The importance of the early years for development throughout life in general is widely acknowledged, particularly for literacy (Catts et al., 2002; Roulstone et al., 2011). The CBI (2016) advises that there should be a focus on developing students' core skills such as communication skills in the time up to age 14. Shiel et al. (2012) recommend that teachers and caregivers intentionally develop monologue in young children. It is suggested that this can be done meaningfully through activities such as answering open-ended questions, recalling, reporting, retelling stories, events and processes, and describing and giving explanations (Snow, 1990). Niedermeyer and Oliver (1972) also suggest beginning public speaking training in the early years of school when young children are imaginative and eager to perform and language experiences can be fun and meaningful.

Hart and Risley (1995) make the point that children from economically deprived backgrounds are likely to have a more limited repertoire of language when they start school because they are less likely to have had a rich talk experience at home. For many children then, schools may offer students "the only second chance for transcending their destinies; but schools will only do so if they provide explicit instruction in the skills of effective spoken communication" (Mercer & Mannion, 2018, p. 19). Primary school intervention is crucial, especially since we know that apprehension associated with communicating increases at about the age of 10 (McCroskey et al., 1981). Biemiller (2010) advises that our chances of successfully addressing vocabulary differences in school are greatest in the preschool and early primary years.

Mercer and Mannion (2018) suggest that from the first year in school, students should be encouraged to share their thoughts and report on what they have done to the teacher and where possible to their classmates. Children will benefit from sensitive, positive and constructive feedback from their teacher about how well they do this. By the time students are in the later primary years, unless they have specific spoken language difficulties, they can be expected to take responsibility for reporting back from group work. Indeed, students with specific spoken language difficulties can choose from a range of other communication options to also report back to peers. All students should be asked to report back sometimes, rather than the most confident and articulate always being allowed to self-select. Mercer and Mannion (2018) report that from observations at School 21 in London, it is clear that students as young as Year 3 (aged 7-8 years) are capable of presenting 5-10-minute speeches from memory to a hall of adults, using a range of effective rhetorical techniques (p. 48).

Typically, students are more likely to be introduced to public speaking and debating in secondary school than primary school. However, early adolescence is a time of heightened vulnerability and anxiety for many students. Several teachers suggest that students, at secondary, are more likely to feel socially anxious (Millard & Menzies, 2016, p. 58). Therefore, there seems to be reasonable evidence to suggest that waiting until this age may not be most beneficial and may present additional challenges in terms of social anxiety. Shafer (2010, p. 279) reported the following reflection of a high school student:

> my public speaking skills are average and I think this is due to the school system and their lack of required courses for public speaking. . . . It is better to be exposed to public speaking at a younger age rather than have the anxiety build up as you go through school.

Summary reflection on why public speaking in primary school

Teaching public speaking skills and providing lots of opportunities for students to practise is a very obvious way to ensure and promote Article 12 of the UNCRC. In this way teachers are helping and empowering students to fulfil and be better prepared to claim this right in many different ways. Even though my study showed a positive impact of explicit public speaking training for students in primary school especially in terms of enhanced self-efficacy and vocabulary acquisition, the surveys, interviews and literature highlighted some ambiguity about the place of public speaking in primary school. This appears to be, in part, due to the use of various terms to refer to the curriculum area of speaking and listening and perhaps, in part, due to the term 'public speaking' not being explicitly used.

Primary school may be an opportune time and place to begin public speaking skill training as my study shows that students are capable of acquiring and using these skills from the beginning of primary school (5 years old). In addition to enjoying the experience, evidenced through certain children's choice to role play public speaking scenarios during 'free play', teachers noted that it achieves many of the learning outcomes of the Primary Language Curriculum in Ireland especially in relation to exploring and using language. Notably, many younger children did not show signs of fear in relation to this experience. To the contrary, it was reported that some seemed to enjoy the attention they got from a larger group when speaking.

Explicitly teaching public speaking skills and providing multiple opportunities to practise to children from an early age can help students to develop confidence in their communication abilities as well as a sense of agency in their own lives. By giving young students the opportunity to practise speaking in front of others, they can build their self-efficacy, self-esteem, establish rapport and relationships with their peers, and feel that who they are and what they have to say is valued. Empowered with the knowledge and practise of the various skills, students are more likely to actively participate in class discussions, ask questions, and take on leadership roles. They are ready and willing to step up, speak out and have their voice and voices heard. Can we facilitate this and listen?

Reference List

Alexander, R. (2003). *Oracy, Literacy and Pedagogy: International Perspectives*.
Alexander, R. (2008). *Towards Dialogic Teaching: Rethinking Classroom Talk*, Fourth Edition. York: Dialogos UK.
Alexander, R. (ed). (2011). *Children, Their World, Their Education: Final Report and Recommendations of the Cambridge Primary Review*, 305–307. Abingdon, Routledge.
Alexander, R. (2012, February 20). Improving Oracy and Classroom Talk in English Schools Achievements and Challenges. Presentation given at the DfE seminar on Oracy, the National Curriculum and Educational Standards.
Alford, C. (2016). *Where Do Stories Live? Building Oral Language Through Storytelling in an Early Years' Context*. eFellow's Research Paper December, 2016. CORE Education Ltd.
Anderson, L. (1997). *Public Speaking Opportunities for Elementary School Students*.
Backlund, P. M., & Morreale, S. P. (2015). Communication Competence: Historical Synopsis, Definitions, Applications, and Looking to the Future. *Communication Competence*, 11-38.
Baker, L. (2008). Representing: Elementary to the Exhibition of Learning. *Horace, Coalition of Essential Schools*, 23(1).
Barnes, D., & Todd, F. (1995). *Communication and Learning Revisited*. Portsmouth, NH, Heinemann.

Bearne, E., Dombey, H., & Grainger, T. (Eds). (2003). *Classroom Interactions in Literacy*. Open University Press, 23–35.

Berman, R. A. (2004). Between Emergence and Mastery. *Language Development across Childhood and Adolescence*, 9–35.

Biemiller, A. (2010). Chapter 3: Teaching Vocabulary in the Primary Grades. *Vocabulary Instruction*.

Boyce, J. S., Alber-Morgan, S. R., & Riley, J. G. (2007). Fearless Public Speaking: Oral Presentation Activities for the Elementary Classroom. *Childhood Education*, 83, 142–150.

Brink, K., & Costigan, R. (2015). Oral Communication Skills: Are the Priorities of the Workplace and AACSB- Accredited Business Programs Aligned? *Academy of Management Learning and Education*, 14(2), 205–221.

Catts, H. W., Fey, M. E., Tomblin, J. B., & Zhang, X. (2002). A Longitudinal Investigation of Reading Outcomes in Children with Language Impairments. *Journal of Speech, Language and Hearing Research*, 45(6), 1142–1157

CBI. (2016). *The Right Combination: CBI/Pearson Education and Skills Survey*. London: CBI.

CCEA. (2007). Northern Ireland Primary Curriculum.

Common Core State Standard Initiative. (2010). Common Core State Standards for English Language Arts & Literacy in History/Social Studies, Science, and Technical Subjects created by The National Governors Association and the Council of Chief State School Officers.

Cregan, A. (2008). From Difference to Disadvantage: 'Talking Posh' Sociolinguistic Perspectives on the Context of Schooling in Ireland. Combat Poverty Agency. Working Paper Services 07/03 ISBN: 978-1-905-48541-1 June 2008

Cregan, A. (2010). *From Policy to Practice. The Oral Language Challenge for Teachers*.

DfES. (2003). *Speaking, Listening, Learning: Working with Children in Key Stages 1 and 2*. London: Department for Education and Skills.

Donaldson, G. (2015). Successful Futures. *Independent Review of Curriculum and Assessment Arrangements in Wales*. Cardiff: Welsh Government.

Edwards, D., & Mercer, N. (1987/2013). *Common Knowledge: The Development of Understanding*. London: Methuen/Routledge.

ESU. (2016). *Speaking Frankly: The Case for Oracy in the Curriculum*. London, English Speaking Union.

Halbhuber, W. (2005). Die Schulstatistik der Kultusministerkonferenz. 14 Migrationshintergrund von Kindern und Jugendlichen: Wege zur Weiterentwicklung der amtlichen Statistik, 67.

Hart, B., & Risley, T. R. (1995). *Meaningful Differences in the Everyday Experience of Young American Children*. Baltimore, MD: Paul H Brookes Publishing.

Hewitt, R., & Inghilleri, M. (1993). Oracy in the Classroom: Policy, Pedagogy, and Group Oral Work. *Anthropology & Education Quarterly*, 24 (4).

Howe, A. (2013) Developing the Talk School: Guidance for Teachers. CfBT Education Trust, 3.

Hunt, S., Wright, A., & Simonds, C. (2014). Securing the Future of Communication Education: Advancing an Advocacy and Research Agenda for the 21st Century. *Communication Education*, 63(4), 449–461.

Killen, M., & Nucci, L. P. (1995). Morality, Autonomy, and Social Conflict. *Morality in Everyday Life: Developmental Perspectives*, 52–86.

McCroskey, J. C, Anderson, J. F., Richmond, V. P., & Wheeless, L. R. (1981). Communication Apprehension of Elementary and Secondary Students and Teachers, *Communication Education*, 30, 122–132.

Mercer & Mannion. (2018). *Oracy across the Welsh Curriculum. A Research-Based Review: Key Principles and Recommendations for Teachers*. EAS, Education Achievement Service for South East Wales.

Millard, W., & Menzies, L. (2016). *Oracy: The State of Speaking in Our Schools*, London: Voice 21.

NCCA. (1999). English Curriculum.

NCCA. (2017). Website – Primary.

NCCA. (2023) Primary Curriculum Framework.

Niedermeyer, C., & Oliver, L. (1972). The Development of Young Children's Dramatic and Public Speaking Skills. *The Elementary School Journal*, 73(2), 95–100. University of Chicago Press.

OAPPG. (2021). The Oracy All Party Parliamentary Group 'Speak for Change' Inquiry Report.

Ofsted. (2005). The Annual Report of Her Majesty's Chief Inspector of Schools 2003/2004, London, The Stationery Office.

Ontario. (2007b). Ontario English Curriculum for Grade 11, 12.

PDST. (2013). *Five Components of Effective Oral Language Instruction*, Professional Development Service for Teachers, Ireland.

Roulstone, S., Law, J., Rush., R., Clegg, J., Pe&ters, T. (2011). *Investigating the Role of Language in Children's Early Educational Outcomes*, Research Report DFE-RR134 (9).

Shafer, S. (2010). Building Public Speaking Skills across the Curriculum. *The International Journal of Learning*, 17, 2.

Shiel, G., Cregan, Á., McGough, & Archer, P. (2012). *Oral Language in Early Childhood and Primary Education (3-8 years)*, NCCA Research Report No. 14.

Smith, F., Hardman, F., Wall, K., & Mroz, M. (2004). Interactive Whole Class Teaching in the National Literacy and Numeracy Strategies, *British Educational Research Journal*, 30(3), 395-411 (408).

Snow, C. E. (1990). Development of Definitional Skill. *Journal of Child Language*, 17(3), 697-710.

Van Ginkel, S., Gulikers, J., Biemans, H., & Mulder, M. (2015). Towards a Set of Design Principles for Developing Oral Presentation Competence: A Synthesis of Research in Higher Education. *Educational Research Review*, 14, 62-80.

6 What Public Speaking in Primary School Looks Like

Now that we've established why it's beneficial and makes sense to begin public speaking training in primary school, we'll take a closer look at what this might look like in practice. What are the skills involved and where does it sit on the curriculum? I'll refer mainly to the Irish primary school language curriculum as it's that which I have worked with more closely over the last few years. This curriculum is evidence-based in research and best practice from across the world and therefore, is likely to have much in common with other country's language curricula.

Implementing public speaking in primary schools

To assist in the advancement of public speaking skills, some states in the US developed knowledge and skill requirements in language arts that include competencies in public speaking and presentations for students in the 4th and 5th grades (9-11 years old) (Combes et al., 2008). The common core standards specified in the literacy standards (Common Core State Standard Initiative, 2010), defining what all students are expected to know and be able to do, aim to prepare students for life outside the classroom, in college, future careers and life beyond formal education. Putting forward a vision of what it means to be literate, prepared for success in the 21st century, standards outlined include: presentation of knowledge and ideas, constructing effective arguments, describing, speaking audibly and at an appropriate pace, expressing thoughts, feelings and ideas clearly, telling a story, recounting an experience, reporting on a topic, requesting clarification, asking questions, discerning a speaker's main points, building on others' ideas, articulating own ideas, adapting communication in relation to audience and task purpose, differentiating between contexts that require formal English and informal discourse, using visual displays and multimedia aids, understanding others' perspectives and cultures and evaluating other points of view critically and constructively.

The most commonly used public speaking tasks in primary or elementary schools in the US were found to be narrating and informing (Common Core State Standards Initiative, 2010; Pabst-Weinschenk, 2005). Giving a narration is already quite familiar to primary school children. The task of giving informative speeches was found to be rather new for elementary school children. Newcomb (1999) encouraged schools to do more to build public speaking skills, explaining that speaking in groups helps students in many ways, including overcoming shyness, testing ideas with peers, and thinking on their feet.

Achieving the oral language learning outcomes of primary language curricula through public speaking

A public speaking approach can meaningfully achieve many of the oral language learning outcomes of the Irish Primary Language Curriculum (PLC) that come under the three elements of oral language; communication, understanding, exploring and using. One progression step (NCCA, 2019, p. 51) identifies how students will "use language with confidence to work collaboratively with others and share the outcomes with familiar and unfamiliar audiences". While the main outcome of a public speaking lesson or series of lessons may be for a student to present, to speak clearly, confidently and competently, the process, preparation and practise involves other students in the classroom at various levels developing at the same time the complimentary, reciprocal skills of listening and evaluating. Thereby, in the classroom context, due attention can be paid to the three important elements of rhetoric Aristotle referred to: the speaker, the speech and the audience. For the presentations phase of the lessons, while one student presents, other students have the opportunity to engage in active purposeful listening and peer evaluation while waiting their turn to speak.

Aspects of public speaking could come under, for example, all three elements of the PLC in Ireland: 'Communicating', 'Understanding' and 'Exploring and Using Language'. It may initially appear more obvious that it might come under 'Exploring and Using language', which prioritises the development of children's ability to explore and use language for a wide range of purposes, in a variety of genres and with a range of audiences, familiar and unfamiliar. Through exploring and using language, the aim is that children's developing sense of voice is nurtured. Speaking activities such as retelling, elaborating, playful and creative use of language, description, explanation and justification are specified. Under the element 'Understanding': "the child's listening and oral comprehension skills are given expression" (NCCA, 2019, p. 33).

The 'Communicating' element focuses on developing children's knowledge and understanding of how we build and share meaning together in communicative relationships, "as listeners and speakers, and as givers and receivers of information" (NCCA, 2019, p. 33), while at the same time, enabling children to develop their own communicative competence. 'Communicating' also includes an awareness of others and social conventions of language use, both of which are central aspects of public speaking. Under the 'Progression Milestones' (p. 58), one milestone specified is: "uses figurative language so that an oral text has particular impact on a listener". Another describes how a student "shows increasing independence in presenting to class on topics, using appropriate manner and topic-specific language". Yet another refers to "provides and justifies opinion about an event".

With reference to the initial oral language emphasis of the PLC, an information leaflet for parents issued by NCCA (2019) informed them that "over the coming years, your child will do lots of talking in class sharing what they think and feel". It further explained to parents that their children would be "helped to learn to talk" as well as having "lots of opportunities to talk in class, give their opinion and express their thoughts and ideas". The PLC also places an emphasis on the transfer of skills across languages. Public speaking is a skill that transfers very obviously and meaningfully.

The PLC specifies developing competencies and skills. These skills are listed in an Appendix on pages 62–64 of the PLC (NCCA, 2019). Skills listed that may be particularly applicable to public speaking are: articulation skills, vocabulary development, joint attention to topic and intentional communication of meaning; intentionality, eye contact, gesture, body language, extra-linguistic skills; audibility, intonation, pitch, pause, emphasis, pace, paralinguistic skills; alertness and responsiveness to others' needs in order to maximise effective communication and awareness of others. Also listed under skills are: creating and understanding narrative text, recount, retell, composing stories and personal narratives, creating and understanding expository text and factual accounts, explanations, descriptions, arguments, using language to ask questions, make requests, express preferences and opinions, narrate, explore, argue, predict, reason about and justify decisions, explanations and outcomes, using language to present information to different audiences.

It is further detailed that many opportunities for children to practise the functions of language are provided through both 'Formal Talk Contexts' and 'Informal Talk Contexts'. Some examples given of 'Formal Talk Contexts' are: debate, dramatic presentations, introducing, thanking, morning news, report, retelling and storytelling. 'Informal Talk Contexts' includes: class discussions, collaborative problem-solving and joint text (oral or written) construction. Notably, although all of these contexts involve speaking in front of others, there is, again, no mention of the term 'public speaking'. If 'public speaking' was named explicitly, I believe it may serve to highlight the clear empowering intention of public speaking training as well as the power of language and communication. It might also help to demystify the skills involved in public speaking, making them more accessible and achievable for all. Public speaking is mentioned and explicitly referred to in the supports' toolkit section of the PLC under 'A Structured Approach to Public Speaking for Children'.

There are many other areas across the primary school curriculum where outcomes related to public speaking skill acquisition are referred to, though notably the term 'public speaking' is, again, not used explicitly. The Social, Personal, Health Education (SPHE) Curriculum of 1999 (NCCA, 1999a) in Ireland explains how SPHE "enables the child to build a sense of self-efficacy" and helps "children to acquire a range of communication skills" (p. 3). Furthermore, it is stated that children "are given opportunities to learn and practise a wide range of communication skills" (p. 5). Also noted is that "children should become aware of the power and the influence of language" (p. 9) developing "in the child a sense of social responsibility, a commitment to active and participative citizenship" and "an appreciation of the democratic way of life" (p. 9). This curriculum area also refers explicitly to "the ability to listen and respond to the opinions and views of others and use verbal and non-verbal behaviour to perform social functions: such as introducing others, expressing thanks, making requests" (p. 21).

Current practice in primary schools

In terms of current practice, even though 70% of teachers who responded to my study survey, replied that they had never received training in public speaking skills, 78% reported that they do teach these skills to their students. These teachers shared that they teach public speaking skills under the following areas which are listed in order of most frequently mentioned:

What Public Speaking in Primary School Looks Like 79

oral language and oral reports (in English and/or cross-curricular), English, Drama, Social, Environmental and Science Education (SESE), Social and Personal Health Education (SPHE), Debating teams, Cross-curricular and even Maths. Certain informal and organically occurring opportunities in school life were also mentioned such as *"readings at Mass", "children presenting at School Assembly", "speaking during philosophical discussions", "presenting as part of project-based learning", "Junior Entrepreneur Programme", "communicating with others", "in infant classes, 'My News' and 'Show and Tell'"* and also *"expressing opinions about a topic to peers and adults informally"*. Public speaking has relevance to other areas of the curriculum, according to 92%. One teacher explained that she had covered it in many subjects, English, Irish, Maths (explaining and justifying a strategy) and SESE. She cautioned that in her opinion, *"it shouldn't be viewed narrowly as how to participate in a specific 'public speaking' exercise"*. Another teacher stated that she encourages children *"to make presentations and I give guidance on eye-contact, pitch etc but I don't specifically teach it"*.

In relation to how much time is spent per week on public speaking skill training, 17% of teacher respondents reported spending 30-40 minutes, 12.5% said 1 hour, 20% said it is integrated across other areas of the curriculum and another 12.5% reported that they spend no time on explicit public speaking skill training. The remaining respondents spend less than 30 minutes per week on public speaking training apart from 2, one of whom reported spending 3 hours per week on these skills and one, 2 hours. One teacher clarified that she spends no time on specific 'public speaking skills' but she said, *"effective oral communication ... is ongoing throughout every subject area"* and another commented that it is *"interwoven within subjects but not explicitly taught"*. Another said that it's given *"no discrete time"*. Two teachers shared that they focus on it for longer in the weeks before a debating competition. School 21, a pioneering school in Stratford, East London has developed, in collaboration with the University of Cambridge, practical methods for teaching a range of oracy skills including public speaking. Students as young as Year 3 (aged 7-8 years) present 5-10-minute speeches from memory to a hall of adults, using a range of effective rhetorical techniques (Mercer & Mannion, 2018, p. 48).

The PLC (NCCA, 2019) in an even more child-centred way moves from curriculum objectives of previous curricula to learning outcomes providing content and experiences that enable all students to develop competence and confidence in using oral language to: become fluent and explicit in communicating ideas and experiences; explore and develop ideas and concepts through talk; identify and evaluate the key points, issues and central meaning of a text or oral presentation and organise efficiently the information gained; justify and defend opinions and present a coherent argument; use oral language to manipulate images in problem-solving; express intuitions, feelings, impressions, ideas and reactions in response to real and imaginary situations through talk and discussion; organise, clarify, interpret and extend experiences through oral language activity; explore and express reactions to poetry, fiction and the arts, refine aesthetic responses through oral language activity; create, develop and sustain imaginary situations through talk, discussion and improvisational drama; compose, relate their own stories and poems; explore, experiment with and enjoy all the playful aspects of language (p. 18).

Other planned for and desired outcomes are that the child should be enabled to: talk about past and present experiences, and plan, predict and speculate about future and imaginary experiences; choose appropriate words to name and describe things and events; experiment with descriptive words to add elaborative detail; combine simple sentences through the use of connecting words; initiate and sustain a conversation on a particular topic; use language to perform common social functions such as introducing oneself and others; greeting others and saying goodbye; giving and receiving messages and expressing concern and appreciation. Also stated on the curriculum is that students become increasingly more aware of the importance of gesture, facial expression, tone of voice, audibility and clarity of enunciation in communicating with others. Furthermore, the child will be enabled to: give and take turns in speaking and experience a classroom environment in which tolerance for the views of others is fostered; initiate conversations; present ideas that are relevant to the subject in a logical sequence; summarise and prioritise ideas; and also discuss and react to local storytellers.

What can be taught in public speaking

First Steps (2013) outlines the following requirements for students to speak and listen effectively for various purposes and to various audiences: an awareness that speakers and listeners make critical decisions when composing and comprehending spoken texts; speakers adjust their speech as they identify with different groups; speakers' and listeners' consideration of different points of view can confirm, broaden or challenge an existing view; the social and cultural background of language users will influence their speaking and listening choices, and speakers consciously select and use linguistic, and rhetorical devices to enhance impact, or to influence particular audiences (p. 102). First Steps (2013) also offers guidance on the teaching of figurative language such as euphemisms, hyperbole, idioms, imagery, metaphor, personification, proverbs and rhetorical questions (p. 102) and prosodic features of language such as pitch, volume, tempo and rhythm (p. 115), repetition, similes and the use of slang (p. 116), all of which play a part in effective, competent public speaking.

In the Irish primary language curriculum context, a variety of speaking genres are taught and practised, as outlined by the PDST (2013). These include: oral reports, storytelling and anecdotes, arguments and informal/formal debates, giving instructions/procedures, partner and small group work, questioning, interviews and conversations. Within this, consideration is given to the many different social contexts of language (formal and informal, familiar and unfamiliar). It is noted that over the course of their time in primary school, the child's oral language should show greater complexity and sophistication as they perform social functions. As specified in the Northern Irish primary school curriculum, students begin to "express themselves with increasing clarity and confidence, using a growing vocabulary and more complex sentence structure" (CCEA, 2007).

As they progress through the primary school, what children will be enabled to do, for example at 5th and 6th class level (age 11-12), requires progressively and incrementally more oral language sophistication. They will be enabled to: discuss issues of major concern; discuss ideas and concepts encountered in other areas of the curriculum; use a discussion of the familiar as the basis of a more formal or objective grasp of a topic or concept; listen to a presentation on a particular topic, decide through discussion which are the most appropriate questions to ask, and then prioritise them; argue points of view from the perspective of agreement and disagreement through informal discussion and in the context of formal debates; justify and defend particular opinions or attitudes and try to persuade others to support a particular point of view; respond to arguments presented by the teacher; discuss the value, truth or relevance of popular ideas, causes and proverbs and also, explore and express conflicts of opinion and historical contexts through improvisational drama.

In terms of public speaking, Martin Robinson (ESU, 2016, p. 101) highlights developing empathy towards other points of view as well as the ability to argue eloquently (p. 102). First Steps (2013) explains how students learn from one another and get to try out their ideas before making them public. The benefits of this technique are increased time on-task and higher-quality contributions to class discussions (p. 169). Specific strategies for planning for formal talks include: determining the purpose of the presentation, deciding on the message, choosing how to present the information, brainstorming and researching, forming the ideas into a plan, anticipating audience questions (and reaction), choosing appropriate vocabulary and determining how the words are going to be said and if any visual aids or notes will be needed (p. 179). It is important to support students by explicitly teaching them the required steps (p. 180). It's also important to ensure that individual students have significant speaking experiences that are commensurate with their abilities sensitive to the 'comfort level' of all students while allowing them to make consistent progress.

Boyce et al. (2007) provide reassurance that confident public speaking can be cultivated by teachers in primary school through engaging students in initial non-threatening activities followed by incrementally more complex challenges across the school year. There are many playful and engaging ways, we can initially engage our students in public speaking activities. Many of these, you may already be using in your classrooms. They include:

- My News: My news is an activity many of us will remember from our childhood where a few children are selected to tell a few items of their news to the whole class. To ensure that more children's voices are heard, children might be facilitated and given a set time to share their news orally in pairs or in small groups. Extending this speaking activity to the home environment, parents can engage their children in conversation asking, for example, what their favourite/least favourite part of their day was, what news they shared or what they learned/discovered from the news shared by their classmates.
- Show and Tell: Show and tell is a classic activity that can help to develop public speaking skills. Students bring an object from home that shows or symbolizes something they are passionate about. They give a short presentation about it to the class. Children benefit from sharing what's special to them and having their interests heard and valued and the teacher and others will gain from getting an insight into something that each student enjoys. Again, to give even more children the opportunity to have their voices heard, one part of 'Show and Tell' could be conducted in pairs or small groups where the students take turns speaking and listening.
- Debate: Debates are, of course, an effective way to practise oral language and critical thinking skills. A wide variety of topics from across the curriculum or of local interest could be selected. Students have the opportunity to more deeply explore and research these topics and prepare arguments for each side. However, I would caution that it is not

advisable to use debate as a first experience of or an introduction to public speaking for all students. While most people may have to engage in public speaking at some stage in their lives, debating is not for everybody.
- Role-play: Role-playing different scenarios can be an engaging way for students to practise public speaking skills. Scenarios such as: accepting or presenting an award, giving a speech, interviewing for a job, giving a eulogy for your pet or a character from History, being a news reporter, being a contestant or a judge on a TV programme such as Master Chef or making a pitch for a new creation. These scenarios help students develop the ability to think on their feet and respond to challenges.
- Public Speaking Games: There are many games that can be used to practise public speaking skills in a playful, creative way, engaging students' imaginations. For example, "Storyteller" is a game where students take turns telling a story, with each student continuing the story where the last person left off. This activity requires that students listen carefully to one another and think on their feet.
- Provide multiple opportunities for children to share and tell their own stories. These stories can be factual or fictitious.
- Practise and rehearsal of speeches, parts of speeches, phrases and words is key. Students can be encouraged to practise their presentations with a friend, parent or relative, practising emphasis and pronunciation of difficult words. Exaggerating pronunciation or emphasis when practising will aid memory. It also contributes to the fun element. Students could practise in a happy voice, sad voice, surprised voice etc. They can also play around with and have fun with facial expressions, body language, hand gestures and eye contact. It's helpful for children to memorize some of the speech, for example the opening or the closing as this may help them relax and interact more freely with the audience.
- Scaffold children to give and receive feedback and also to apply feedback to their speeches and presentation so that they learn to embrace constructive feedback in a positive way.
- Together, analyse, evaluate and discuss historical and contemporary speeches or excerpts from them, which are freely available on YouTube including TEDx speeches. There are even some delivered by other children and teenagers from around the world.

When you begin to look for public speaking opportunities and activities, you will be amazed how many you will find in the course of your day.

I mentioned before how the activity of public speaking can work well across the whole curriculum with the content of the various curriculum areas providing plenty of material to speak about once specified skills of public speaking have been explicitly taught. Teachers participating in my study found it necessary to distinguish between the explicit teaching of skills and activities that provide opportunities to practise public speaking. Providing the latter without the former is akin to playing matches of a particular sport without having training and skill building sessions. Not only is it not advisable to provide the opportunities for speaking in front of groups without related training, findings from my study's survey responses revealed that for some adults, their life-long fear of public speaking was linked to an initial negative, unprepared-for experience of public speaking as a child. Explicit teaching and training are required.

Explicit teaching of public speaking skills

Whereas engaging in various public speaking activities may lead to a more confident disposition for some, specific skills have to be taught, learned and practised to ensure that all children get equal access to this skill training. If left to chance, some children and students (few) will progress in the development of these skills, in part due to encouragement they may be receiving from home and opportunities that are being provided elsewhere. It's important to explicitly explain and discuss unspoken and broad rules for communication in terms of socially acceptable speaker and audience behaviours as well as respectful interactions and turn-taking. It's not okay to assume that all children will already have a similar level of understanding or experience in relation to this. In my experience, we can assume very little when it comes to children's communication skills.

So, under what area of the curriculum, does the explicit teaching of public speaking take place? There are three main areas identified in Irish primary schools where oral language development can occur: oral language across the curriculum, oral language in literacy and discrete oral language. In my opinion, this is the same for public speaking. Discrete oral language time refers to a timetabled class, taken out of the suggested weekly time allocated for language during which "specific oral language skills are taught and practised" (NCCA, 1999c, p. 70). Following explicit instruction, "children's language learning is increased through opportunities to produce language orally, non-verbally and in writing, in meaningful contexts, throughout the school day" (NCCA, 2019, p. 35; Ó Duibhir & Cummins, 2012, pp. 37-58). Speaking and listening skills that can be taught explicitly include: use of voice (volume, tone, pitch, stress, pronunciation, pace and pause), use of body (body language, hand gestures, eye contact, proximity), use of props and visual aids including but not limited to technology, language features, different genres of public speaking including argument and debate and oral reports.

Assessment of public speaking and oral language skills

Assessment is an important necessary element of primary school curricula to enable progress to be measured and next steps in learning ascertained. It is "the process of gathering, recording, interpreting, using, and reporting information about a child's progress and achievement in developing knowledge, skills and attitudes" (NCCA, 2007, p. 7). Appropriate and relevant assessment is necessary to progress learning in a particular area. Mercer and Mannion (2018, p. 60) outline three main challenges for the assessment of oracy:

1. the fact that spoken language is ephemeral and does not leave a paper trail
2. restrictions on the number of students that can be assessed at one time
3. the context specificity of speech acts.

In relation to assessment of spoken language, assessment arrangements should give priority to their formative role in teaching and learning (Mercer & Mannion, 2018) using information gathered as 'Assessment for Learning' (AfL) data by the teacher to draw skill profiles of individual students, to plan and develop relevant teaching on the use of spoken language and move all students' learning forward. Not knowing how or if oral language and public speaking skills can be assessed may present as a barrier to oral language and public speaking instruction for some teachers. It may be helpful, therefore, for teachers to know, first and foremost, that oral language and public speaking can be assessed to progress learning and teaching and guidelines are available. It is suggested that oral language/oracy is more likely to be recognised as an important part of the school curriculum if it can be and is assessed (Mercer & Mannion, 2018).

When considering assessment, it's important to be clear on what the purpose of the assessment is? Assessment should help the teacher to further support the child to make progress. Assessment in primary school is ultimately about putting together a picture over time of a child's learning progress, how and what the child is learning. The teacher gathers information and evidence through whatever means possible and relevant. This information helps to show what the child has already achieved, is managing well and where additional support may be needed. It helps to signpost and inform the next steps in the child's learning. The Primary Language Curriculum (PLC) in Ireland, through its learning outcomes, describes the expected language learning and development for primary school children at the end of a period of time. 'Progression continua' are provided as supports to help teachers plan for children's progress in their language learning, assisting them to identify where the child is at and suggesting possible next steps.

The Assessment of Performance Unit (APU) in the UK demonstrated that it is possible to carry out reasonably robust and valid assessments of oracy (APU, 1985). Oracy Australia provides oracy assessments in which the tasks of oral presentation, reading aloud, memorised oral interpretation of literature, and listening and responding are rated (Education Department of Western Australia, 1997). In Ireland, some of the guidance on oral language assessment advises that oral language ability can be measured in terms of the success with which the child is able to listen, talk about experiences, present ideas, give and take turns, initiate and conclude conversations, and perform social functions using language. Listening and talking skills are included in Scotland's Curriculum for Excellence (CfE) as important uses of language skills in everyday life. The Scottish Survey of Literacy, a sample survey measuring national performance in literacy and numeracy, aligned to the Curriculum for Excellence (CfE) levels, included an assessment of Listening and Talking using Group Discussion tasks at ages 8, 11 and 13 (SSLN, 2014). This was the first large scale national assessment of these skills in Scotland. Students were graded within five performance categories assigned to each student performance: performing very well, performing well, performing beyond the level, working within the level and not yet working within the level. Among the findings were that students from the least disadvantaged areas performed better than students from the most disadvantaged areas.

Students' oracy skills (even if informally) can be assessed using the Oracy Skills Framework (Cambridge University, 2014) to identify strengths and establish which sub-skills might need to be developed further in order for students to participate more fully in their learning

(Mercer & Mannion, 2018, p. 15) and make progress. The Cambridge Oracy Assessment includes: the Oracy Skills Framework; a set of oracy tasks, which provide the basis for assessment; and a rating scheme for assessing performance on tasks and giving feedback (Mercer & Mannion, 2018, p. 45). The Oracy Skills Framework subdivides oracy skills into four domains: physical, linguistic, cognitive, emotional and social. The Oracy Assessment Toolkit was created through a partnership between the University of Cambridge and School 21, funded by the Education Endowment Foundation (EEF) and although designed for Year 7 students (10-11-year-olds), Donaldson (2015) explains that it can be easily adapted for use with students, ages 10-14. Further research could possibly investigate if it may be adapted for other age groups also, including younger primary school students.

Rubrics are a helpful and efficient form of assessment which can also be used for peer and self-assessment. Rating scales and descriptive or analytic rubrics are the two main types of rubrics used to assess public speaking performance. Marcotte (2006) suggests that not providing assessment tools like rubrics is unfair to students as when teachers do not explicitly articulate the qualities they are looking for when assessing, learning becomes a hit-or-miss endeavour (p. 3). According to Gschwend (2000), the main purpose of rubrics should be to enrich learning by providing students with specific feedback about the strengths and weaknesses of their performance. Descriptive rubrics "replace the checkboxes of rating scale rubrics with brief descriptions of the performances that merit each possible rating" (Suskie, 2009, p. 142).

The following is an example of the 'LET's Stand' public speaking assessment rubric where twelve different skills within public speaking can be assessed on a scale of 1-5 that indicate the levels of Beginner, Developing, Average, Competent and Very Competent.

Table 6.1

Skill	Beginner	Developing	Average	Competent	Very Competent
Structure	No evidence of sequencing	Beginning, middle or ending clear, but not the rest	Beginning and ending clear, but not enough body	Clear beginning, middle and ending, but transitions from one part to the next unclear	Excellently structured. Beginning, middle and ending, with language to indicate each, e.g. Firstly/In conclusion
Voice	Speaks in a monotone voice	Uses some intonation	Uses some intonation and different expression	Uses loud voice, soft voice, expression and emphasis, but not always appropriately	Uses vocal variety, expression, intonation and emphasis to great effect

(LET's Stand, 2021)

Some studies have examined the reliability of publicly available rubrics used to evaluate public speaking competence (Morreale et al., 2007; Schreiber et al., 2012). The Public Speaking Competence Rubric (PSCR), for example, assesses eleven competencies or dimensions: 1. Topic selection, 2. Introduction, 3. Organization, 4. Supporting materials, 5. Conclusion, 6. Word choice, 7. Vocal expression, 8. Non-verbal behaviour, 9. Adaption to audience, 10. Visual aids and 11. Effectual persuasion (Schreiber et al., 2012, p. 214). The Public Speaking Competence Rubric (PSCR) provides students with a clear description of what is expected in advance of their speech assignment. Teachers can then use the PSCR rubric not only to grade and provide feedback on speech presentation, but also to train students to use the PSCR independently as a means of self and peer evaluation (p. 223).

Other areas that could be included in a rubric are: energy level and enthusiasm, length of presentation and adherence to time limits, pace and transition to different segments and points, use of cue cards or notes (appropriate, helpful or distracting), accuracy and presentation of facts, details and research. Using these lists as a guide, the teacher may exercise their own agency in selecting the areas they wish to focus their assessment on and include these areas in their own teacher-designed checklist or rubric. Morreale et al. (2007) suggest that a speaker is perceived as competent if their public speech is effective and appropriate. A speech is considered effective when the communicational intention is appropriate and observed as achieved and when the speaking behaviour is adequate to the specific context. Other possible assessment methods include conferencing, conversations and interviewing involving teacher-child, peer-to-peer and small groups, whole class portfolios, work samples (e.g., video and voice recordings), concept and mind mapping before/during/after questioning, teacher observation, informal/formal observation notes, teacher designed tasks and tests, listening and speaking checklists (First Steps, 2006) and questionnaires (First Steps, 2013).

With more specific reference to public speaking assessment, Backlund and Morreale (2015) advise that the appraisal of public speaking competence depends on the speaker's actual demonstrated performance within a specific speaking context, which would explain why public speaking competence is not assessed on just the content of the presentation. A Competent Speaker speech evaluation form, designed by Morreale et al. (2007) and a speech evaluation form by Lucas (2007) assess presentational competencies and public speaking performance under detailed specific areas. Speeches require expertise in a number of areas, including researching an idea, crafting the content of the idea, and delivering the idea in a way that is well adapted, dynamic and understandable to the audience. Thomson and Rucker (2002) explain that it is possible that individuals may be proficient in one area (such as delivery dynamism) but lacking in another (such as content craftsmanship). Individuals may be significantly better at presenting than writing the speech or vice versa. While Joe et al. (2015) acknowledge that research on public speaking competence assessment is limited (p. 2), public speeches can be evaluated reliably and validly using evaluation forms as long as the forms address the age-old speech constructs of content and delivery.

Regular, positive, constructive feedback is a vital part of public speaking instruction. A 'feedback loop' helps students polish, progress and refine their efforts. Students can be taught how to self-evaluate, evaluate their peers and embrace constructive feedback in a positive way, receiving it, responding to it and applying it to progress on their speaking journey. Coaching and confidence building are very important. Pointing out a speaker's unique strengths to them gives them a strong foundation to build on. The efforts of all speakers should be praised and reinforced while providing students with challenges that are within their zone of proximal development. Although children often receive guidance and feedback on oral reading skills and writing tasks, they get little, if any, feedback on their oral language and public speaking skills (Anderson, 1997). It's said that 'we measure what we treasure'. Assessment has a very important role to play in ensuring that all of our students can progress through their speaking journeys.

In addition to student skills to be assessed, First Steps (2006) recommends checklists for looking at and setting up the environment (p. 64) and conducting an audit of existing classroom contexts for speaking and listening (p. 65). These checklists enable and support teachers to take a detailed look at the classroom environment in terms of optimising the learning, practising and teaching of speaking and listening skills and ensuring a safe space in which all students can speak up. A recurring issue for those teaching public speaking is how to evaluate students' speech performances fairly and objectively. The goal of assessment has to be, above all, to support the improvement of teaching and learning (Frederickson & Collins, 1989). The aim here is not to overwhelm teachers with the variety of assessment tools and methods for assessing public speaking and oral language skills. It's simply to clarify and highlight that literature reveals evidence that oral language and public speaking skills can be assessed in a robust, reliable way, using a range of assessment methods, purposeful rubrics and frameworks that will inform, enable and empower progress.

Embedding public speaking in your school

Embedding public speaking in your school could be further supported by holding an annual school public speaking event. A committee of mainly students could take responsibility for planning the event which in itself, would provide an organic opportunity to facilitate and shine a light on 'student voice'. This committee could be encouraged, guided or supported to come up with an event theme. Next, a call could be put out for speakers to volunteer or speakers nominated from amongst the student body at large. Teachers could also be given an opportunity to nominate speakers and perhaps parents too. The speakers could consist of a mix of students, parents, community leaders and community residents who speak in public as part of their careers. Other possible speakers might be parents, staff, a local politician, senior citizens, celebrity residents and members of local organisations. Conscientiously including a speaker or speakers from a minority group or seldom-heard voices will send a very powerful message.

It's important to be strict and fair on the time limit you allow for each presentation. In addition to the speakers who prepare speeches, the event would naturally provide many other speaking opportunities, such as Master of Ceremonies (MC). Perhaps students, in pairs or alone, could recite poetry and tell jokes between the presentations or at the beginning to warm up the audience. The event could be a real celebration of the spoken word in all of its forms. The committee should try to give all speakers a few opportunities to practise on the stage before the event and when the committee knows the content of the speeches, its members can organize the agenda so that there is a balance of light-hearted and serious material.

This event could be integrated with the school awards' ceremony or perhaps, the organizing committee might consider presenting a surprise award on the day or paying a special tribute to someone in the audience. A panel discussion (on a topical issue or an issue of school or community concern) is another interesting way to involve more speakers. An important goal of this event is to involve as many speakers as possible in a non-competitive, meaningful way. This doesn't have to rule out the possibility of including a debate, as long as plenty of time has been spent building the participating debaters' speaking confidence and competence before they are expected to perform on the debating stage.

At other school events that already form part of the school year, attention might be paid to how to include some students as speakers, providing speaking opportunities in very natural, organically arising ways. On 'Open Nights', students can take the lead, as they already do in many schools I am familiar with, in certain areas, for example, taking on the responsibility of welcoming and showing visitors around, answering questions and reporting on certain subjects. With a certain degree of scaffolding and support where needed, students could lead weekly school assemblies. Older students leading assemblies is a visible example to younger students of what they can aspire to and achieve. Never underestimate the power of role-models and the influence students can have on one another. Graduation speeches could become a natural and expected part of the school's Graduation ceremony. When you begin to think along these lines, you will, most likely, see lots more speaking opportunities that are present in your own school context.

Findings from my research, especially the example of how students were motivated to set up a student council following their engagement with public speaking training would suggest that perhaps public speaking can add another element here in terms of the possibility of representation of voices from all backgrounds in public forums. It is worth noting also that there are other alternatives to student councils in terms of facilitating all students to have their voices heard. Some schools have begun to explore the option of child advisory panels (CAPs). It's also important to be alert to opportunities that may arise for students to speak outside the school and bring these opportunities to their attention like the example from my study of a 10-year-old student who spoke confidently, presenting a prepared speech on the topic of 'Health in my school' to a large audience of unfamiliar adults at a 'Functional Medicine' conference. This girl is from the Travelling community, a minority ethnic group that "experiences extreme levels of disadvantage in every facet of their lives, i.e. education, employment, housing and health" (ESRI, 2017). She certainly showed how capable she is of speaking out once she had learned and practised the skills. Let us not forget that all children from all backgrounds have something special and unique to share.

Summary reflection on what public speaking in primary school looks like

Alexander (2012, p. 6) acknowledges that a certain degree of confidence is a precondition for articulating ideas in front of others. Public speaking skill mastery has the potential to develop meaningful confidence, and provide more equal access to available opportunities for all students. Having the desire to teach public speaking skills and knowing how to are slightly different matters. Public speaking skill and oral language training are both a curricular and pedagogical matter requiring knowledge of what to teach and how to teach it. Hopefully, this chapter will guide and support teachers to implement public speaking in their classroom and school for the good of all of their students. In the next chapter, I will detail the public speaking intervention we used in my study, how we approached the teaching of public speaking skills as well as other approaches to public speaking skill training.

Reference List

Alexander, R. (2012, February 20). Improving Oracy and Classroom Talk in English Schools Achievements and Challenges. Presentation given at the DfE seminar on Oracy, the National Curriculum and Educational Standards.

Anderson, L. (1997). *Public Speaking Opportunities for Elementary School Students*.

APU. (1985). *Assessment of Performance Unit. Practical Assessment in Oracy at Age 11*. London, DES.

Backlund, P. M., & Morreale, S. P. (2015). Communication Competence: Historical Synopsis, Definitions, Applications, and Looking to the Future. *Communication Competence*, 11-38.

Boyce, J. S., Alber-Morgan, S. R., & Riley, J. G. (2007). Fearless Public Speaking: Oral Presentation Activities for the Elementary Classroom. *Childhood Education*, 83, 142-150.

Cambridge University. (2014). Oracy Skills Framework. Assessing Oracy.

CCEA. (2007). Northern Ireland Primary Curriculum.

Combes, B. H., Walker, M., Harrell, P. E., & Tyler-Wood, T. (2008). PAVES: A Presentation Strategy for Beginning Presenters in Inclusive Environments. *Teaching Exceptional Children*, 41(1), 42-47.

Common Core State Standard Initiative. (2010). Common Core State Standards for English Language Arts & Literacy in History/Social Studies, Science, and Technical Subjects created by The National Governors Association and the Council of Chief State School Officers.

Education Department of Western Australia. (1997). *Oral Language Resource Book*. Rigby Heinemann

ESRI. (2017). *A Social Portrait of Travellers in Ireland*. Dorothy Watson, Oona Kenny, Frances McGinnity.

ESU. (2016). *Speaking Frankly: The Case for Oracy in the Curriculum*. London, English Speaking Union.

First Steps. (2006). *Second Edition Speaking and Listening Map of Development*. West Australian Minister of Education and Training: Harcourt Education.

First Steps. (2013). *Speaking and Listening Resource Book FIRST005 | Speaking and Listening Resource Book*. Department of Education, WA.

Frederickson, J., & Collins, A. (1989). A Systems Approach to Educational Testing, *Educational Researcher*, 18(9), 27-32

Gschwend, L. (2000). Every Student Deserves an Assessment Tool That Teaches. *Communication Teacher*, 14, 1-5.

Joe, J., Kitchen, C., Chen, L., & Feng, G. (2015). Research Report ETS RR-15-36 A Prototype Public Speaking Skills Assessment: An Evaluation of Human-Scoring Quality. ETS Measuring the Power of Learning.

LET's Stand. (2018, 2021). http://www.letsstand.ie/

Lucas, S. E. (2007). *Instructor's Manual to Accompany the Art of Public Speaking* (9th ed.). New York: McGraw-Hill.

Marcotte, M. (2006). Building a Better Mousetrap: The Rubric Debate. *Viewpoints: A Journal of Departmental and Collegiate Teaching, Learning and Assessment*, 7(2), p. 111.

Mercer & Mannion. (2018). *Oracy across the Welsh Curriculum. A Research-Based Review: Key Principles and Recommendations for Teachers*. EAS, Education Achievement Service for South East Wales.

Morreale, S. P., Moore, M. R., Surges-Tatum, D., & Webster, L. (2007). *The Competent Speaker Speech Evaluation Form* (2nd ed.). Washington, DC: National Communication Association.

NCCA. (1999a). SPHE Curriculum.

NCCA. (1999c). English Curriculum.

NCCA. (2007). Assessment in the Primary School Curriculum: Guidelines for Schools.

NCCA. (2019). Primary Language Curriculum.

Newcomb, A. (1999). Finding a Voice. *Christian Science Monitor*, 91(55), 13.

Ó Duibhir, P, & Cummins, J. (2012). *Towards an Integrated Language Curriculum in Early Childhood and Primary Education (3-12 years)*. Research Report No. 16. NCCA: Dublin.

Pabst-Weinschenk, M. (2005). Freies Sprechen in der Grundschule: Grundlagen-Praktische Übungen. Scriptor.
PDST. (2013). *Five Components of Effective Oral Language Instruction*, Professional Development Service for Teachers, Ireland.
Schreiber, L. M., Paul, G. D. & Shibley, L. R. (2012). The Development and Test of the Public Speaking Competence Rubric. *Communication Education*, 61(3), 205–233.
SSLN. (2014). The Scottish Survey of Literacy and Numeracy.
Suskie, L. (2009). *Assessing Student Learning: A Common Sense Guide* (2nd ed.). San Francisco, CA: Wiley.
Thomson, S., & Rucker, M. L. (2002). The Development of a Specialized Public Speaking Competency Scale: Test of Reliability. *Communication Research Reports*, 67, 449459.

7 Pedagogical Approaches to Public Speaking Training

If public speaking skills are being taught explicitly in their child's school, the parents I surveyed gave no indication of knowledge of this in their responses aside from a few mentions of "plays and debates". The main experience of public speaking noted by parents and teachers in relation to themselves was that of debating during their own teenage years. It appears that explicit teaching of public speaking skills happens only in some primary schools and can depend on the vagaries, interests and values of individual teachers and schools. One teacher survey respondent clarified that she spends no time on *"specific public speaking skills"* but *"effective oral communication is ongoing throughout every subject area"*. She said that no discrete time was allocated to it. More teachers shared that they cover it *"informally"* across the curriculum and in infant classes through 'show and tell'. In the absence of explicit teaching, there is a risk that, as Mercer and Mannion (2018) suggest, students' oral language skills are "too often left to chance", leading to some students developing and progressing their skills while others do not.

While many of the teachers in my study expressed an interest in teaching public speaking skills, they also shared the associated challenge and concern. The majority had not been trained in public speaking skills themselves and none had received training in how to train others in public speaking skills. It is rare to expect teachers to teach something they have neither been taught themselves nor taught how to teach. In spite of the fact that 24% of teachers responding to my research survey, indicated that they did not know if public speaking was on the Irish primary school curriculum and 26% stated that it was not, 78% of teachers replied that they do teach their students public speaking skills across the curriculum and under the following areas and subjects: Literacy, English, Drama, Maths, SESE, SPHE, Religious Education, debating teams taking part in in-class, in-school debates as well as inter-school debates organised by agencies external to the school, presenting projects to the class, and speaking at whole school assembly. It is unclear as to whether skills are being explicitly taught or being planned for all students in a systematic way or simply, opportunities being provided for some to practise. So, let's take a look at some pedagogical approaches that support public speaking and oral language skill development while empowering students to have their voice and voices heard.

Dialogic teaching

Alexander (2008), Bruner (1983, 1986) and Cazden (2001) have all written about the concept of 'dialogic teaching' looking at ways in which the immense cognitive, affective, social and educational potential of talk can be better exploited in classrooms between teacher and students and where more authentic questions are posed (Nystrand et al., 1997), classroom exchanges extended and students' contributions explored and built on where students learn to talk and talk to learn. It is about pedagogy across the curriculum and how teachers as well as students use talk to maximum effect to progress learning.

Alexander (2003, p. 33; 2008, pp. 112–113) outlines five principles of dialogic talk: collectivity, reciprocity, support, cumulation and purposefulness. Collectivity refers to the dialogue being a shared experience where students and the teacher address learning activities together. Reciprocity involves both parties listening when the other is speaking and demonstrating this listening by asking questions, sharing and respectfully challenging ideas. Support refers to the safe, supportive environment in which all contributors are encouraged to input with all contributions given value and respect. Cumulative dialogue involves building on one another's ideas and contributions, with open-ended questions and inputs aimed at deepening the learning and understanding. Finally, purposefulness refers to the teacher's broad plan for this approach which will have taken into careful consideration in planning such elements as topic, time, relationships, space and organisation. Lefstein (2006) added two more principles—criticality and meaningfulness—to account further for different viewpoints.

Dialogic teaching methods championed by Alexander (2003) are based on a Vygotskian, sociocultural conception of education. Skidmore (2000) distinguished between pedagogic dialogue, the most conventional classroom discourse, and dialogic pedagogy. According to Skidmore, pedagogic dialogue tends to be teacher-controlled with closed interaction and limited opportunities for participation, reflection or extended contributions on the part of the students. In contrast, dialogic pedagogy is a participatory mode in which the dialogue is all-important; the teacher manages the interaction and encourages children to voice their own evaluative judgements.

While dialogic teaching aims to improve students' powers of communication, "harnessing the power of talk to stimulate and extend pupils' thinking and advance their learning and understanding" (Alexander, 2003), it achieves even more than that. It causes teachers to reflect on and rethink not just the teaching methods used but also the classroom relationships fostered and the balance of power within the class. It focuses on four main areas: talk for everyday life, learning talk, teaching talk and classroom organisation. Talk for everyday life includes: transactional talk, expository talk, interrogatory talk, exploratory talk, expressive talk and evaluative talk. Learning talk in dialogic classrooms goes way beyond just using talk to answer questions. It consists of learning to: narrate, explain, analyse, speculate, imagine, explore, evaluate, discuss, argue, justify and question. In learning, as in life, all of these forms of talk are necessary. Students in dialogic classrooms also learn to listen, think about what they hear, give others time to think and talk, and respect alternative viewpoints.

In dialogic teaching, how students and teachers use talk is jointly important so focused attention is also paid to the teacher's use of talk. In dialogic classrooms, teachers tend to intentionally use a broader range of talking styles. They use the frequently used modes of teaching talk: rote, recitation and short questions; instruction to inform students of what is to be done and how; and exposition to explain new information and concepts. However, they also regularly and intentionally use discussion and dialogue. Students benefit hugely from discussion and dialogue where they are required to listen, think, engage, negotiate, make and contribute to decisions about their learning and where they feel truly and deeply listened to.

Through discussion, more student talk input is encouraged and the opportunity is provided to think in different ways. The aim of discussion and dialogue is to empower learners both cognitively and socially. Included in discussion are questions and comments that require deeper thought and contemplation to extend contributions and build on one another's input. The teacher scaffolds and supports students' contributions especially with language to bridge the gap between present and intended understanding so that they can more accurately and authentically express their view. Throughout the interactions, the teacher is modelling very important communication skills for the students. Dialogue and discussion are purposeful in that they are planned and structured with specific learning goals in view while allowing space for new insights to emerge.

Classroom organisation, climate and respectful relationships play a seminal role in making dialogic teaching possible and productive. In dialogic classrooms, students have opportunities to work in a variety of ways. Teachers engage students in group work that is sometimes teacher-led and other times, student-led. Opportunities are also created for students to work and collaborate in pairs and one-to-one with the teacher on occasion. Students feel safe to express their ideas freely, they are listened to and they listen respectfully to one another, in part because of ground-rules for speaking and listening that were co-created with the teacher.

Talk as pedagogy

The Bullock report (1975) states that talk as curriculum cannot be considered in isolation from talk as pedagogy. Vygotsky (1978) suggests that for a teacher to teach and a learner to learn, they must use talk and joint activity to create a shared communicative space, an 'intermental development zone' (IDZ). In this 'intermental zone', reconstituted constantly as the dialogue continues, the teacher and learner negotiate their way through the activity in which they are both collectively involved (Vygotsky, 1978, p. 128). This pedagogy derives from social constructivism. Edwards and Westgate (1987) make the point that "most of our everyday life depends on skills in talking and making sense of the talk of others, as we work or trade or simply pass the time of day" (p. 6). Teachers use talk every day in their classrooms and practice as a medium to communicate, share information, brainstorm ideas, explore opinions, influence, motivate, inspire, organize students' understanding, perception of and participation in classroom activities and to promote problem-solving strategies. They mediate the curriculum, in large part through talk.

The skilful teacher is like an orchestra conductor in control of the contributions and interactions, determining who contributes and when and ensuring all students have an input. They facilitate classroom discussions where students can, through structured and cumulative questioning and commenting, negotiate and achieve common understandings and deeper learning. The teacher asks different kinds of "quality" questions (Corden, 2000), encouraging, clarifying and extending student contributions to promote higher levels of cognitive engagement through appropriate challenge, enabling all students to gain from the discussions and dialogue and make progress. Teachers also choose vocabulary and phrases carefully to provide meaningful feedback for the class as a whole as well as to individual students.

Vygotsky also formulated the theory of the zone of proximal development (ZPD) as the gap between a child's existing knowledge and means to solve problems unaided and the understanding he or she can reach with the guidance of a more capable peer or teacher. This pedagogical concept is well known amongst educators and encourages the process of 'scaffolding', which Bruner (1983, 1986) termed to describe the intervention and guidance that can be given to the learner to span this learning gap. Subtle but sufficient—this support is just enough so that the student can advance, seemingly on his or her own. Scaffolding is applicable to the acquisition of speaking skills in so far as students can be guided by the teacher to become more independent and proficient as speakers.

Talk as content

Alexander (2012) identified six vital functions of classroom talk: for thinking, learning, communicating, democratic engagement, teaching and assessing (p. 4). In addition to asking their own questions, students need to be able to use talk to narrate, explain, speculate, imagine, hypothesise, explore, evaluate, discuss, argue, reason and justify. Mercer et al. (1999) defined exploratory talk as talk in which "partners engage critically but constructively with each other's ideas", challenging and counter-challenging views, providing justifications and alternative hypotheses. Mercer et al. (1999) report research (p. 98) that found that the incidence of talk of an 'exploratory' nature in primary classrooms was very low with more regular interactions of a competitive, uncooperative nature generating 'disputational talk'. Exploratory talk embodies the principles of accountability, of clarity, of constructive criticism and receptiveness to well-argued proposals which are highly valued in many societies (Mercer, 1995).

In relation to public speaking, instead of just expecting some students to speak in public or debate, teachers can engage all students in the study of tools and techniques that can empower and enable them to speak in public or debate to the best of their abilities. Students learn about and practise specified skills. They become aware of how different social settings require adapted talk. They can learn by studying and evaluating speeches together. Students will need to know the purpose of their presentation and the range of messages their speech can convey and also have knowledge of a range of vocabulary and grammatical constructs in relation to their chosen speech topic and be able to choose them appropriately. They will also need to know how to plan, construct and structure a speech or presentation using their knowledge of rhetorical techniques and other public speaking skills as well as giving evidenced reasons to support views. Every student should have the opportunity to develop a rich repertoire of knowledge, skills and dispositions relating to spoken language and communication.

Although commonly described as skills, there is a significant body of knowledge that underpins the development of spoken language and communication. Additionally, unlike some other skills, it's not a skill we can choose because we may or may not need to use it at some stage in our lives. It's a fact of life that every day, people, young and old, face the prospect of speaking in some type of a public forum. Therefore, some might say that oral language is more than a skill because life experience can be diminished or enhanced by our ability or inability to develop proficient oral language skills.

Gradual Release of Responsibility Method (GRR)

The Gradual Release of Responsibility method (GRR) (Pearson & Gallagher, 1983) is an effective teaching approach that can be used to teach public speaking skills. The GRR method involves a gradual shift of responsibility from the teacher to the student, allowing the student to take more control of their learning. In the context of public speaking, the teacher can begin by modelling effective speaking techniques and providing direct instruction on how to, for example, structure a speech, use effective body language, use voice projection and variation to maximum effect, etc. Then, the teacher can guide the student in preparing and practising their speech and providing feedback. Finally, the student can deliver their speech independently, with the teacher providing support and feedback as needed. This approach allows students to build confidence and develop their skills in a safe and supportive environment, in an incremental way.

Explicit teaching of public speaking and oral language skills

The focus on explicit teaching of oral language including public speaking skills is particularly important given that "there is evidence that some teachers may have struggled to implement" oral language "because the underlying framework was unclear to them" (NCCA, 2012, p. 10). Rarely addressed on its own merit, and even more rarely, explicitly taught or assessed, oral language has been most often used as a tool to support and guide reading and writing across the curriculum. As Cameron (2003) points out, "In the modern era, talk has more often served as the medium of instruction rather than as its object".

Effective speaking and listening skills need to be explicitly taught and applied purposefully in order for all students to use them independently for effective communication (Cregan, 2019, p. 26). First Steps (2013) cautions that in relation to formal oral reporting, the process of preparing to speak must be explicitly taught and preparation time allocated before asking students to present formally. By explicitly teaching students how to use spoken language more effectively, they will develop their empathetic capabilities and social confidence, as well as their thinking and reasoning skills (Mercer, 2016, p. 24).

"Presentational oracy skills need to be taught explicitly and not just as an implicit part of a more general attempt to improve students' emotional sensitivity and social confidence" (Mercer & Mannion, 2018, p. 23). The aim is to teach students to choose behaviours that will equip them to express themselves effectively in a variety of contexts (Eisenhart, 1990). To have a collection of skills to choose from, students need to have been explicitly taught and acquired those skills, with plenty of opportunities to practise them. The relevant skills can be explicitly taught in discrete oral language lessons with the opportunities for practise and development organically arising across the curriculum and at whole school events.

Importantly, on a practical level, the starting point is to create that safe, supportive environment in the classroom. Zenger and Folkman (2017) recommend creating a safe environment so that difficult and complex issues can be discussed openly and also recommend clearing away all distractions so that full attention can be given to the speaker. Students listening to the speaker are made aware that they are playing an active role, i.e., actively listening to provide feedback. A motivating and supportive environment where a variety of communication styles are valued, accepted and accommodated is also important (PDST, 2013, p. 42). Skills training at an early age is one way of addressing and trying to mitigate the fear of public speaking. Research shows several reasons for fearing public speaking and confirms that adequate preparation and practise can alleviate most of them as can a focus on skill acquisition.

How public speaking skills are developed

Shafer (2010) recommends "an experience-based learning approach to public speaking in education" (p. 280). Noting that, as many students are required to speak in front of their peers at seemingly younger ages, teachers should provide the basic skills necessary to complete an oral presentation as opposed to assuming that students will be able to muddle through a required oral report. Remember, that 'muddling through' experience could have long lasting implications for some students. A simple structure Shafer (2010) recommends is the 'Three Ts': *T*ell the audience what you are going to tell them (The Introduction), *T*ell them (The Body), and finally, *T*ell them what you told them (The Conclusion). Shafer (2010) recommends that practising an active set of skills can be approached using a fun, yet strategic, methodology (p. 281).

Mercer and Mannion (2018) claim that developing students' presentational group working skills is best done by focusing on the development of one skill at a time, using tried and tested teaching methods such as (a) modelling the skill either through the use of video or role-play: Through modelling, teachers demonstrate "the behaviours, skills and competencies that students are to learn" (Collins III & O'Brien, 2003, p. 224). (b) explaining the skill, rationale for the use of a particular skill and when it should be used, (c) providing opportunities for deliberate practise and (d) combining the use of different skills over time. This informs a structured approach similar to the First Steps (2013) structured approach of 'Model, Share, Guide and Apply' and the Gradual Release of Responsibility Model (GRR) of Pearson and Gallagher (1983) mentioned previously.

Public speaking is, by nature, an active exercise. There is no such thing as a passive public speaker. Therefore, children have to be actively involved, learning by doing and progressing in their efforts by receiving and applying feedback. Feedback plays a vitally important role in the skill building process, pointing out strengths as well as areas for improvement. When it comes to skill building, for example, in the case of public speaking, "to achieve results, one has to use all the available strengths" (Seligman, 2002, p. 60). Strengths become a speaker's fuel, giving them the tools to both distinguish themselves from other people and connect with them (Lopez, 2008, p. 11).

'LET's Stand' public speaking programme

Morreale et al. (2007), acknowledged that very few teaching interventions, materials and supports were available to foster public speaking skills for primary school children. 'LET's Stand' (2021)–'**L**isten, **E**valuate, **T**alk and **S**tand'–is a structured public speaking programme for primary and secondary school students. It aims to empower students to develop their communication skills and build their confidence in public speaking. The structured programme facilitates the explicit development of listening, speaking and communication evaluation skills. Twelve specified public speaking skills are introduced to students incrementally, one skill at a time. *"This programme is all about enabling and empowering our students to pitch and present their ideas and thoughts to their class"*, said Múinteoir Valerie (teacher's review).

The skills covered in the programme include: standing up, speaking out, body language, eye contact, hand gestures, voice, pause, storytelling, facial expressions, visual aids and 'lovely language'. There are ten speaking projects for students to complete in a year at their own pace and level. Topics for each project are taken from across the curriculum with titles sufficiently open to be tailored to content covered in a particular class and/or students' own interests. Student agency and choice are key features as students may choose/adapt a topic or decide how long they wish to speak for (in consultation with the teacher of course).

The teaching approach follows the structure of the GRR method of teaching (Pearson & Gallagher, 1983) and the model, share, guide, apply sequence (First Steps, 2013). Teachers reported that having a clear structure is a very helpful support. Guidance is provided for teachers on how to create a safe, supportive learning and speaking environment that enables students to freely express themselves confidently in a safe, non-judgmental space. Students are also taught how to give positive and constructive feedback to their peers. Practical tips and techniques are provided to help students overcome anxiety and nervousness when speaking in public, if and where it arises. The programme comprises student workbooks, a teacher manual and online programme support resources. It is designed to be flexible, so that if a school decides to implement the programme in a particular year level, they can easily revisit the skills taught in previous years with the help of 'LET's Stand' workbooks using the teacher manual and online programme resources. Student books are titled: A for Able, B for Brave, C for Confident and D for Daring.

The structure of a speech

The structure of a speech is important to know because it provides additional support for speech writing and delivery, and helps the speaker to organize their thoughts and ideas in a way that is clear, coherent and effective, keeping the audience engaged and helping them to remember the key points that the speaker is making. Knowing the structure of a speech may also add to teachers' confidence when engaging their students in public speaking. There are a few different ways that a speech can be structured, usually depending on the purpose and audience of the speech. Probably the most common layout of a speech is the three-part structure, which consists of an opening, a middle or body, and a conclusion. An opening might consist of a quotation, a statistic or a rhetorical question carefully chosen to capture the audience's attention. It's very similar to how teachers plan to capture students' attention at the beginning of a lesson. The middle or body of the speech may consist of three points or three examples related to the message of the speech or a compelling story. An effective ending would be to summarize the main points and circle back to the opening. The ending should leave the audience clear on your message and perhaps with a call to action. Teachers will notice a clear link here between structuring a speech and laying out a piece of writing in other areas of the curriculum.

Another way to frame a speech is to use the problem-solution structure. This structure works particularly well for persuasive speeches where the speaker is trying to persuade the audience to adopt a particular viewpoint or take a specific action. The problem-solution structure begins by identifying a problem or challenge that the audience is facing, and then presenting a solution or course of action that can help to address that problem. An example of a speech that uses the problem-solution structure is US President John F. Kennedy's 'Ask Not What Your Country Can Do for You' speech. In this speech, Kennedy identifies the challenges facing the country and then presents a vision for a more engaged and active citizenry that can work together to address these challenges. Another effective structure for a speech is the chronological structure. This structure works particularly well for speeches that are telling a story or recounting a historical event. Telling stories is always effective and can really add to a speech. It is said that storytelling is one of the most powerful ways to put ideas into the world. The speaker should ensure that the choice of story is appropriate and emphasizes the point of the presentation. The chronological structure starts at the beginning of the story or event, and then moves forward in time to the end. It is relatively easier for the speaker to memorize speeches with this structure as details are recounted in the order in which they happened.

Regardless of the structure a speaker chooses, a speech needs to have some structure. Some key elements that should be included in every effective speech include: a clear introduction that engages the audience, a main body that presents the speaker's key points with clarity and conviction, and a conclusion that summarizes the main message of the speech and leaves a lasting impression on the audience. Whether using a three-part structure, a problem-solution structure, or a chronological structure, the key is to organize the speech in a way that helps the speaker to present their message with power and purpose, cognisant also of making it easy for the audience to receive, understand and be impacted by the message of the speech.

Here are some additional tips to consider when putting a speech together to enhance its quality and impact. Think multisensory. Use descriptive language that connects with the senses: sight, sound, smell, taste, touch. This engages more of audience members' whole being in receiving the speech. To ensure and enhance understanding, the speaker will also need to consider matching their language to that of their audience. Speakers can sometimes be tempted to end their speeches quickly. When concluding a speech, don't just let it trail off or end abruptly. American poet and educator Henry Wadsworth Longfellow explained, "great is the art of beginning but greater is the art of ending". Ease the audience into the ending and finish a speech purposefully. Using a quotation that a famous person has said to end your speech can have the effect of adding authority and credibility while reinforcing the speech's message. Accessing relevant quotations is made even easier nowadays with internet search engines. However, remember, it's more impactful if the audience recognizes the person being quoted.

And finally, don't be a 'time bandit'. Keep to the time allowed for the presentation. For example, if the audience has graciously given 1-2 minutes or 5-7 minutes of their precious time, do not try to steal more. Time is precious. The audience is likely to prepare themselves, and the teacher will have prepared the audience in the classroom, to listen attentively for the time the speaker has been allocated but no longer. The speaker wants to be remembered for their presentation not for having gone over time.

How general speaking skills are developed

Cregan (2010) found that teachers tend to feel that 'day-to-day' strategies rather than more 'one-off' activities are important for teaching oral language along with exposure to high quality literature and poetry, and experience of drama and play. Children must encounter high quality language from a range of sources, and have increased opportunity to use oral language in the classroom accompanied by appropriate feedback (NELP, 2008). Structured and scaffolded opportunities are recommended for children to develop and practise independent student talk.

Northern Ireland's curriculum documents (CCEA, 2007) point to how speaking skills are acquired: through observing modelled behaviours; understanding non-verbal signals; talking with adults and other students; adopting or assuming a role relevant to context; thinking through and talking about experiences, pictures and stories; students talking about their work, play and things they have made; recalling, sequencing, predicting, describing, explaining; sharing their thoughts, feelings and ideas with different audiences; taking part/contributing to group oral language activities; developing an extended vocabulary through listening to and responding to adults and peers; and through focused experiences to introduce and generate new vocabulary. Millard and Menzies (2016) reported that the oracy strategies most used by class teachers were: modelling good oracy, setting expectations for oracy, initiating pair/group activities, feeding back on what students say, feeding back on how students talk, scaffolding students' oracy, initiating students' presentations, initiating debating activities, assessing oracy as a discrete skill, and initiating drama-based activities.

Opportunities to practise

Once the skills of effective spoken communication have been taught, organic and intentional opportunities schools can provide for public speaking can be availed of and maximised for practise. Some such opportunities mentioned by Mercer & Mannion (2018) include: philosophical enquiry/community enquiring (Topping & Trickey, 2007); structured debates (Mezuk et al., 2021); speech days (Sherrington, 2016, p. 45-46); speaking assemblies (Earnshaw, 2016, p. 11); democratic activities such as the model United Nations (Engel et al., 2017); enquiry-based pedagogies, such as 'Mantle of the Expert' (Swanson, 2016), Project Soapbox, (Smith & Foley, 2015) and conflict resolution using peer mediators (Sellman, 2011). Mercer and Mannion (2018) stress that these are not methods for teaching oracy skills and do not obviate the need for explicit oracy teaching.

Oral storytelling is a learning opportunity which, according to Alford (2016), provides children with a fun and meaningful way to expand their oral language. As part of a research project into how the arts and creativity could play a role in encouraging engagement in storytelling in early childhood, Alford (2016) observed that when telling stories, children were exploring and experimenting with language more, using language not normally used in conversation. Secondly, Alford observed that children become more expressive when telling stories, both verbally and non-verbally. In addition, the more stories children told, the more their confidence increased and the clarity of their voice improved. Storytelling is at the core of who we are. It has been a feature of human life for millions of years. A very effective and powerful strategy in public speaking, research indicates that story-telling activities can help to promote speaking proficiency and literacy skills and can generalise easily and meaningfully to other areas of the child's learning and the curriculum.

The use of debate as a teaching strategy dates back at least as far as 411 BC in Athens (Huryn, 1986). Moorghen (ESU, 2016) outlines three key outcomes of debating as critical thinking, confident communication and empowered citizenship. Cambridge University (2014) describes how during debating tasks, students use a range of public speaking skills. It would appear that debating skills and public speaking skills are closely linked. However, debating is one genre of public speaking and may represent a difficult initial experience of public speaking for students as what they say will be refuted and argued against. Further exploration of the topic of debating can be found in chapter 8.

Socratic Circles can also be used whereby a text is examined or a concept explored by the students using a series of questions and answers connecting new knowledge with prior knowledge. In the Socratic Circle, students engage in clarifying concepts, probing assumptions, reasons, implications and consequences and questioning viewpoints. Dating from the 4th century BC, Socrates cultivated critical thinking through thoughtful questioning, and he was adept at posing questions that challenged his learners.

When asked about potential opportunities within school for public speaking skill training, amongst the teachers who responded to my survey, debating was the most commonly mentioned. This was followed by presentation of projects, school assemblies, student council, school committees, philosophical discussions during oral language lessons and oral language across the curriculum as well as under the curricular subjects of Drama, Social Environmental and Scientific Education (SESE), English; and Social, Personal and Health Education (SPHE). Some teachers suggested that it's an important choice for differentiation to give students the option of feeding back what they have learned orally, in this way integrating with all subject areas. It was shared that *"certain types of learners"* may prefer to feedback orally what they have learned. Some students who may struggle with aspects of writing may show compensating strengths in the area of oral language. Specific occasions and events in the day-to-day and annual life of a school were also identified as potential opportunities for practise, e.g., delivering messages to classes and teachers, weekly school assemblies, Grandparents' Day, school celebrations, occasions when special visitors come to the school, Open Days, graduation ceremony and inter-school debating competitions.

Some teachers I surveyed stated that confidence building goes far beyond literacy and numeracy and confidence building is a significant contributing factor to motivation and engagement. Many teachers surveyed made the point that very young children are *"not afraid to talk"*. They *"have no inhibitions"* and will benefit hugely from the *"the confidence they'll get from achieving something that's that little bit outside their comfort zone"*. When a child is given the opportunity to deliver a speech, they are literally being given the gift of the audience's attention for the duration of that presentation. It's very important not to interrupt a speaker in the middle of a speech. It's rude, it models bad behaviour and for the speaker, it distracts them and the flow of thoughts and speech.

Cross-curricular opportunities

Once speaking skills have been taught, there are many opportunities to practise them across the whole curriculum. Mercer and Mannion (2018) recommend that similar to literacy and numeracy, oracy should be embedded in the teaching and learning of all subjects. The Northern Ireland curriculum also refers to investigating and talking with confidence about Art, History and Science and more. Requiring students to make oral presentations in content areas outside of the speech class may enhance the learning of that content (CCEA, 2007). Students could role play and act out famous characters from across the curriculum, from scientists to historians explaining their inventions and theories. They can use descriptive language and competent speaking skills to reflect on and appreciate a work of art and of course, stories, as mentioned earlier, permeate the curriculum.

Groupwork

The ESU (2016) and Voice 21 recommend that encouraging students to work and present in pairs or groups can help build confidence (p. 59). Cregan (2010) also suggests an increased pedagogical emphasis on group work and exploratory learning through talk (p. 35). According to Corden (2007, p. 112), the essence of constructivist learning is that students gain through social interaction with others, where they share perceptions and sometimes conflicting views of the world. For effective group work, two key conditions must be met: first, there should be a clear group goal; and second, there should be individual accountability within the group (Black & William, 1998; Slavin, 1988).

Howe and Abedin (2013) found that children's language use is richer during collaborative group work than the language they tend to use during traditional 'Initiation – Response – Evaluation' (IRE) interactions. In collaborative groupwork, where children are using accountable talk (Michaels et al., 2008), children are required to: take turns, ensure that everybody is included and that all voices in the group are heard, speak directly to others, express themselves clearly, listen actively to the views and contributions of others, respond to what others say, respect the ideas of others whether they agree with them or not, agree and disagree respectfully, ask questions including clarifying questions, offer encouragement to others and check that others have understood what they have said.

Challenges to note and overcome

Now that we've discussed the powerful possibilities and potential pedagogies for teaching public speaking, as well as some tips and tricks for preparing speeches, it is important to consider some of the challenges we may be required to overcome along the way. Teachers who took part in my action research study shared some of the challenges that presented while implementing a public speaking intervention. Some of these challenges included:

- hearing **every** child speak
- training students in how to deliver helpful, positive evaluations to their peers
- training younger students to actively listen and take turns
- providing opportunities for students to speak outside the classroom
- ensuring inclusion for all students, especially some students with certain SEN challenges
- while allowing and encouraging students to use the language they come to school with, knowing when to intervene and make suggestions regarding more socially acceptable language for particular contexts
- keeping the focus of these lessons as predominantly oral when some of the older students in particular were more inclined to want to write down their entire presentations
- managing and becoming comfortable with the noise level in the classroom.

Hearing every child speak was a challenge. The teachers reflected on whether or not the teacher actually needed to hear each child speak on each project. As a group within our school, it was agreed that through careful differentiation, for some projects, some students could speak to smaller groups. One teacher suggested that this could be done during 'in-class support' time when another teacher would be in the classroom for station teaching. In consultation with the children, the class teacher would decide which students the smaller audience would be best suited to and differentiate and scaffold accordingly, increasing the size of the audience for that particular child as the child became ready for it. This could be a child with a particular Speech and Language challenge, a shy child, an EAL child, a child showing nerves or a reluctant-to-speak child. It was agreed that the important goal to keep in sight was that each student got the opportunity to speak to an audience, with the size of the audience varying from one to fifty. During our research project, ten students who wanted the additional opportunity were also supported to speak in front of the whole school at School Assembly.

It's worth noting that all students in the Junior Room, aged between 4 and 6, were eager to speak on topics which included, talking about themselves, their family, their favourite toy, retelling a story and reciting a nursery rhyme. This eagerness was evident when they explicitly asked for 'Speaking Time', gesturing towards the lectern. When it came to the presentations part of the lesson, eight out of ten students put their hands up to go first. When they stood behind the lectern and began to speak initially, they appeared content to stay there and continue speaking until they were given a prompt, a hand signal from the teacher, to begin to finish up. The challenge here lay more in teaching them to listen to one another, take turns and give positive, specific feedback.

Some other challenges to be aware of, mentioned by teachers surveyed, include: supporting students who may already have a fear of public speaking in how to manage it, the prevalence of a school culture which places more emphasis on written homework rather than oral homework and encouraging and facilitating students to speak and present proudly in their own dialect or language using their own accents. Some teachers found that assigning part of the speech presentations as homework actually actively engaged some parents and family members in supporting the child to prepare. Here, some parents who did not often help their children with their written work seemed more interested and confident in helping them with their oral presentation practise. In relation to shy children, one teacher mentioned that there's a *"delicate balance between encouraging them outside their comfort zone and making them feel uncomfortable"*. More information on how to support shy children can be found in chapter 10. Other solutions that were found to support teachers to move beyond challenges that presented include: a supportive school ethos that values and endorses talking in lessons, setting ground rules for talk with students, explaining clearly why talk-based activities are important (Millard & Menzies, 2016) and gathering different forms of assessment evidence as outlined in the paragraph below. Teachers are expert at coming up with creative solutions to challenges they observe in the areas of teaching and learning. Identifying and being aware of the challenges is an important first step.

Assessment

As teachers, we like to feel confident in how we assess knowledge and skills so that we can ensure and enable progress. Teachers in my study informed that what worked well for them in terms of public speaking training, was to introduce one new skill at a time and then build on the skills incrementally. Teachers said it was easy to assess students' understanding of the skills through a combination of watching students perform and apply them, student conferencing, student self-evaluation and peer evaluation. Assessment data can also be collected from video footage, photographs and diary logs. A range of assessment data can also be gathered using the range of assessment methods outlined by the NCCA (2007). Literature (Cambridge University, 2018; Schreiber et al., 2012) reveals evidence that oral language and public speaking skills can be assessed in a robust, reliable way, using a range of assessment methods, purposeful rubrics and frameworks that will inform, enable and empower progress. Public speeches and presentations can be evaluated reliably and validly using different evaluation forms as long as they address the age-old constructs of content **and** delivery.

Summary reflection on pedagogical approaches to public speaking training

To ensure that oral language/oracy is taught, it is "recommended that school leaders write oracy into their school's development plan, curriculum, or teaching and learning policy to position oracy at the heart of their school's practice" (ESU, 2016, p. 73). Oral language is most definitely on the curriculum as also is public speaking even if the term 'public speaking' is not used. In terms of methodology and pedagogies for oral language and public speaking, literature recommends explicit teaching, a structured approach with clear rules and routines, many opportunities for student practise and constructive feedback in a supportive environment. Public speaking skills can be taught to all students in a fun, engaging, and effective way empowering all children to build their confidence and progress their communication skills.

Reference List

Alexander, R. (2003). *Oracy, Literacy and Pedagogy: International Perspectives*.
Alexander, R. (2008). *Towards Dialogic Teaching: Rethinking Classroom Talk*, Fourth Edition. York: Dialogos UK.
Alexander, R. (2012, February 20). Improving Oracy and Classroom Talk in English Schools Achievements and Challenges. Presentation given at the DfE seminar on Oracy, the National Curriculum and Educational Standards.
Alford, C. (2016). *Where Do Stories Live? Building Oral Language Through Storytelling in an Early Years' Context*. eFellow's Research Paper December, 2016. CORE Education Ltd.
Bearne, E., Dombey, H., & Grainger, T. (Eds). (2003). *Classroom Interactions in Literacy*. Open University Press, 23-35.
Black, P., & William, D. (1998). Assessment and Classroom Learning, *Assessment in Education*, 5(1),1-74.
Bruner, J. (1983). *Child's Talk: Learning to Use Language*. New York: WW Norton & Co.
Bruner, J. (1986). *Actual Minds, Possible Worlds*. Cambridge, MA: Harvard University Press.
Cambridge University. (2018). *The Development of Oracy Skills in School-Aged Learners*. Part of the Cambridge Papers in ELT series November 2018.
Cameron, L. (2003). Challenges for ELT from the Expansion in Teaching Children. *ELT Journal*, 57(2), 105-112.
Cazden, C. B. (2001). *Classroom Discourse: The Language of Teaching and Learning*, Portsmouth, NH: Heinemann
CCEA. (2007). Northern Ireland Primary Curriculum.
Collins, III, J. W., & O'Brien, N. P. (2003). *The Greenwood Dictionary of Education*.
Corden, R. (2000). *Literacy and Learning through Talk: Strategies for the Primary Classroom*. Open University Press: Philadelphia
Corden, R. (2007). *Literacy and Learning Through Talk*. Open University Press: McGraw Hill Education.
Cregan, A. (2010). From Policy to Practice: The Oral Language Challenge for Teachers.
Cregan, A. (2019). *Promoting Oral Language Development in the Primary School*. NCCA and Primary Developments.
Earnshaw, B. (2016). Start Talking at the Back . . . Middle and Front of Class. In *Speaking Frankly: The Case for Oracy in the Curriculum*, 10-17. London: English Speaking Union.
Edwards, A. D., & Westgate, D. P. G. (1987). *Investigating Classroom Talk*. London: The Falmer Press.
Eisenhart, C. (1990). Oral Language Development: The Foundation for Literacy. PHD dissertation, The University of Virginia.
Engel, S., Pallas, J., & Lambert, S. (2017). Model United Nations and Deep Learning: Theoretical and Professional Learning. *Journal of Political Science Education*, 13(2), 171-184.
ESU. (2016). *Speaking Frankly: The Case for Oracy in the Curriculum*. London, English Speaking Union.
First Steps. (2013). *Speaking and Listening Resource Book FIRST005 | Speaking and Listening Resource Book*. Department of Education, WA.
Howe, C., & Abedin, M. (2013). Classroom Dialogue: A Systematic Review across Four Decades of Research. *Cambridge Journal of Education*, 43(3), 325-356.
Huryn, J. (1986) Debating as a Teaching Technique. *Teaching Sociology*, 14, 266-269.
Lefstein, A. (2006). *Dialogue in Schools: Towards a Pragmatic Approach*. Working Papers in Urban Language and Literacies, Kings College, London.
LET's Stand. (2018, 2021). http://www.letsstand.ie/
Lopez, S. J. (2008) *Positive Psychology. Exploring the Best in People*, Vol . 1, 2,3 and 4. Greenwood Publishing Group – Praeger Perspectives, Westport, Connecticut, London.
Mercer, N. (1995). *The Guided Construction of Knowledge: Talk Amongst Teachers and Learners*. Clevedon, Multilingual Matters.
Mercer, N. (2016). Oracy and Thinking Skills. In *Speaking Frankly: The Case for Oracy in the Curriculum*. London, English-Speaking Union.
Mercer & Mannion. (2018). *Oracy across the Welsh Curriculum. A Research-Based Review: Key Principles and Recommendations for Teachers*. EAS, Education Achievement Service for South East Wales.
Mercer, N., Wegerif, R., & Dawes, L. (1999). Children's Talk and the Development of Reasoning in the Classroom. *British Educational Research Journal*, 25(1), 95-111.
Mezuk, B., & Ko, T. M. (2021). *Debate Participation and Academic Achievement among High School Students in the Houston Independent School District: 2012-2015*.

Michaels, S., O'Connor, C., & Resnick, L. B. (2008). Deliberative Discourse Idealized and Realized: Accountable Talk in the Classroom and in Civic Life. *Studies in Philosophy and Education*, 27, 283-297.

Millard, W., & Menzies, L. (2016). *Oracy: The State of Speaking in Our Schools*, London: Voice 21.

Morreale, S. P., Moore, M. R., Surges-Tatum, D., & Webster, L. (2007). *The Competent Speaker Speech Evaluation Form* (2nd ed.). Washington, DC: National Communication Association.

NCCA. (2007). Assessment in the Primary School Curriculum: Guidelines for Schools.

NCCA. (2012). *Literacy in Early Childhood and Primary Education (3-8 years)*, Research Report No. 15, Kennedy et al.

NELP. (2008). National Early Literacy Panel 2008, Developing Early Literacy: A Scientific Synthesis of Early Literacy Development and Implications for Intervention.

Nystrand, M., Gamoran, A., Kachur, R., & Prendergast, C. (1997). *Opening Dialogue: Understanding the Dynamics of Learning and Teaching in the English Classroom*. New York: Teachers College Press.

PDST. (2013). *Five Components of Effective Oral Language Instruction*, Professional Development Service for Teachers, Ireland.

Pearson & Gallagher. (1983). *The Gradual Release of Responsibility in Literacy Research and Practice*. Literacy Research, Practice And Evaluation, Volume 10.

Schreiber, L. M., Paul, G. D. & Shibley, L. R. (2012). The Development and Test of the Public Speaking Competence Rubric. *Communication Education*, 61(3), 205-233.

Seligman, M. E. P. (2002). *Authentic Happiness: Using the New Positive Psychology to Realize Your Potential for Lasting Fulfillment*. New York, NY: Free Press.

Sellman, E. (2011). Peer Mediation Services for Conflict Resolution in Schools – What Transformations in Activity Characterise Successful Implementation? *British Educational. Research Journal*, 37(1), 45-60.

Shafer, S. (2010). Building Public Speaking Skills across the Curriculum. *The International Journal of Learning*, 17, 2.

Sherrington, T. (2016). Oracy in the Secondary Curriculum: Our Journey at Highbury Grove. In *Speaking Frankly: The Case for Oracy in the Curriculum*, pp. 40-47. London: English Speaking Union.

Skidmore, D. (2000). From Pedagogical Dialogue to Dialogical Pedagogy. *Language and Education*, 14(4), 283-296.

Slavin, R. (1988). Cooperative Learning and Student Achievement. *Educational Leadership*, 46(2), 31-33.

Swanson, C. J. (2016). *Positioned as Expert Scientists: Learning Science through Mantle of the-Expert at Years 7/8*, (Thesis, Doctor of Philosophy, PhD). University of Waikato, Hamilton, New Zealand.

The Bullock Report. (1975). *A Language For Life*. Report of the Committee of Enquiry Appointed by the Secretary of State for Education and Science under the Chairmanship of Sir Alan Bullock. Her Majesty's Stationery Office, London.

Topping, K. J., & Trickey, S. (2007). Collaborative Philosophical Enquiry for School Children: Cognitive Effects at 10-12 Years. *British Journal of Educational Psychology*, 77, 271-288.

Vygotsky, L. (1978). *Mind in Society: The Development of Higher Psychological Processes*. Cambridge, MA: Harvard University Press.

Zenger, J., & Folkman, J. (2017). *What Great Listeners Do*. Harvard Business Review.

8 Debate Is Great but WAIT

I am so grateful for the opportunity I got to take part in debating when I was in secondary school. It was the only public speaking opportunity that was available to me at school, and I know for sure that it has helped to shape who I am today. Amongst other benefits, debating gave me the opportunity to develop and use public speaking skills and to explore a range of topics on a deeper and more lateral level. It also helped to develop my confidence and sense of self-efficacy. In a very real and meaningful way, debating helped me to experience that my voice had impact. Across the trajectory of my life since, I believe that my debating experience helped to open certain doors of opportunity to me simply because I was, at times, less afraid and more prepared than others in the room to speak up and put myself forward when opportunity came knocking. However, on reflection, I am not sure that debating is the best place to start when it comes to developing public speaking skills for children.

Debating

Debating is one genre of public speaking. It's competitive, persuasive public speaking. Some might say, debating is a combination of proving your argument right and your opponent's argument wrong. A feature of the world we live in, it's a significant part of politics and how people come to power in our society. The process of debating involves defining the motion, clarifying the topic or question, and quoting research, statistics, stories which are presented as true, whether they are or not. Speakers debate by carefully using the art of rhetoric to persuade and convince the audience that their side of the motion is right. In competitive debates, judges judge what is said and how it is said, the quality of the arguments, the evidence provided to back them up and the performance of the debater. Sometimes the audience has the power to decide, by vote, on the outcome of a debate.

Experienced debaters have a variety of tactics and speaking strategies they use to try to win over the audience. Some refer to presenting their own argument in the most powerful and compelling way possible and some refer to intentionally discrediting and refuting the reason in their opponent's argument. With little time for lengthy explanations, many debaters become masters of rhetoric, impactful one-liners, repetitions and compelling stories and statistics, all carefully selected and strategically curated to validate their side of the argument. One common tactic used when refuting the opponent's arguments is to pick out the weakest part of their argument, focus the audience's attention on that and claim that this weak point discredits the whole opposing side as if that smaller part represented the larger position. The goal of a debate is not necessarily to arrive at the truth or to provide and present a detailed, cogent, well-researched answer to an important question, no matter how much we'd like to think it is. The end goal is to win.

Benefits of debating

There are many positive reasons for and benefits to engaging young people in debating. Some studies in high schools in America have connected debating with better school outcomes, including graduating from school, better scores on SAT tests, getting in to 'better' colleges and performing better in college. Debate experiences have the potential to develop and practise the five "Cs" of 21st-century skills: critical thinking, communication, collaboration, creativity and civic awareness. Participation in debate has been linked to improved critical thinking skills and academic performance (Mezuk & Ko, 2021). Other benefits include enhanced self-efficacy and various indicators of positive social and emotional development (Kalesnikava et al., 2019). These benefits correlate with school engagement and are relevant across the curriculum emphasising the salience of debating for student engagement with learning both inside and outside the classroom (Louden, 2010).

Most obviously, debaters build confidence speaking in public and expressing their ideas eloquently. Debating enhances the ability to structure and organize thoughts as well as improving learners' analytical, research and note-taking skills, their ability to form balanced, informed arguments and to use reasoning and evidence. It's a very active process where the learner learns by doing. Attention and focus and keen listening skills are required for the duration of the debate so as to pick up on the arguments made by teammates and the other team. In addition, oral and written communication skills are practised and improved, helping students to build links between words and ideas that make concepts more meaningful. Through analysing the appropriateness of their information and arguments and anticipating the arguments of their debating opponents and synthesizing wide bodies of complex information, students become astute at discovering information related to their side of an argument. Debating provides the opportunity to explore, research and examine a range of interesting, relevant and controversial topics. Students collaborate and consult with teammates to divide up the points of their team's argument developing vital skills of collaboration and teamwork.

Students then have to organize their information in a structured, cohesive, compelling way so that it may be presented in the most impactful way possible. Speakers learn how to become more persuasive speakers. The art of oral persuasion practised in debating links with persuasive writing and many skills developed through debating can be meaningfully transferred to writing and other areas of the curriculum at school. Facing any fear or nerves they may have in relation to public speaking, students are gaining in confidence every time they step outside their comfort zone to debate. Students learn much through an element of competition, putting in extra practise sessions, in order to compete to the best of their ability.

Debating is not easy. A challenging activity on many levels, it takes effort, skill and resilience to elaborate on your own arguments in a clear and structured way, to listen to and take on the rebuttals of your opponents and to challenge the points of others. By realizing, in a very real way, that you can do hard things, this leads to students believing more in themselves and their abilities, thereby enhancing their sense of self-efficacy. It provides the opportunity to practise active citizenship, investigating, exploring and debating matters of local, national and even international concern, highlighting the importance of having a seat at decision-making tables. You experience in a real way how you can have an influence on the debate when you step up and sit at the bargaining table.

Competitive debating programmes are a feature of school life across the world and are possibly more prevalent in secondary schools, consisting of in-class, in-school or inter-school competitions. Millard and Menzies (2016) reported that teachers from independent (46%) and grammar schools (69%) indicated they are more likely than those in local authority schools or academies to have debating clubs (p. 49). Some schools offer after-school debating clubs as enrichment programmes. Debating skills can prepare young people for future roles such as politicians, public representatives and advocates. However, the fact that not all students receive the same training or opportunities to participate in debating points perhaps to an inequality of opportunity and access. This is problematic in education systems that are underpinned by principles of inclusion and equality of opportunity.

Debate teaches useful skills for other academic pursuits and life more generally. There are many occasions in life when persuasive speaking and debating matters. We are all often faced with situations in which we need to argue a point, whether we're standing up for ourselves or others, pitching to an investor or competing for a position or contract. If students have not heard, as well as practised in meaningful roles with supportive models, the kinds of language they will need to deliberate and contest existing injustices and necessary reform, they may remain subject to social, economic and political exploitation (Brice-Heath, 2012). Through debating, young people have a structured opportunity to explore, research and have their voice heard on topics of significance to them. Some very important topics I've heard primary school children debate include: homework, mobile phones in school, every child should have a pet, bullying, climate change, free music and more. When students are preparing for a debate, they have to consider and anticipate the arguments that their opponents may make. They may even have to propose a topic or motion they initially disagree with. This helps students to better understand opposing viewpoints.

Attending and participating in debate has the potential to challenge and overcome biases. While each team debates one side of a motion, debates viewed in their entirety, as an event, allow for a more well-rounded exploration of a subject with arguments on at least two sides, for and against, being presented. Because two sides of an issue are presented, usually in close succession, any potential bias that a single presenter may have can be effectively countered by the opposing arguments. Those observing the argument are presented with two or more sides of an issue. It's a major positive if opposing views can be expressed and presented in a calm, peaceful manner. This can be a strong example to children and students of how disagreements may be negotiated and settled in a respectful way. Debates can replace confrontation and aggression with logic and reason. On the other hand, some of the political and presidential debates we have become used to seeing on television in recent years can serve as a poor example of the benefits that debating can reap. These debates can begin to introduce us to some of the less favourable qualities and skills debating can also develop. We often see candidates disrespectfully interrupting, deflecting and ridiculing. These kinds of performances can give debating a really bad name.

It's clear that there are many benefits to debating. What merits consideration, however, in the school context, is whether or not all students are given the same opportunities to access, participate in and benefit from this activity. Debating can channel the "natural dogmatism of teens" (ESU, 2016) into effective spoken communication, giving students better access to a range of school experiences. It can make a significant difference in their choices after school transcending any social limitations of their backgrounds, thereby, potentially being "an engine for social mobility" (ESU, 2016, p. 51). Geoff Barton, Headteacher at King Edward VI School, described debating as "an act of social liberation" (ESU, 2016, p. 53). Providing the opportunity to research and look at topics of social concern, debating can potentially educate students in discussions and debate about values and society.

Drawbacks of debating

At present we live in polarized times with an apparent increase in extreme views. Is it helpful to encourage our youth to think in binary ways? Might an over-emphasis on debating encourage this? Lack of understanding of the views and an unwillingness to listen to the opinions of others can be perpetuated through polarizing styles of debate. Matters can be viewed in very binary ways with little tolerance or desire to explore the vast amount of grey area in between. Learning to debate is a very valuable skill but it is not, in my opinion, the best place to begin public speaking skill training for children. Some of the reasons for suggesting this are: debating is confrontational, it pits students against one another in determination to argue their point or defend their side to the bitter end and win. In debates, there are usually winners and losers. This is seldom decided by who is actually right, but rather by who is the best at debating and persuading the audience. Deconstructing and undermining the arguments of others is a significant part of debating. This doesn't require any effort at mutual understanding but rather, the opposite.

Debates are timed. The pace of debating is often quite fast and therefore, debates may favour students who have more of a competitive, aggressive style. There is little time for detailed descriptions. This side-lines students who also have very valid points to make but may need slightly longer to formulate and structure their responses and input to help reach a more measured and balanced understanding of a topic. This fast pace and aggressive nature can make debates more heated and emotional, often resulting in less clarity of thought and so increased polarization may occur when winning at all costs is the objective. Add to this the pressure of having what you're saying and how you're saying it judged by judges and the audience and torn apart by the opposition. Not only that but also being scrutinized for how you're performing as a member of a team. Furthermore, the language of debates is usually very formal and follows the pattern of the "literate language" of schools which Cregan (2010) writes about. This is not language that children from all backgrounds may be used to.

Bearing all of this in mind, you need a pretty thick skin to choose to debate in the first place. Debates can be hurtful. You are an 'opponent'; and already a 'loser' in the eyes of the debaters arguing the other side of your argument. What's more, in debating contests, once the winners are announced, there is often very little time for reflection before moving on to the next topic, the next debate. It is as if the act of winning and losing settles the debate. It is important to learn not to take any of the arguments personally even if they are intended to be. No matter how valid your points may be, the opposing team cannot allow themselves to be swayed or persuaded by your arguments. Some debates can serve to confirm pre-existing biases. While debaters need to be good listeners, it's important to bear in mind that there are different types of listening. It is difficult to listen well when you are talking, or when you are constantly thinking of a response or rebuttal. Debating opponents are often listening with ear blinkers or ear filters on, if such things exist, filtering information that confirms their side of the argument.

Does debating serve the goal of reducing polarization or does it in fact increase it? Does it solve any of the problems it addresses? Winning a debate comes down to who is the most persuasive, who is best at looking suave and using simple rhetoric. A debate is a competition. Various learned and practised, deliberate tactics called 'logical fallacies' can be used to win a debate. The use of logical fallacies has more to do with devious tactics than robust research and evidence. These types of debates are unproductive and unlikely to help anyone to learn. Some common logical fallacies used in debate are: oversimplifying an argument; over-exaggerating a line of reasoning to the point of absurdity; quoting an argument out of context; attributing a weak case to a non-existent group; arguing against an opponent that doesn't exist; using vague, non-specific language without explicitly giving any sources; responding critically to arguments that nobody on the opposing side has made as the audience may not even remember; making your own stance so vague that you can claim anyone who disagrees didn't understand your position. When debating against someone who is using logical fallacies, the best course of action is to point it out, call the opponent out on it, explain what they're doing and why it isn't helpful. We're all susceptible to debating with logical fallacies. It has little content of substance but can be quite persuasive for an audience who is not alert to the tactics being used.

As previously mentioned, debates, by their nature tend to focus on polarizing and binary issues. This can have the effect of making some complex issues seem trivial. It is counterproductive to even try debating certain issues such as hate-related questions and racism if debating just provides a platform for the expression of hateful, harmful and offensive views. In cases like this, one side may just be looking for publicity. This informs us of the importance of carefully choosing topics that warrant a debate. "Let's discuss it" and "let's debate it" are two very different approaches. Why not bring together people impacted by certain issues to explore causes and to collaboratively devise solutions and a plan to implement them? By positing only two sides to highly complex issues, debate may actually exacerbate rather than diminish polarization, even creating it where it shouldn't exist in the first place. Taking the time to research two sides (and the many other sides that often exist) of a debate can provide a wonderful learning experience but this is ideal and is not, in reality what happens with many debates. If we are genuinely curious about the other person's perspective and open ourselves to trying to see matters from another's point of view, we discover that multiple other perspectives exist and can co-exist. Looking at just the pros and the cons of a topic or question does little or no service to the vast amount of grey area between both poles.

Some people may find debating entertaining and enlightening. Some may see debating as a way to prove that they are smarter than someone else and some may just love arguing and be addicted to the thrill of winning an argument, at all costs. They may misrepresent the views of the person they are debating with and this can be humiliating and embarrassing, leading to the other person feeling attacked. This experience at a young age can have a detrimental effect on both parties as one may intentionally avoid all debating and public speaking opportunities in the future and the other may end up alienating themselves from constructive discussions and debates with people who have caught on to the tactics they choose to use.

Debate is not the most effective tool for solving actual problems

Almost always negative, debating is not usually solution-oriented. Most of the debates we have are not rationally thought out, they're emotionally driven. We most often hear about two sides of the problem without touching on solutions or the middle ground. The focus is more on tearing down arguments rather than building on ideas. In many ways, it is a waste of the profound, powerful opportunity for solution-oriented thinking. What is the purpose of debate? Most of us might say wishfully that it's about getting to the truth, helping someone with an incorrect, harmful idea see the light. Much of the time, we're really debating because we want to prove ourselves right and our opponent, the 'other', wrong. If we're really honest, the self-serving interest in debating is not to get to the truth. Perhaps, 'we can't handle the truth'. Perhaps we can't handle the thought that there is a possibility that our opponent might be correct in some respects.

Nobody likes to be proven wrong. It's painful especially if it's in relation to a topic that you're passionate about. Uncertainty is shaky ground so people often unconsciously shield themselves from expressing their views because they don't want to be proven wrong. Even if a certain opinion does not serve us, many of us prefer not to change our mind. Sometimes, changing your mind can be too challenging. In fact, changing your mind may be perceived by some as a sign of weakness. We'd almost prefer to ignore anything that may challenge our beliefs. There's an expression that states, "if you don't stand for something, you'll fall for anything". However, what this statement ignores is that it's healthy to change some of what we stand for as we naturally change across our lifetime.

Experience of debating at school

I was first given the opportunity to join the debating team in secondary school. There was no audition. My teachers suggested that I be on the debating team and I believe now this was because two of my siblings before me were on debating teams and I was reasonably good academically. Out of eighty students in my year, five of us got the opportunity to make up the debating team. Others may not have wanted to debate but the point is, they weren't given the opportunity to try or decide. They were neither asked nor informed of what debating was. Having debated for three years, I entered my first public speaking competition at the end of my third year. This was an impromptu speaking competition where we had to pick a topic out of a bag. In preparation for this, I was advised to consider the many sides of the topic picked, the pros and cons, positives and negatives and everything in between. In three years of taking part in debates, I'm not sure I had done that before.

Results from my research survey suggest that debating is the most common form of public speaking currently and traditionally done in primary schools and more so, secondary schools. Some teachers used the term 'debating' to represent the full extent of public speaking in their school while some expressed the awareness that debating is only *"one genre of public speaking"*. Referring to debating, one teacher mentioned that it's not best practice to *"focus on three or four pupils who may be on the debating team at the expense of whole class participation"*. Debating is competitive public speaking and as teams usually consist of three or four people, importantly, not every child in every class will have an opportunity to have this experience. Having said that, some teachers said that they engage the whole class in the preparation phase for a formal debate which may be somewhat of a consolation. Some teachers can be very skilful in how they do this.

Andrew Fitch (ESU, 2016) points out that debating seems like the most democratic of activities, on the surface. He questions whether oracy events and competitions at the elite level reflect the democratic potential of debates. Fitch mentions specifically the World Schools' Debating Championships where students from the best private schools across the world, come together to celebrate their skills and represent their countries "as members of the educational 'crème de la crème'". Debating itself is not a problem but it may become an issue if a few students getting the opportunity to take part in debates constitutes public speaking opportunities for a whole school. Three teachers mentioned in my survey that public speaking was being covered in their schools by providing competitive debating opportunities. As the ESU (2016) suggests, this "risks oracy becoming the preserve of a self-selecting few, exacerbating inequality" (p. 14), if some students have access to this training while others do not. This should be a concern for education systems and establishments that present themselves as being underpinned by the principle of inclusion.

As mentioned, it can be problematic when debates are presented and used by schools as the only form of public speaking. In some schools and universities, where debate teams may be ubiquitous, it can be the same self-selecting few that always make the team. It is problematic if some students get the message, no matter how inadvertently that they are not and will never be good enough to make the debating team. This may lead to them feeling that their voice is not valued as much as others' and that what they have to say doesn't matter. Some people may be turned off public speaking because of an initial negative experience of debating. Not everyone has a disposition or inclination to argue topics or a need to 'win' a discussion.

Mezuk et al. (2011) found that differential self-selection of students with stronger academic performance in middle school onto the high school debate programme was a common practice in the US. There are many students who do not get to avail of the opportunities that debating provides. While one parent in my research study suggested that debating is a *"far more useful skill"* than public speaking, another parent surveyed pointed out that debating competitions have limited value as *"'at risk' children fall to the wayside"*. This may be due to debating teams being made up of a select few of the class or school's "best speakers" in spite of some teachers' best efforts to include all of the students in preparing for a debate. Grice (2014) advises that it is worth reflecting on the fact that the development of presentational and debating skills are often prioritised in elite, independent schools whose alumni are disproportionately represented in establishment professions such as politics, media and the judiciary (Stanford, 2015).

There are many occasions in life when persuasive speaking and debating matter. But it is important to bear in mind that there are also many more occasions in life when it really doesn't. Not every topic needs to be argued. Not everybody will be interested in debating or even public speaking for that matter. That is not to say that they don't have a unique perspective that they may choose to express through a different format. They will still benefit from public speaking training. A combination of open public speaking and debating opportunities is possibly, a good approach. Not everyone needs to become a skilled debater but everyone can benefit from improving and developing their speaking skills in a variety of contexts. For the majority of students in our classrooms, it may be more helpful to support students' understanding of how to engage in dialogue, discussion and negotiation.

There are many alternative oral language activities to debating in which we can engage our students in our classrooms and schools before or if we are to consider debating. It may make more sense to engage students in these activities before debating is even mentioned. This may level the playing field somewhat, giving more of a chance to all students to build their confidence having had the experience and support of public speaking work before being expected to argue or defend a side of a topic. Instead of pitting intelligent debaters against one another in our classrooms, what if we created opportunities for them to work together to solve actual problems? What if we trained them to negotiate rather than debate? When we listen to another with the aim of understanding, we may just change our mind or at least develop or broaden our thinking on a certain issue and learn something new. This is a slight but significant shift in perspective and intention. Skills of creativity and innovation are triggered when we may catch ourselves saying, "*I never thought of it like that before*".

Most of the studies about and commentaries on debating refer to debating in secondary schools although many primary schools engage in debating activities too. However, there has been little systematic enquiry by researchers into the effectiveness of the training techniques used. What is clear is that debating is not an opportunity available to all and even in schools where debating is available either as an in-class or extra-curricular activity, self-selection or selection of the 'best speakers' can occur. If no other form of public speaking opportunities is offered and practised, there may be even 'better speakers' present in the class who just never got the chance, encouragement or the training to develop their voice and have it heard.

Dialogue rather than debate

Targeting the development of dialogue in an explicit way improves speaking and active listening skills. Dialogue is based on working at understanding one another's views rather than undermining them. The pace of dialogue allows more time for students to think and consider their next response in a less pressurized environment. Even if they disagree, don't like or don't understand the other person's view, students are encouraged to listen actively and attentively to one another, to ask for clarification, to summarize another's views, to dig deeper and try to understand. The goal is understanding and acceptance, not agreement. It's okay to disagree but we actively practise respect for another's views. This creates a space in which to cultivate empathy.

There are no winners or losers in the collaborative process of dialogue. The process is the important element. Students are encouraged to explain and rationalize their views for others, but not present them as fact. Both parties also become stronger and clearer at expressing their own views in a way that others can better understand. In this way, a strong foundation is laid for the skills of negotiating to develop. The act of speech itself manifests our thoughts, our ideas, who we are and what's important to us into the world. We become aware in a very real, experiential way that, 'we don't see things as they are, we see them as we are'.

When students identify important points of agreement within their dialogue, they can be guided and supported to begin to build on each other's ideas to reach new, co-constructed ideas and concepts. Setting challenges or problems for students to solve or work on possible solutions collaboratively, builds a myriad of positive teamwork and negotiating skills. Yes, they can apply their fact-gathering skills and critical thinking but a further step is achieved in how they address complex problems collaboratively. Students can spur one another on and trigger even more creative thinking in one another. I suggest that we could devise a new, playful word for a new activity—'complabboration' (competitive collaboration). Imagine students working together on solution-focused teams, with a healthy amount of competition between and within teams, to tackle the problems they face in their communities, country, and world. The competition could be decided by which groups are able to solve the problems in the most sustainable, humane, innovative and effective way. They could then be provided with the opportunity to present their work not only to their school community, but to the wider community also.

What we can learn from Toastmasters in terms of communication skills

When I joined Toastmasters in 2004, my main fear was that it might be a debating club, that I might be putting myself and my ideas in front of what I thought of as a firing line, setting myself and my views up to be shot down. However, I quickly realized that debating had little to do with it. On the contrary, Toastmasters is a worldwide non-profit educational organization that promotes and supports the development of public speaking, communication and leadership skills. The safe, supportive environment of a Toastmasters meeting provides members with an ideal space in which to improve their public speaking, communication and leadership skills and receive constructive, personalized feedback along the way as members work their way through Toastmasters' education programme at their own pace.

We can learn from Toastmasters in terms of how to set up that safe, supportive environment in which all speakers can develop their skills and maximize their speaking and communication potential. Toastmasters also helps members to manage the fear of public speaking, learning and practising skills that will help them be more successful in life, becoming a better listener, team player, leader and communicator. The point is I would never have joined Toastmasters if it was about debating, and since I joined, I've experienced first-hand that there's so much more to public speaking than debating.

Alternatives to debating

Philosophy for Children (P4C)

Philosophy for Children (P4C) can be a very effective way of encouraging and facilitating students to explore topics and questions on a deeper level, stimulating a range of deep thinking skills including creative, critical and rigorous thinking. Not an additional subject, it is an approach to learning and teaching that explores the big ideas that arise in all areas of life and education by engaging children in related philosophical dialogue and enquiry. P4C uses philosophical dialogue and enquiry to help learners to think, to speak, to listen, to learn and to live together more effectively.

P4C gives voice and expression to the ideas that are already in the room, focusing on what is and what could be. It can positively impact active citizenship and demonstrates in a very real way that students' thoughts and ideas matter while promoting dialogue for change. Sometimes opinions just need to be expressed and listened to, neither agreed nor disagreed with. Questions are formulated around concepts and big ideas to try to capture what is most interesting and curious to the participants in relation to the concepts. P4C provides a structured philosophical approach for investigating these questions in a safe and satisfying way. P4C sessions conclude with individual and class reflection on the skills and dispositions that P4C develops.

Students also learn to disagree respectfully increasing their acceptance and understanding of themselves and others. Concepts and topics can be inspired by, as well as integrate and connect with curriculum content and therefore, students are helped to make valuable connections between their learning and life experiences. In many ways, P4C can bring the curriculum to life helping students to further develop their vocabulary and thinking about topics through listening to others. Student voice is prioritized as students choose the concepts for exploration and they have a meaningful experience of having their voice valued and heard. It can be fun and playful with students having the freedom to be as imaginative as they choose, considering a range of 'What if . . .' possibilities.

P4C shifts the traditional power dynamics in the classroom in which teachers usually ask all of the questions and are thought to know all of the answers. P4C activities can be conducted in the form of circle time discussions which indicate a sharing of power. Children benefit from P4C by having time-tabled time and encouragement to think deeply. They have an opportunity to develop creative, critical, caring and collaborative thinking. Creative thinking develops through giving examples, considering alternatives and making connections. Critical thinking skills involve weighing up the evidence, reasoning and questioning. Caring thinking is developed through showing interest and sensitivity, listening carefully, thanking other students for sharing their thoughts and waiting your turn. Collaborative thinking is evident when students build on one another's ideas, share tasks and negotiate. Mutual understanding is encouraged throughout.

More alternatives to debating

Peer mediation and restorative practice approaches to behaviour management also open the door to compassionate communication, deepening listening skills and mutual understanding.

Other alternative activities to debating which can support the development of speaking, listening and reasoning skills present through dramatic role play of certain roles such as broadcaster, reporter, auctioneer, narrator, tour guide, show host and master of ceremonies. Reciting classic, contemporary or favourite poems, nursery rhymes and prose also provides an opportunity for students to play around with aspects of their voice and delivery style. More ideas are simulated phone conversations, leaving a message, buddy reading and discussing books, telling a joke or humorous story, comedy skits and stand-up comedy, show and tell, interview about a favourite book/chapter/character, award acceptance speeches, leading assemblies and maximizing speaking opportunities at other school events.

Edward De Bono's 'Thinking Hats' approach is another great way to challenge students thinking and talking about topics in a range of ways from a variety of different perspectives. Exploring a range of public speaking genres will give all students the opportunity to practise, for example, telling or retelling a personal experience, making a political speech, a graduation speech or a speech to convince, persuade, entertain, inform, inspire. Students could also gain practise through being given the responsibility and opportunity to make announcements on the school intercom.

Hearing children express their thoughts on issues that affect them and topics that interest them benefits the teacher in important ways also. It provides a unique window into a child's world, their joys, concerns, imaginations and inner lives, informing the teacher about how and what they think about. It has the potential to enhance a teacher's practice as, apart from the expressed thoughts and ideas they hear, they learn in a very practical way to facilitate meaningful discussions as well as other strategies that can be used in other areas of their teaching. Teachers develop their own listening skills as well as many of the skills that students develop. Their relationship with students becomes stronger as they begin to know them better and students actively witness the respect the teacher is showing towards their voice.

Debate is great but 'WAIT'

Personally and professionally, I have a lot to be grateful to debating for. If I hadn't been given the opportunity to debate in secondary school, there was no other option for developing my public speaking skills available to me. I am certain that finding my voice through debating impacted the rest of my life in terms of confidence, self-belief, self-efficacy and a deep sense of the importance of using my voice. I developed a love of words and rhetoric and what I regard as a healthy curiosity about issues in my local area and the world at large. I went on to debate in university and was a member of the university team that won a trip to Kenya in a 'Debates for Development' competition. My experience of public speaking through debating was, I believe, a significant part of what drove me to become a teacher and a school leader. I am now passionate about empowering all of my students to develop their speaking skills and voice so that they are ready to debate, **if they wish**, when the opportunity arises. In recent years, I've been volunteering as a judge for secondary school debates where I get the privilege of listening to talented and passionate speakers who have either self-selected or been selected from amongst their peers to represent their school. I'm still unsure as to how fair or inclusive this selection process is.

Through public speaking training, children can learn and practise many skills and rhetorical techniques which they can eventually effectively use in debating. They can also develop their reasoning and thinking skills, all skills that again will stand to them when and if they choose to debate. Furthermore, aspects of debating can be woven in and out of all children's public speaking training in a supportive, non-competitive way so that confidence can be built first. Conscientiously focusing on building confidence first should be a priority.

Summary reflection on debating in school

As outlined in this chapter, debating can be a very worthwhile activity with many benefits. Experienced, well-prepared speakers, skilled at engaging audiences are best placed to reap these benefits. It should be borne in mind that, as an educational activity, debating also has some drawbacks and limitations. What if debating activities are contributing to polarizing individuals at a time when we could be doing more to encourage and prioritize mutual understanding, active listening, curiosity and respect? Rather than simply winning an argument, what if we focused more on co-constructing solutions to current issues with others whose views may be different to ours? Nobody likes to lose an argument but sharing opinions is a very natural desire. If we are choosing to debate or engage our students in debating activities, we need to be clear about our intentions. What are we trying to achieve?

I have heard some schools say, "*yes, we do public speaking with our students. We have a debating team*". Debating, in my opinion, is not the best first experience of public speaking for all young people. Debating is only one genre of public speaking and a competitive genre at that. Although many teachers can go to great lengths to include the whole class in the preparation for a debate, the message is still very clear. Only those regarded as the 'best speakers' will represent the class. Debating itself is not a problem but it may become an issue if a few students getting the opportunity to take part in debates constitutes public speaking opportunities for a whole school.

I am very aware that it is not advisable to stifle debate. Debates can be planned or they can arise naturally in the course of conversation. Debating has a place and purpose. We want to encourage free, respectful expression of authentic voices upholding everyone's right to freedom of speech. Competitive debating is usually the domain of more experienced, proficient speakers. Therefore, my point is simply that debating is neither the most inclusive approach nor a good starting point at which to begin public speaking training for all young people.

In conclusion, all children should be empowered to find and practise using their voice and have had structured experiences to hear and consider many viewpoints before being expected to propose or oppose a topic as part of a debate, presenting an argument that others will pick apart. Imagine all the problems we could solve if we became better at listening to and understanding one another and more clearly articulating our own views. Debate can be powerful. Debate can be great but my advice is to WAIT. Before we launch our children into competitive debating, I believe that it would be more helpful for students to have been introduced to public speaking and on an incremental basis '**W**eave **A**spects of debate **I**n and out of **T**opics' (WAIT) explored from a multitude of viewpoints.

Reference List

Brice-Heath, S. (2012). *Words at Work and Play: Three Decades in Family and Community Life*. Cambridge University Press, 2012.

Cregan, A. (2010). *From Policy to Practice. The Oral Language Challenge for Teachers*.

ESU. (2016). *Speaking Frankly: The Case for Oracy in the Curriculum*. London, English Speaking Union.

Grice, A. (2014). Old Boys' Club Still Dominates Public Life, According to Major New Report. *The Independent*, 28 August.

Kalesnikava, V. A., Ekey, G. P., Ko, T. M., Shackelford, D. T., & Mezuk, B. (2019). Grit, Growth Mindset and Participation in Competitive Policy Debate: Evidence from the Chicago Debate League. *Educational Research and Reviews*, 14(10), 358-371.

Louden, A. D. (Ed.). (2010). Navigating Opportunity: Policy Debate in the 21st Century: Wake Forest National Debate Conference. IDEA.

Mezuk, B., Bondarenko, I., Smith, S., & Tucker, E. (2011). Impact of Participating in a Policy Debate Program on Academic Achievement: Evidence from the Chicago Urban Debate League. *Educational Research and Reviews*, 6(9), 622-635.

Mezuk, B., & Ko, T. M. (2021). *Debate Participation and Academic Achievement among High School Students in the Houston Independent School District: 2012-2015*.

Millard, W., & Menzies, L. (2016). *Oracy: The State of Speaking in Our Schools*, London: Voice 21.

Stanford, P. (2015). Who Needs a Designer Debating Hall? *The Telegraph*, June 13.

9 Fear of Public Speaking and Communication Apprehension

Mark Twain advises, "do the thing you fear the most and the death of fear is certain". There are many common phobias that adults suffer from, for example: arachnophobia: fear of spiders, claustrophobia: fear of enclosed spaces, agoraphobia: fear of crowded public places, atychiphobia: fear of failure, thanatophobia: fear of death, aerophobia: fear of flying, aquaphobia: fear of water, xenophobia: fear of the unknown and even hippopotomonstroses quipedaliophobia: fear of long words. Acrophobia, fear of heights, and glossophobia, fear of public speaking, consistently feature among the most common (Pertaub & Barker, 2002). However, it may be suggested that we could live quite well never having to go near a high place, while avoiding public speaking situations and opportunities may be significantly more difficult to avoid and their avoidance may have a lifelong-lasting, limiting impact.

Fear of public speaking

Literature describes the fear of public speaking as a prevalent phobia, one of society's most widely suffered anxieties (Blöte et al., 2009), the prevalence of which varies depending on measurement (Martin-Lynch et al., 2016). For some people, the thought of public speaking produces more anxiety than the thought of death (Mancuso, 2014). In a US national survey, approximately 21% of respondents reported a lifetime social fear of public speaking. They reported that this fear caused considerable distress or avoidance of certain situations where speaking might be required (Ruscio et al., 2008). Other reports suggest that public speaking anxiety may affect up to as much as 75% of the adult population to varying degrees (Motley, 1997). Literature and research (McCroskey, 1977; Stewart & Tassie, 2011; Nash et al., 2016) reveal a pervasive, debilitating fear of public speaking that can have a severe negative impact on a person's experience of formal education and opportunities within and beyond school. Furthermore, McCroskey (1977) points out that intense fear or high levels of communication apprehension (CA) is highly associated with ineffective communication.

The idea that some people severely struggle when delivering a speech, address or presentation in public, also known by some as stage fright, came into question many centuries ago, early on in the study and teaching of rhetoric. Fast forward to the 21st century when we are still trying to understand why some people may be more apprehensive and fearful to speak. Stein et al. (1996) suggest that approximately 10% of those who suffer from fear of public speaking report significant distress which interferes with their life (specifically work, education and social life). Therefore, addressing this fear is of significant importance to the individual and society at large, as it is clear that it can have a detrimental impact on people's lives, interactions and opportunities. Taking a closer look at the fear of public speaking or glossophobia, is an integral part of the study of public speaking.

It's interesting to note how some students who report having difficulty delivering speeches in a classroom may have what seems to be little hesitation communicating through other means, e.g., posting on social media and speaking with their friends. I wonder, therefore, is it really a fear of speaking? We speak every day, one-to-one, in our families, in small groups and sometimes slightly larger groups. Speaking seems like such a natural activity. It seems more likely that fear of public speaking may be a fear of being the centre of attention, a fear of making a mistake or appearing foolish and a fear of being judged.

Communication apprehension

McCroskey (1970) writes about the construct of communication apprehension, which he explains has been central to the study of communication avoidance since 1970. McCroskey began to use the term 'communication apprehension' in 1968 and defines it as "a broadly-based anxiety related to oral communication" explaining further that it is "an individual's level of fear or anxiety associated with either real or anticipated communication with another person or persons" (McCroskey, 1977). Interesting here is the fear-evoking potential of even "anticipated communication". McCroskey believed that communication apprehension is most likely the single best predictor of someone's willingness to communicate.

Bodie (2010) defined public speaking fear as a "situation-specific social anxiety that arises from the real or anticipated enactment of an oral presentation" (p. 7). A critical word in these definitions is 'anticipated', and it is important to note that the anxiety regarding a future communicative encounter can be as powerful as or in some cases, more powerful than the real interaction itself. This anxiety is further heightened when individuals go beyond basic everyday communication interactions to deliver public speeches.

Public speaking anxiety

Public speaking anxiety (PSA) is classified in the Diagnostic and Statistical Manual of Mental Disorders (DSM-5) as a social anxiety disorder (American Psychiatric Association, 2013) in which fear of negative evaluation is a core aspect. Reviews by Bippus and Daly (1999) and Pearson et al. (2007) of public speaking apprehension reveal numerous contributing factors including perceived skill deficiency, fear of evaluation and audience scrutiny, lack of experience in public speaking situations, poor preparation, introversion, a low level of self-esteem, below-average abilities and achievement and even a genetic predisposition. Other common sources of speech anxiety include "the speaker's previous public speaking experiences and fear of being in the spotlight," (Thomas, 2007, p. 5). Public speaking anxiety is considered a specific type of social phobia but among individuals with social phobia, it is the most commonly feared social situation (Furmark et al., 2000).

What does fear of public speaking physically look and feel like

In terms of the internal impact of the fear of public speaking, a feeling of discomfort and dread is common. A variety of symptoms, physical and psychological, can be experienced in a public speaking situation, including palpitations, sweating, gastrointestinal discomfort, diarrhoea, muscle tension and confusion (North & Rives, 2001), increased heart rate and shallow breathing, negative covert verbal behaviour and comments to oneself, such as "I must appear unintelligent," and trembling hands (Daly et al., 1997). While a certain amount of nerves in a public speaking situation may be helpful, it moves into the realm of fear when it begins to cause considerable discomfort, distress and becomes debilitating. Other behaviours reported are swaying back and forth, shaking, mumbling, fidgeting, quivering voice, heavy breathing, speaking in a monotone voice, lack of eye contact, panic attacks, fainting and unwanted urination (Mulac & Sherman, 1974). Some less obvious physical symptoms include speech blocks, blurry vision, memory loss and dry mouth. In terms of psychological impact (Barlow, 2002), some fear that others will judge them negatively (Pertaub & Barker, 2002), and even though they recognize that this fear is irrational, they still experience extreme discomfort and anxiety and seek to avoid the social encounter whenever possible.

Nerves

Even for those who don't have a deep debilitating fear of public speaking, the act of speaking in public brings with it its own fair share of nerves. Nervousness is a very normal aspect of all forms of performances in public. A small amount of nerves is manageable and many might say that nerves are a sign that you care but there are times when nerves can get the better of us and for some people, this can happen more often than others. Mark Twain famously suggested, "there are only two types of speakers: the nervous and the liars". While presenting speeches, many people engage in 'nervous habits' that can decrease the effectiveness of their presentation and negatively impact their credibility as a speaker (Mancuso, 2014). 'Nervous habits' are defined as repetitive behaviours that have a negative social impact on the individual exhibiting them (Miltenberger et al., 1998). Examples of 'nervous habits' that occur during public speaking include shifting weight from one foot to the other, nail biting, hair pulling, thumb sucking, tic disorders (both motor and vocal), looking at the floor or ceiling, decreasing speaking volume, trailing off at the end of sentences, making clicking noises with the tongue, stuttering and using filled pauses instead of silent ones (Spohr, 2009). Stuttering and filled pauses are both types of speech disfluencies that cause a temporary disruption in the flow of speech. Filled pauses are considered indicators of "preparedness problems" and can lead to a decrease in the speaker's credibility (Clark & Tree, 2002) and impact.

Strategies for managing nerves

Thankfully, there are many recommended tools and techniques that we can learn to help us manage our nerves. These can be trialled for ourselves and our children. What works for one may not work for another but once we find a few exercises that work for us, to help us settle ourselves and self-regulate before a presentation in public, this is invaluable learning that can support us and our students in many areas of life. Some possible strategies include:

- Relaxation techniques, e.g., deep breathing, mindfulness and grounding. Try, for example, breathing in for 5 seconds, hold for 5, out for 7 (at least five times). Through simple mindfulness practices, we can become more acutely aware of our immediate surroundings, the sights, sounds, smells, feeling of safety in this space. Grounding is a self-soothing technique that brings us into the 'here and now', the present moment, helping us feel more connected to our bodies and the earth. The aim here is to give ourselves a sense of how strong and connected we are.
- Question and challenge how you think about public speaking. Do you see it as an opportunity and a skill set that you can learn, practise and master, step-by-step, an opportunity that can potentially open doors for you or do you see it as an activity that is imposed on you, that you are forced into? Be aware that your personal perception of public speaking makes the world of a difference.
- Intentionally label your nervous reaction as 'excitement' rather than nerves. The same physiological reaction occurs in your body for both but again, it makes a significant difference which label you choose. Your body believes what you say.
- Repeat affirmations or positive statements to yourself before you speak. Choose affirmations that mean something to you, e.g., *I am strong, confident, brave. I am ready, I have prepared. I have something to say that only I can say. My message is important. This is a wonderful opportunity. This is it. I matter and what I have to offer the world matters. I make a difference.*
- Start with small audiences if you think this will help. However, be aware that some people actually find it easier to speak to larger audiences.
- The first few times you speak in public, choose topics that you are familiar and comfortable with.
- Practise in front of a mirror, your friends, a pet. Practise as you walk or exercise.
- Visualize the parts of your speech/presentation as you practise.
- Take a drink of water (with lemon and/or honey if you can, these are good for your voice) and keep a drink of water close to hand when speaking. It's important to stay hydrated, remembering that nerves can sometimes cause your mouth to become dry.
- Visualisation is powerful. Picture yourself standing proud, succeeding, speaking to a very supportive audience who are listening attentively and enjoying your speech.
- Learn to see the opportunity to speak in public as a gift that you've been given, the gift of your audience's attention and time. With this gift, you have the opportunity to impact/entertain/inform/persuade/inspire your audience for the duration of your presentation.
- Be grateful for the opportunity, it's difficult to be nervous when you're expressing gratitude.
- Focus on your message, not on yourself.
- Make it more about the audience than you.
- Tell yourself that your audience wants you to succeed and they're willing you on.
- Think communication rather than performance. Imagine that you are having a conversation with the audience.

- Prepare and practise, practise, practise. Then, remind yourself of how much preparation and practise you have done.
- Remind yourself that nobody in the world knows everything about everything, and each one of us knows something that others don't know. This is a fact.
- Say 'yes' to every opportunity and chance that you get to speak. Experience builds confidence and with every experience your skills are improving.
- Use the energy/adrenaline of your nerves/excitement as positive energy.
- Remember, nerves are a sign that you care.

Longer term impact of fear of public speaking

Other impacts of a fear of public speaking can include some of the following behaviours: communication avoidance, withdrawal and disruption, and even excessive communication. Long-term effects can include avoiding certain courses and career paths where oral presentations are required (Kostić-Bobanović, 2006), never speaking in class and choosing not to speak up for oneself. Young people may have paths for promotion in the work place closed to them, resulting in considerable personal distress, frustration, underachievement and depression. They may settle for careers or jobs very different to their original passion or interest. Students who are very anxious about public speaking in class may sometimes avoid social events that they would otherwise like to attend. They may not talk to classmates they would like to get to know and may drop out of school rather than face a feared situation (Kostić-Bobanovic´, 2006). Public speaking anxiety is associated with low income and increased likelihood of unemployment (Stein et al., 1996). Conducting a randomized telephone survey of residents in Canada, Stein et al. (1996) found that respondents with substantial public speaking fears were less likely to be employed and more likely to have lower education attainment than those with lower levels of public speaking anxiety. Clearly then, allowing a fear of public speaking to develop and prevail has serious implications. Poignant and serious is Aristotle's advice: "Criticism is something we can avoid easily by saying nothing, doing nothing, and being nothing".

Reasons for fear of public speaking

Choi (1998) suggests that "most often, students are scared and reluctant to present because they have neither had experience nor learned the rules" (p. 30). Fear of negative audience feedback and judgment and perceived skill deficiency also play a role. Research shows several reasons for fearing public speaking (Field et al., 2003; Kostić-Bobanović, 2006; McCroskey, 1977) including an initial negative unprepared-for experience of speaking in public in childhood. Adequate preparation and practise can alleviate or mitigate the negative impact of most of these as can a focus on skill acquisition (Martin-Lynch et al., 2016). As discussed in previous chapters, evidence-based supports and strategies are available that can be implemented at primary school in order to support the development of oracy and public speaking skills.

The impact of negative audience feedback was measured by Pertaub and Barker (2002) who conducted an experiment to assess the anxiety responses of university students giving five-minute presentations to virtual audiences consisting of eight male avatars displaying three different types of audience behaviour: an emotionally neutral audience that remained static throughout the talk, a positive audience that exhibited friendly and appreciative behaviour towards the speaker, and a negative audience that exhibited hostile and bored expressions throughout the talk. The results show that the negative audience clearly provoked an anxiety response irrespective of the normal level of public speaking confidence of the subject. This confirms that the speaker's response is affected by the behaviour of the audience even though they know it to be virtual (Slater et al., 1999). A further finding was that, despite the fact that real audiences are rarely so overtly hostile, the negative audience was described by the participants, as being the most realistic of the different scenarios. Perhaps, this finding could be generalized to classroom practice and challenged at an early stage by explicitly creating and emphasizing that safe, supportive environment for public speaking training with the audience giving supportive, positive feedback from the outset in an intentional effort to mitigate or negate the perception of the negative audience.

How to manage and overcome the fear of public speaking

What can be done to support students and to address fear of public speaking and communication apprehension? Ashlock et al. (2015) propose that by recognizing students' communication apprehension as normal, teachers can use teaching techniques to help students manage feelings of apprehension (Robinson, 1997). Similar strategies to those mentioned above for dealing with nerves could be encouraged and practised. Treatments for public speaking anxiety (PSA) include numerous variations and combinations of cognitive restructuring, cognitive behavioural therapy (CBT), feedback, relaxation training and skills training (Mancuso, 2014). Cognitive restructuring refers to noticing, challenging and changing negative thought patterns. Other recommended techniques to reduce CA include self-monitoring, visualisation, video-taped feedback, impromptu speeches, sensitisation and practising speeches.

Ashlock et al. (2015) investigated whether intensive public speaking courses (three- and four-week summer courses) actually increase students' communication apprehension instead of helping lower students' apprehension, as compared with fifteen-week courses. There were 722 undergraduate university students involved in this study. Students enrolled in longer courses experienced significantly reduced CA, less than those enrolled in shorter, more intensive courses. Evidence such as this demonstrates the potential for public speaking training to reduce communication apprehension with longer courses with more regular sustained practise being more effective in this regard.

It appears that experiencing anxiety and engaging in nervous habits are the two most common problems that people experience when making a formal presentation in public. Techniques can be taught and used to address these nervous habits. A study of six participants conducted by Mancuso (2014) evaluated the effectiveness of simplified habit reversal in reducing three nervous habits: filled pauses, tongue clicking and inappropriate use of the word 'like'. Habit reversal training consisted of awareness training and competing response training, i.e., becoming aware of the nervous habit and substituting it with another behaviour. The competing responses for each target behaviour Mancuso introduced the study participants to were: for filled pauses, a three-second silent pause; for tongue clicking, the participant placing his or her tongue against the inside of the bottom front teeth in their mouth holding this position for three seconds; for saying 'like', beginning the sentence again with an appropriate phrase (e.g., 'for example', 'such as') or simply without the inappropriate 'like'. During the study, the participant was asked to raise their left hand when becoming aware that they were about to engage in any of the three target behaviours. All six participants exhibited an immediate decrease in all three target behaviours. Four out of the six participants exhibited an 80% decrease in the target behaviours during their first speech suggesting that for some people, awareness training alone may be sufficient to decrease habit behaviours.

While this work may have focused on a small sample of participants, it is proposed that it may offer insights into supports regarding strategies that could be tried with children who are being limited and adversely affected by the impact of unhelpful habits. A recommendation of Mancuso's work (2014) was that future research should also focus on methods of skill development to improve the overall skills of speakers including eye contact, posture, voice projection, and use of inflections. Beatty (1988) suggests using cognitive restructuring as a way to lower anxiety. Cognitive restructuring is based on the assumption that people often label situations incorrectly and think that things are worse than they actually are (Fremouw & Scott, 1979) and aims to change irrational beliefs by substituting more realistic positive ones. By encouraging students to talk about and acknowledge their fears, including their fear or nervousness concerning public speaking, with teachers and one another, anxiety they are experiencing can be alleviated (Nicosia, 1997) or at least lessened.

Despite the importance of competent public speaking, very little research has been conducted in the area of public speaking skill acquisition within schools. According to Mancuso (2014), a number of studies aimed at reducing PSA examined public speaking skills as a secondary measure (Bennett, 1984; Hayes & Marshall, 1984) and very few studies have focused solely on skill acquisition. Studies that have examined skill acquisition as an antidote to fear have examined two main techniques: skills training and video feedback. Skills training typically involves instructions, modelling, rehearsal and feedback (Miltenberger, 2012), methods similar to those outlined in the chapter on relevant pedagogies. Video feedback in classroom settings increases desirable public speaking behaviours and decreases behavioural indicators of anxiety (Deihl et al., 1970). Ayres et al. (2009) reported that the level of public speaking anxiety of at-risk students lessened after exposure to a videotape intervention designed to reduce speech anxiety.

Kostić-Bobanović (2006) found that students experienced significantly less anxiety before and during public speaking after they had been taught how to manage their distress, by means of affective strategies. To deal with nerves, Kostić-Bobanović (2006) recommended using relaxation techniques and making encouraging statements to oneself. This is consistent with the idea of using affirmations. Honeycutt et al. (2009) recommends that imagined interactions can help reduce fear of communication in which mental imagery is used before and after to prepare and review communication. This is consistent with the concept of visualization.

Addressing the pervasive fear of public speaking is important as Nash et al. (2016) confirm that public speaking and oral assessments are a common assessment type in university (p. 585). Public speaking assessment tasks may exacerbate the already normal anxiety experienced in relation to assessment. If they cannot avoid such situations, students are potentially enduring them with some distress (Cornwell et al., 2006). Therefore, this has serious implications for students' transition into, out of and through university, as well as their capacity to achieve successful outcomes (Martin-Lynch et al., 2016) and their overall well-being. Presently in Ireland, students in secondary schools present projects as Class Based Assessments (CBAs) which are assessed towards their Junior Certificate Examination. The degree to which they are prepared with the oral presentation skills necessary for this is unclear and can vary from school to school. Noteworthy is that social phobias, such as fear of public speaking, develop and are most pronounced during early adolescence (10-14 years) (Field et al., 2003). Field et al. (2003) suggest that this fear is likely to begin during the child's elementary school years. Might this suggest a case for early intervention and early training in the skills of public speaking?

Chesebro et al. (1992) suggest some ways that teachers might direct their attention to reducing levels of CA, which include providing opportunities for students to develop their self-esteem, especially in the area of self-perceived communication competence and helping students improve their general communication skills. Many sources offer tips to help students prepare successful speeches and presentations (DeVito, 2009; Keenan Fitzgerald, 2018; Lucas, 2007; Osborn et al., 2009). Beatty (1988) advises that "every effort should be made to ensure that nonperforming classmates are present, attentive, responsive and supportive of student speakers" (p. 37). This points to the importance of preparing the 'audience' to actively listen and carefully setting up that safe, supportive environment in the classroom. McKenzie and Saunders (2007) offer two important learning objectives for the initial lessons of a public speaking course: to help students realise that fear of public speaking can be managed effectively; and to create a non-threatening environment in which students receive positive feedback about their performances (p. 53).

Martin-Lynch et al. (2016) also noted that despite the experience of anxiety in certain public speaking situations, for some at potentially debilitating levels, most participants in their Australian based pilot study of six university students, had not received any skills training in public speaking, an aspect they suggest speaks to the broader equity issues which may be present and unacknowledged (p. 6). Martin-Lynch et al. propose that the equity issues may be felt even more strongly by individuals who experience social anxiety more generally, or more severely. Strahan (2003) suggests that students, who are socially anxious, not only achieve poor grades, but avoid situations, and potentially units and career choices, which might require public speaking.

Feedback in relation to fear of public speaking from my study

Given the widely reported, pervasive fear of public speaking, it was essential to include questions on this in my own research study. In response to the direct question, "Do you have a fear of public speaking?", 46% of teachers surveyed answered 'yes'. On a scale, 68% of those who reported a fear of public speaking indicated that they were *"a small bit nervous but not afraid"*, 26% said *"very nervous and afraid"* and 6% reported that they were *"petrified"* of public speaking. When asked where they thought this fear may have come from, the responses included the following and are listed in order of the most frequently stated: *"low confidence"*, *"lack of practise"*, *"lack of opportunity"*, *"lack of experience"*, *"negative childhood experiences of speaking"* (*"being told my argument/delivery was wrong as a child"*), *"being shy"*, *"being an introvert"*, *"no training"*, *"no support"*, *"fear of making a mistake"*, *"fear of being judged", "fear of someone laughing", " intrinsic pressure to perform well especially in front of others"* and a *"poor performance when I first had to speak in public"*. One teacher recalled, *"I remember reading at Mass when I was younger but I had to stop reading because I would be sick with nerves"*. Another teacher interviewed offered the following insight: *"I feel it's a daunting task–even though I am happy to speak in front of thirty students, I would not feel confident speaking to a different audience."*

In response to the survey question "Do you think your students have a fear of public speaking", 60% of teachers responding answered 'yes' and 40% 'no'. The main reasons given for thinking their students would have a fear, in order of the most frequently stated, were: *"lack of confidence", "have not been taught the skills", "lack of opportunity to practise", "lack of experience", "lack of preparation", "anxiety issues", "peer pressure", "shyness", "fear of ridicule and being judged", "poor language skills", "lack of vocabulary development", "being self-conscious", "the older they get, they are more self-conscious", "unsure about what they should say", "nerves"*, and *"personality type"*. One teacher suggested that this fear may be greater if a student struggles with other areas of the curriculum too. Another teacher replied that *"most people hate being in the lime-light. A lot of very bright people are extremely articulate but don't need to be heard on a public platform"* and yet another suggested that fear *"can be picked up from others"*. Other elaborations offered included: the *"majority see it as something for the academic and confident children"* and *"I think some pupils have a fear of public speaking because it is not something they are used to doing"*.

The reasons offered for surveyed teachers' opinion that students may not have a fear, in order of most frequently mentioned were: *"confidence", "frequent experience of speaking, lots of practise", "they have done a little of it on a continual basis", "support", "they want to talk and be heard", "they have so much to say", "some children enjoy being the centre of attention", "encouraged by parents and teachers", "experience speaking and being spoken to in their homes and other settings", "comfortable in their environment", "the process and practice is normalized", "children love a challenge", "they don't know it's something to fear yet"* and *"they actually enjoy it"*. One teacher elaborated that *"they get the message early that they have something important to say. They are so young they don't associate it with any fear so I feel strongly that this is the most opportune time to begin. Then they never will have the crippling fear that some of us adults are overcome with until we go and do something about it"*. It was also suggested that *"a minority of pupils have a natural gift for public speaking"*. One teacher shared the perception that *"fear is instilled and created. They don't have the inhibitions, we can project ours onto them or create an ability to speak confidently"*.

Although teachers stand in front of groups of students every day and relatively naturally use some of the skills of public speaking, it's interesting how many of the teacher respondents in my study reported experiencing a fear of public speaking with a few categorising it as *"petrifying"*. Notably, there was initially no mention of fear by teachers in response to the term 'children public speaking' and only a few mentioned nerves as compared with comments regarding fear in response to their own experience of public speaking. Perhaps teachers view speaking in front of children on a day-to-day basis very differently to speaking in front of another audience. On reflection, I wonder might this, in any way, be connected with the perception of being in a position of power in one situation and less so, in the other.

In my study surveys, 48% of parents from a range of professional backgrounds reported having a fear of public speaking. One parent added, *"I did but with training overcame it"*. The most common reasons given for the fear by parents who responded to the survey were *"no practise or not enough"*, *"lack of preparation"*, *"lack of opportunity"*, *"lack of knowledge of the subject"*, *"being shy"* and *"fear of making a mistake"*. In the survey, 94% of parents and 98% of teachers responded that they have been called on to speak in public at some stage throughout their lives. Ninety different occasions were mentioned including: reading at Mass, taking part in group projects, debates, speaking at a meeting, chairing or facilitating a meeting, asking a question at a meeting, family gatherings and parties, weddings, speaking at charity events, sporting events, disagreeing clearly with someone, communicating a message to a doctor, a policeman, standing up in front of a group to speak at school, university project presentations, workplace presentations, awards ceremonies and funerals. One parent shared her view that *"the earlier children begin to develop public speaking skills the easier it will be for them. It is a crucially important skill as it now feeds into the new Junior Cycle (in secondary school in Ireland) where pupils are required to do oral CBAs (Class-Based Assessments)"*.

It would appear that a first initial negative experience of public speaking can have a long-lasting, and in some cases, a life-long-lasting negative, limiting impact on individuals. For some research participants, the term 'public speaking' quickly connected them with their own, most often, negative childhood experiences of speaking in front of a group unprepared, evident in the example of the response of this teacher interviewed: *"for me, public speaking brings me right back to standing up there and not having any notes"* or for some survey respondents, *"being told my opinions don't matter"* and *"being told that girls should be good listeners and not vocal in public spaces"*. In these cases, unfortunately, the message was communicated somehow that their voices didn't matter. This message can, unfortunately, be communicated in more subtle and indirect ways also when and if little effort is made to facilitate children to speak up, communicate their opinions and needs and have their voices heard.

What parents and teachers and indeed students think and perceive in relation to the topic of public speaking and the related fear really does matter as our perceptions and what we believe can have a significant bearing on our reality. Bandura (1977) hypothesized that expectations and perceptions of personal efficacy indicate and determine whether coping behaviours will be initiated, how much effort will be made and how long that effort will be sustained in the face of challenges. Dweck's (2015) discussion of 'tenacity' would also indicate the importance of what we think we can and cannot do. How we behave in the face of fear has relevance here also. There's a Japanese proverb that states, "fear is only as deep as the mind allows". Do we fall in the face of fear or do we feel the fear and face it? Parents and teachers play a very important role in supporting and empowering children to face their fears.

Summary reflection on fear of public speaking

Let's not forget that fear kills more dreams than failure ever does. Fear of public speaking is one of the most common fears in our world today. Its impact on individuals and on society is far reaching and profound. Marie Curie famously said, "nothing in life is to be feared. It is only to be understood. Now is the time to understand more so that we may fear less". Perhaps with enhanced understanding of public speaking and all that it entails, we may all begin to fear it less. This chapter will have reminded us of strategies that we can use for ourselves and in schools that help to mitigate or lessen this fear. These supports can enable and empower individuals to face the fear in a very practical and meaningful way, overcome it and become more resilient in the process.

But what if fear of public speaking is being passed on when we don't name activities that quite clearly involve public speaking as 'public speaking' in school? What if there is a fear of even addressing the topic for people who have never been taught public speaking skills themselves? In my experience, the term 'public speaking' is rarely if ever used in the school setting. Does perhaps, even the term 'public speaking' itself engender fear?

There are certain occasions in life on which we are called to speak when we may easily and understandably be overcome with emotion, for example, on family occasions such as weddings, funerals, milestone birthdays, retirement or leaving parties, accepting or presenting an award or even speaking up in a courtroom situation. Given the sudden and often unexpected nature of some of these events, there may be little or no time to prepare. These occasions can be marked with deep and raw emotions and if we are not somewhat prepared, through having learned and practised relevant skills at some stage in our lives, nerves can numb us. However, if we have the support of a skill-set that was studied and acquired over a period of time and practised on regular occasions, this would surely go a long way towards empowering us to represent ourselves and what we want and need to say in the best possible way. We can, perhaps, in this way, fall back on a habit that's been formed over years.

Have you ever had that niggling, numbing knot in the pit of your stomach? When you knew that you had something to say, but didn't say it. When you were at a meeting and you had a question to ask, but didn't ask it. An idea to share that could have made all the difference but you just didn't share it. Why? Because of fear? If unexpressed, where do all of these thoughts, ideas, feelings go? This loss of unexpressed ideas, thoughts and feelings may be not just our loss, but society's also. It's important that we, educators, parents and all who have the privilege of working and living with children do not project any fears we may have onto our young people. Let's remember that we are in a privileged position to support them to face and rise above their fears in safe, supportive environments so that they can have their voices heard.

Reference List

American Psychiatric Association. (2013). *Diagnostic and Statistical Manual of Mental Disorders*, 5th Edition. Arlington VA: American Psychiatric Association.

Ashlock, M. Z., Brantley, W. A., & Taylor, K. B. et al. (2015). Comparisons of Speech Anxiety in Basic Public Speaking Courses: Are Intensive or Traditional Semester Courses Better? *Basic Communication Course Annual*, 27 (13).

Ayres, J., Hopf, T., Hazel, M. T., Sonandre, D. M., & Wongprasert, T. K. (2009). *Visualization and Performance Visualization. Avoiding Communication: Shyness, Reticence, and Communication Apprehension*, 375-394.

Bandura, A. (1977). Self-efficacy: Toward a Unifying Theory of Behavioral Change. *Psychological Review*, 84(2), 191-215.

Barlow, D. H. (2002). *Anxiety and Its Disorders: The Nature and Treatment of Anxiety and Panic* (2nd ed.) New York: Guilford Press.

Beatty, M. (1988). Situational and Pre-Dispositional Correlates of Public Speaking Anxiety. *Communication Education*, 37, 28-39.

Bennett, L. J. (1984). Teaching Speech Delivery Skills to Reduce Speech Anxiety (Unpublished doctoral dissertation). Drake University, Iowa.

Bippus, A. M., & Daly, J. A. (1999). What Do People Think Causes Stage Fright. Naïve Attributions about the Reasons for Public Speaking Anxiety. *Communication Education*, 48, 63-72.

Blote, A. W., Kint, M. J., Miers A. C., & Westenberg, P. M. (2009). The Relation Between Public Speaking Anxiety and Social Anxiety: A Review. *Journal of Anxiety Disorders*, 23(3), 305-313.

Bodie, G. (2010). A Racing Heart, Rattling Knees, and Ruminative Thoughts: Defining, Explaining, and Treating Public Speaking Anxiety. *Communication Education*, 59(1), 70-105.

Chesebro. J. W., McCroskey, J. C., Atwater, D. R., Bahrenfuss, R. M., Cawelti, G., & Gaudino, J. L., (1992). Communication Apprehension and Self-Perceived Communication Competence of At-Risk Students. *Communication Education*, 41, 345-360.

Choi, E. Y. (1998). Through Another's Eyes: Student Fear Number One - Presenting. *Gifted Child Today Magazine*, 1(4), 30-31.

Clark, H. H., & Tree, J. E. F. (2002). Using Uh and Um in Spontaneous Speaking. *Cognition*, 84, 73-111.

Cornwell, B.R., Johnson, L., Berardi, L., & Grillon, C. (2006). Anticipation of Public Speaking in Virtual Reality Revels a Relationship Between Trait Social Anxiety and Startle Reactivity. *Biology Psychiatry*, 59(7), 664-666.

Daly, J. A., McCroskey, J. C., Ayres, J., Hopf, T., & Ayres, D. M. (1997). *Avoiding Communication: Shyness, Reticence, and Communication Apprehension* (2nd ed.). Cresskill, NJ: Hampton Press.

Deihl, R. E., Breen, M. P., & Larson, C. U. (1970). The Effects of Teacher Comment and Television Video Tape Playback on the Frequency of Non-Fluency in Beginning Speech Students. *The Speech Teacher*, 9, 185-189.

DeVito, J. A. (2009). *The Essential Elements of Public Speaking* (3rd ed.). Boston: Pearson Publishing

Dweck, C. S., Walton, G. M., & Cohen, G. L. (2015). Academic Tenacity: Mindsets and Skills that Promote Long-Term Learning. Paper prepared for the Gates Foundation.

Field, A. P., Hamilton, S. J., Knowîes, K. A., & Plews, E. L. (2003). Fear Information and Social Phobia Beliefs in Children: A Prospective Paradigm and Preliminary Results. *Behaviour Research and Therapy*, 41, 113-123.

Fremouw, W. J., & Scott, M.D. (1979). Cognitive Restructuring: An Alternative Method for the Treatment of Communication Apprehension. *Communication Education*, 28, 129-133.

Furmark, T., Tillfors, M., Stattin, H., Ekselius, L., & Fredrikson, M. (2000). Social Phobia Subtypes in the General Population Revealed by Cluster Analysis. *Psychological Medicine*, 30, 1335-1344.

Hayes, B. J., & Marshall, W. L., (1984). Generalization Effects in Treating Public Speakers. *Behaviour Research and Therapy*, 22, 519-533.

Honeycutt, J. M., Choi, C. W., & DeBerry, J. R. (2009) Communication Apprehension and Imagined Interactions. *Communication Research Reports*, 26(3), 228-236.

Keenan Fitzgerald, S. (2018). *A Structured Approach to Public Speaking for Children*. NCCA, Curriculum Online. Primary Language Toolkit.

Kostić-Bobanović, M. (2006). *Coping with Public Speaking Anxiety*. Head of Department of Foreign Languages, Faculty of Economics and Tourism, University of Zagreb.

Lucas, S. E. (2007). *Instructor's Manual to Accompany the Art of Public Speaking* (9th ed.). New York: McGraw-Hill.

Mancuso, C. J. (2014). Using Habit Reversal to Decrease Filled Pauses and Nervous Habits in Public Speaking. University of South Florida Scholar Commons – Graduate Theses and Dissertations.

Martin- Lynch, P., Correia, H., & Cunningham, C. (2016). Public Speaking Anxiety: The S.A.D. Implications for Students, Transition, Achievement, Success and Retention. In *Students Transitions Achievement Retention & Success* (STARS) Conference 2016, 29 June-2 July 2016, Pan Pacific Hotel, Perth, WA.

McCroskey, J. C. (1970). Measures of Communication-Bound Anxiety. *Speech Monographs*, 37, 269-277.

McCroskey, J. C. (1977). *Human Communication Research*, Vol. 4:1.

McKenzie, L., & Saunders, J. (2007). Facing the Fear: Methods for Addressing Speech Anxiety in Public Speaking Class. *Texas Communication Journal*, 31(1), 53-54.

Motley, M. T. (1997). *Overcoming Your Fear of Public Speaking: A Proven Method*. New York: McGraw-Hill

Mulac, A., & Sherman, A. R. (1974). Behavioral Assessment of Speech Anxiety. *Quarterly Journal of Speech*, 60(2), 34-143.

Nash, G., Crimmins, G., & Oprescu, F. (2016). If first-Year Students Are Afraid of Public Speaking Assessments What Can Teachers Do to Alleviate Such Anxiety? *Assessment & Evaluation in Higher Education*, 41(4), 586-600.

Nicosia, G. (1997). Implementing Public Speaking Skills across the Curriculum. *Community Review*, 15, 74.

North, M., & Rives, J. (2001). Virtual Reality Therapy in Aid of Public Speaking. *International Journal of Virtual Reality*, 3, 2-7.

Osborn, M., Osborn, S., & Osborn, R. (2009). *Public Speaking* (8th ed.). Boston: Pearson.

Pearson, J. C, DeWitt, L., Child, J. T., Kahl, D. H., & Dandamudi, V. (2007). Facing the Fear: An Analysis of Speech-Anxiety Content in Public-Speaking Textbooks. *Communication Research Reports*, 24, 159-168.

Pertaub, D. P., & Barker, C. (2002). An Experiment on Public Speaking Anxiety in Response to Three Different Types of Virtual Audience. *Presence*, 11(1), 68-78.

Robinson, T. E. (1997). Communication Apprehension and the Basic Public Speaking Course: A National Survey of In-Class Treatment Techniques. *Communication Education*, 188-197.

Ruscio, A. M., Brown, T. A., Chiu, W. T., Sareen, J., Stein, M. B., & Kessler, R. C. (2008). Social Fears and Social Phobia in the USA: Results from the National Comorbidity Survey Replication. *Psychological Medicine*, 380(1), 15-28. doi: 10.1017/S0033291707001699.

Slater, M., Pertaub, D-P., & Steed, A. (1999). Public Speaking in Virtual Reality: Facing an Audience of Avatars. *IEEE Computer Graphics and Applications*, 19(2), 6-9.

Spohr, C. (2009). Public Speaking Skills Are Key to Successful Public Relations. *AAILL Spectrum,* 14, 8-9.

Stein, M. B., Walker, J. R., & Forde, D. R. (1996). Public-speaking Fears in a Community Sample: Prevalence, Impact on Functioning, and Diagnostic Classification. *Archives of General Psychiatry*, 53(2), 169-174.

Strahan, E. (2003). The Effects of Social Anxiety and Social Skills on Academic Performance. *Personality and Individual Differences*, 34(2), 347-366.

Thomas, C. (2007). *Conquering Speech Anxiety. Confidence in Public Speaking*. Oxford University Press.

10 Supporting ALL Children to Have Their Voice Heard

From the outset, let's be clear. Just because a child is shy, doesn't speak the language of instruction in the school fluently, or has special education needs (SEN), does not mean that they don't have something unique and important to say and contribute. I was a very shy child and still am a shy adult. I also lived, for a period of time, in a country where I didn't speak the language of daily communication and often felt unintelligent, limited and frustrated that I could not explain myself more clearly and communicate with those around me. Throughout, I've always felt that I have something meaningful and uniquely mine to contribute. I believe that this is the case for everybody, no matter what their challenges may be.

In hindsight, I know that as a child, I needed, probably slightly more than others, to be gently pushed and encouraged to speak out in front of others from a young age. As a middle child of seven, I liked my own company and was very comfortable fading into the background. However, as a thinker and somebody who began to enjoy poetry, I also became acutely aware that I had something to say that was often different to what others around me at that time were saying. I knew that if I didn't find some way of expressing it, nobody else could do it for me and worse still, I risked having others who didn't know, understand, or represent my views, speak up for me.

Newcomb (1999) encourages schools to do more to build public speaking skills, explaining that speaking in groups helps students overcome shyness, test ideas with peers, and think on their feet. With regard to supporting the shy, 'reluctant to speak' child or a child with SEN, Vries and Rentfrow (2016) make the point that schools should support all students to develop the self-confidence and social skills that will enhance their life chances, stressing that it's not about teaching all students to be extroverted. Amy Gaunt, Head of Oracy in School 21, cautioned that there is a worrying tendency for students' low confidence and ability in oracy to result in teachers avoiding oracy-based activities, which does nothing but further exacerbate the problem resulting in a self-fulfilling prophecy (Millard & Menzies, 2016). Millard and Menzies (2016) also make the point that "children who find making verbal contributions in lessons hard get a sense of achievement when they do" (p. 31).

To avoid oral language and public speaking activities based on a flawed assumption that it may be counter-productive for some children, I believe, is a seriously consequential, very limiting and dangerous decision to make on somebody else's behalf. Millard and Menzies (2016) caution that there is a real risk that shy students are simply excused from oral participation without any action being taken to help them overcome their anxiety. As mentioned in a previous chapter, Mercer and Mannion (2018) state that research is clear that these communicative behaviours (for interviews, telephone conversations, presentations, debating, acting roles) can be taught, practised and mastered to a significant degree for all students from all backgrounds.

Shyness and supporting children who are shy

What is shyness? Gaining a deeper insight into this personality trait might help us better understand our students and children who are shy. Being shy is often considered a negative personality trait in today's society. People who are shy are often misunderstood, stereotyped as timid and assumed to be lacking in confidence. However, being shy is not inherently negative. Shyness can actually have several positive aspects. Shy people are often highly empathetic, creative, imaginative and perceptive, as they spend a lot of time observing and analysing their surroundings. Shyness is a natural and valid personality trait. Attempting to cure shyness would be like trying to change a person's fundamental nature, which is not only impossible but also unfair and disrespectful to the individual. Supporting students who are shy to access, participate in and benefit from opportunities on a par with their peers, while being who they truly are, is possibly a better approach.

Shyness is a common human experience that can affect anyone regardless of age, gender, or social status, and it affects different people in different ways. It is a natural response to unfamiliar or uncomfortable situations, often characterized by feelings of awkwardness, nervousness and self-consciousness or simply shying away from certain social situations and not being as talkative or visible as some peers. It may be a protective mechanism to protect us from being exposed to negative or hurtful feedback but it's not usually a conscious decision. It's very deep in our nature and natural responses to our environment. The origins of shyness are complex and multifaceted, stemming, it is believed, from a combination of genetic, environmental, and cultural factors. Opportunities for children who are shy should not be limited by others merely on the basis that they are shy.

Some individuals may experience shyness in social situations, while others may feel shy about expressing themselves creatively or sharing their ideas. Certain personality traits have a genetic component and can be inherited. It is thought that shyness may be one of those although genes alone does not explain why some siblings are shy and others not. Life experiences, particularly those that involve rejection or embarrassment, can contribute to shyness. A person who experiences embarrassment or humiliation in a social situation may become shy in similar situations in the future. Shyness may be context specific. It is important to bear in mind that, as a teacher in my research shared, *"even children who are shy have at least one place where they are not shy"*.

Shyness often develops in childhood. Children who are raised in environments where they are not encouraged to interact with others or are exposed to traumatic experiences such as bullying or rejection, are more likely to develop shyness. Additionally, children who are naturally introverted or highly sensitive may be more inclined to be shy. Children who are shy may have difficulty interacting with others and making friends, which can further reinforce their shyness. Shy children are typically quiet and introverted, and they may struggle with speaking in front of a group. However, they might quite simply, on occasion, prefer not to speak. They may be trying to think and they may prefer to listen for a period of time first before they offer their opinion. This is not a negative. The world surely needs more listeners and considered thinkers. It's important to know and accept when not speaking is a choice.

Positives of being shy

While shyness is possibly, most often perceived as a negative trait, it is important to recognize that there are also strong positives to being shy. It can be a valuable trait in many situations. Shy individuals tend to be more observant and reflective, which can lead to greater creativity and problem-solving abilities. Shyness can also be a sign of humility and a lack of ego, which are important qualities in leaders and influencers. Shy people tend to be great listeners, very thoughtful and empathetic, and as good listeners they make for great discussion facilitators, mediators and negotiators. They often possess a heightened sensitivity to others' emotions and are skilled at reading nonverbal cues. In leadership roles, shy leaders tend to be more democratic and collaborative, seeking and facilitating input regularly from others and valuing different perspectives. They are also more likely to be approachable and open to feedback. Shyness can lead to greater caution and thoughtfulness in decision-making, which can often result in better outcomes.

Despite the challenges of shyness, many famous people throughout history have achieved great success despite their shyness. These individuals serve as examples of how shyness can be overcome and even used to one's advantage. Mahatma Gandhi was a famously shy and introverted person, but he was able to make a significant impact on the world through his humility and dedication to his principles. A political and spiritual leader who led India to independence from British rule, he famously once said, "In a gentle way, you can shake the world". Albert Einstein, one of the most brilliant minds in history, was a shy and introverted person, and was known for his social awkwardness. Einstein was able to make ground-breaking discoveries in physics due to his ability to think deeply and reflectively, which was likely aided by his introverted personality. J. K. Rowling, author of the *Harry Potter* series, has also described herself as shy and introverted.

Shyness as a cultural trait

Shyness may also be thought of as a personality trait, more common in some cultures than others. Cultural factors also play a role in the development of shyness. In some cultures, shyness is viewed as a positive trait, associated with humility and modesty. In other cultures, shyness may be viewed as a negative trait, associated with weakness or social ineptitude. Cultural norms and expectations can influence how individuals perceive and experience shyness. Shyness can even be used as a strategic mode of communication in some cultures. Chaidaroon (2003) details a cultural interpretation of shyness in terms of Thai culture, and explains that appearing to be shy or reluctant to ask for favours, being humble and not responding too quickly in interactions are strategic modes of communication to gain social respect and recognition in Thai society.

Disadvantages and limitations of being shy

While being shy is not inherently a negative trait, it can come with certain disadvantages that can hinder and limit an individual's personal and professional growth. If teachers and parents are aware of these potential limitations, they may be in a better position to help, encourage and support children in these situations. One of the most significant disadvantages of being shy is difficulty in building relationships. Shy individuals may struggle to approach new people or engage in social situations, which can lead to feelings of isolation and loneliness. They may struggle with asserting themselves and setting boundaries.

Being shy can also lead to opportunity and career limitations. Shy individuals may be naturally self-effacing and have difficulty in networking and promoting themselves, which can lead to them not volunteering for opportunities in class or school that are open for volunteers. Longer term, it can limit opportunities for career advancement. Shy individuals may avoid trying new things or taking risks in public situations, which can prevent them from pursuing new experiences and opportunities. While some quietly confident shy people may well discover their niche and opportunities within their own areas of interest, being shy and unsupported in challenging situations may lead to fewer opportunities for personal growth, development, fulfilment and self-actualization.

Shyness can be a sign of low self-esteem. Many shy individuals also experience social anxiety, which can be debilitating in social situations. Social anxiety can manifest in physical symptoms such as sweating, trembling, nausea and even nose bleeds, making social situations even more challenging and uncomfortable when these symptoms occur. Shy people may also struggle with public speaking or presenting, which can impact their ability to take on leadership roles, orally express their needs or engage in important family and business meetings. This might suggest more of a need or impetus to support children who are shy as best we can to develop these skills in a safe, supportive environment before they will be called on to use them in the more critical, unforgiving, competitive environment of the 'real' world.

Important considerations when training children who are shy in public speaking skills

When training all children in public speaking, while it is important to create a safe and supportive environment, this safe supportive environment is even more important for children who are shy. This points to the importance of the principles of 'Universal Design for Learning' (UDL). An adaptation or consideration that's good for one child experiencing a particular challenge in class has the potential to be good for all children. Teachers and parents can play a vital role in encouraging and supporting shy children to build their confidence by encouraging them to begin practising their speaking skills in a comfortable setting. This could be in front of one person, a small group of friends or family members, moving intentionally and considerately towards incrementally bigger audiences as the child's confidence begins to grow.

Another consideration when training shy children in public speaking is to focus on their interests and passions. If children are given a topic that they are passionate about, they are more likely to engage with the subject matter and feel more comfortable speaking about it. Teachers and parents can also encourage shy children to use props or visual aids when presenting, as this can help to take the full force and focus of the audience's attention off the child and onto the content. It is also worth bearing in mind that even when a child may be experiencing difficulty in terms of the presentation of a speech, shy people can be exceptional speech writers. Perhaps in the initial stages, students could work in pairs on speech projects. The child whose main strength lies in the area of presenting will learn from their partner who may excel in putting the content together, while the shy child will benefit from working closely with a classmate who is a strong presenter. It's important to praise and validate the gifts and importance of both sets of talent. This could also provide a natural, relevant opportunity to alert children to the fact that many politicians, presidents and public figures do not actually write their own speeches but have communication teams working with them to help them refine and present their messages.

Children who are shy may be afraid of being judged or criticized, and so positive feedback can help them identify their own strengths, what they can concretely build on and thereby, feel more confident and motivated. Positive feedback and plenty of encouragement will help significantly. When providing feedback, it is important to focus firstly on the child's strengths rather than their weaknesses. Once a certain level of confidence has been built, suggestions can be offered as to where improvements can be made. In my research, what teachers found helpful in the case of a nervous, younger child was to give them the opportunity to speak to a puppet or group of puppets, one or a few close friends or one trusted adult. It was agreed that the class teacher, knowing the students and school-based options best, is best-placed in consultation with the student and perhaps the parent, to decide what might work best for each student who exhibits nerves.

Attempting to cure shyness can have negative consequences. Shy individuals may already feel marginalized or misunderstood, and attempts to "cure" their shyness may reinforce feelings of inadequacy or shame. As mentioned, shyness is often accompanied by anxiety, and attempting to cure shyness may exacerbate anxiety. Rather than trying to cure shyness, individuals can be supported to learn social skills that can help them feel more comfortable and confident in social situations. For example, shy individuals can practise assertiveness skills or engage in activities that align with their interests, allowing them to connect with others who share similar passions. There are very practical ways in which children who are shy can be supported.

School is an ideal environment in which we can consciously create that safe, supportive environment. Students can be encouraged to start with small, achievable goals such as initiating a conversation. Shy students are bound to benefit from being shown and exploring the range of different ways they can express themselves and choosing the form of expression that is most comfortable for them. Helping shy students to see the positives in this personality trait can also be empowering, helping them experience that their uniqueness is valued. Bear in mind that when you are providing training and opportunities for children who are shy to speak to the best of their abilities, you are empowering them, equipping them with skills that they can draw on when need be to talk, but you are not requiring them to talk. Encouraging, preparing and gently coaching and coaxing, yes. But not requiring or forcing. The choice is always theirs.

In conclusion, shyness can come with certain disadvantages that can impact an individual's personal, social and professional life. However, with the right support and practise, it is possible to embrace, overcome and/or accept and manage shyness to lead a fulfilling and successful life. By understanding the causes, challenges and benefits of shyness, shyness can be seen as a natural and valid personality trait that should be accepted and respected rather than stigmatized or cured. We can develop a more nuanced understanding of this common trait and support individuals who experience shyness allowing them to navigate their shyness in a healthy way and not be limited by it. At the same time, we must remember as Cregan (2010, p. 94) cautions, "the silent child may not just be shy—he/she may have great difficulty communicating as communication may not be done at home" or there may be other reasons why a child does not or cannot communicate.

Supporting children from disadvantaged backgrounds

Cregan (2019) makes the observation that children learn to talk by talking, and that in diverse classrooms all children must feel that they have something worthwhile to say; that their talk is valued and contributions welcomed. Clarke et al. (2016) have found inequitable distribution of talk time in classrooms, generally favouring students from advantaged backgrounds. Therefore, there is a need to conscientiously and equitably support students from disadvantaged backgrounds with opportunities to improve their speaking skills. Evidence suggests that the impact of poor oral language skills is extremely serious, and can be limiting and long-lasting for children from disadvantaged backgrounds (Alexander, 2012; Cregan, 2010). The Communication Trust, UK (2015a) explains that children who struggle with language at age 5 are six times less likely to reach the expected standard in English at age 11. In general, students from economically deprived backgrounds are less likely to have had a rich talk experience in their home environment (Mercer & Mannion, 2018).

About 1 million children in the UK have long-term, persistent speech and language difficulties (The Communication Trust, 2015a, p. 5). In addition, the Trust reports that in areas of social deprivation, more than 50% of children start school with delayed language. The Department of Education and Skills (DES) in Ireland reported in 2005 (p. 25) that teachers often remark on "the fact that children come to school with a significant oral language deficit". Cregan (2010) explains that research shows that a focus on oral language can hold considerable power in bridging the gap, improving access to the curriculum and improving these students' readiness to avail of opportunities within school and beyond. Cregan reported that children who most need classroom-based, oral language development intervention were too often the least likely to get it "making it considerably more difficult for them to achieve their potential through the school system than is the case for their more privileged, mainstream counterparts" (2010, p. 23). The value ascribed to certain patterns of language variation is closely aligned with the social status of people. The "accepted norm for the oral variety of language is accorded prestige, higher value, power and authority" (Wolfram et al., 1999, p. 12). For those children whose language use is different, unconscious but biased negative judgements are made (Michaels & Cazden 1986). All teachers may need to be aware of this in terms of encouraging and supporting all of their students from diverse socio-economic and cultural backgrounds to speak up in their classrooms.

Fairclough (2001) claims that "language has become perhaps the primary medium of social control and power" (p. 2). Bourdieu (1991) cautioned that "one must not forget that the relations of communication 'par excellence' are also relations of symbolic power" (p. 37). Bourdieu argues that the standard variety of the official national language becomes the dominant language, which is used as an instrument of power and functions as "cultural capital". According to Bourdieu this "linguistic capital" is unequally distributed among people from different social classes, the less linguistic capital a speaker possesses, the greater his/her disadvantage (Cregan, 2008, p. 14). Considering social equity or lack of social equity, it is worth reflecting on the fact that the development of presentational and debating skills are often prioritised in elite, independent schools (Stanford, 2015) whose alumni are disproportionately represented in establishment professions such as politics, media and the judiciary (Grice, 2014). Millard and Menzies (2016) reported that teachers from independent and grammar schools highlight they are more likely than those in local authority schools or academies to have debating clubs (p. 49). The fact that not all students receive the same training points perhaps to an inequality of opportunity and access.

Supporting children with special education needs

We would never intentionally exclude any child from an opportunity that might benefit them in life. There are no two children with special needs who have exactly the same needs. Therefore, it's important to look at the strengths and needs of each individual child to ascertain how best to support them. Children with special needs may have physical, cognitive, or emotional disabilities or a comorbidity of challenges that may impact their ability to communicate effectively. Parents and professionals working with the children can provide very valuable input. The best results will be achieved when teachers and parents work closely with the child's therapists and specialists and of course, the child themselves, to understand their unique challenges and strengths.

Many young people with significant special education needs have overcome what at one time, may have seemed like insurmountable challenges to leave their unique mark on the world and have their voice heard. Joanne O' Riordain, born without all four limbs, is now a well-known Irish activist and sports journalist. Mattie Stepanek, born with a rare mitochondrial disorder, was an American poet, philosopher, peacemaker and motivational speaker and published seven best-selling books of poetry and peace essays before his death at age 13. Christopher Nolan, Irish writer and advocate for the disabled, was born in 1965 with severe cerebral palsy. He could neither control his limbs nor speak. His mother, Bernadette, taught him to read and spell by associating letters with her drawings. His father read and recited poetry to him, telling him stories which Christopher later wrote about using his sole means of communication, his eyes through which his parents helped him work out a system of signals. He later learned to type with his forehead, using a 'unicorn stick'.

Temple Grandin, American academic and animal behaviourist, is author of eight books, many of them at least partly autobiographical. An autism spokesperson and advocate who did not learn to talk until she was three and a half years old, she is one of the first autistic people to document the insights she gained from her own personal experience of autism. She has created systems to counter stress in humans and animals including the Temple Grandin 'hug machine' which she invented in 1965 at age 18. Born in 1947, she continues to speak frequently at autism conferences and events across the world on animal science and welfare. American author, Helen Keller, born in 1880, also defied the odds, triumphing over the limitations of both blindness and deafness to become a disability rights advocate, political activist and lecturer.

Recalling "the frustration of not being able to talk", Temple Grandin shares, "I knew what I wanted to say, but I could not get the words out, so I would just scream". She said, "If I could snap my fingers and be non-autistic, I would not. Autism is part of what I am. . . . I am different, not less." There are countless more examples of inspiring individuals with SEN from across the world who may have struggled to have their voice heard but when they did, made a unique and profoundly valuable contribution within and beyond their communities. Joanne O'Riordan, Mattie Stepanek, Christopher Nolan, Temple Grandin and Helen Keller are simply a sample, albeit a sample of profoundly inspirational individuals.

If we want to create truly inclusive learning environments in our schools, we would be wise to invite and facilitate the voices of those with additional needs who are arguably more aware of the challenges posed by environments that are not inclusive. If we want to get relevant feedback and input regarding, for example, UDL, surely we should ask someone with SEN, consult with them and their parents and include them in the decision-making process. The chances are they may be able to point out where barriers exist quicker than anyone else. Ellen Notbohm, author of 'Ten Things Every Child with Autism Wishes You Knew' writes, "presuming that a non-verbal child has nothing to say is like presuming an adult without a car has nowhere to go". The message in these paragraphs is to never underestimate or disregard the potential of any child with SEN but rather serve to facilitate their learning, development, progress and self-expression as we aim to do with all of our students.

Speech and language difficulties

Speech and language difficulties are a common problem in childhood. Some children may also have speech and language difficulties as a secondary part of another diagnosis. Speech is something that develops gradually in children, and this can be different in everyone. Speech and language difficulties may be deemed present if a child's skills are significantly behind those expected of someone in their age group. Speech and language difficulties can affect all children in different ways and may include stammering, stuttering, dysfluency, cluttering, delayed language development, difficulties understanding or processing language or difficulties with articulation. Some speech disorders may require specific intervention and support as directed by a speech and language therapist.

Stammering, stuttering or dysfluency affect how fluently we talk. These difficulties can affect a person's ability or struggle to say some words all together. It takes a significant amount of courage to speak up in class when you know that you may stammer. In the classroom context, a stammer requires the listener to be patient and aware, giving more time to the speaker without causing additional pressure. Speech cluttering also makes it difficult to understand what someone is trying to say. This affects fluency and articulation. The rhythm of speech is also affected. Speech cluttering is characterized by fast bursts or choppy segments of speech, or extended pauses resulting in the speaker appearing disorganized and difficult to understand. The speaker can be aware or unaware that they are cluttering their speech. In the classroom context, it is likely that the confidence of the child with a stammer will be affected by the reactions of others. Giving a person with a stammer the time and space to express themselves is often one of the most effective ways of supporting them. Conferencing with parents, speech therapist and very importantly, the child, will help the teacher ascertain the child's level of comfort and ability in terms of speech contributions in class.

Specific difficulties with articulation and articulation disorders refer to difficulties articulating a range of speech sounds. These can involve substituting different sounds at the beginning of words such as 'w' and 'r' or difficulty pronouncing certain sounds at the beginning or end of words, for example, 'sc' at the beginning and 'ck' at the end. Sometimes, children with articulation disorders may omit sounds from the beginning of words altogether, or add sounds that don't exist to the middle of words. A lisp is another type of articulation disorder affecting how words with 's' and sometimes 'z' sounds are said. This can be a feature in early childhood that some children grow out of naturally. As mentioned, speech and language difficulties affect different children in different ways. Some may find it difficult to understand spoken language including specific vocabulary and concepts. As a result, they may find it challenging to follow instructions. Visual aids and gestures are usually helpful supports here. Attention and listening skills can also be affected. Consider how you might feel when listening to a language you don't understand, or only partially understand, being spoken. Now, imagine if this was your only language for communication. I'm not saying it's exactly the same experience, just that, relating to a similar frustration and challenge might help us to better empathise with the struggles of the child with speech and language difficulties.

For some children, the difficulty may be in speaking itself, producing speech as explained above in relation to difficulties articulating certain sounds and cluttered speech. Some children may feel very self-conscious and hyper-aware of their difficulties and may very intentionally either try to cover them up, distract or shy away from situations where speaking is expected. In their view, it may be easier for them to not even try to express themselves in conversation, during class or when playing with peers. Their confidence in speaking can be, understandably, adversely affected and they may experience difficulty having their needs met. Helping them to discover the mode of communication and expression with which they feel most comfortable will be of huge benefit to them.

Supporting children with speech and language difficulties

Communication is very obviously impacted by speech and language difficulties. Education and learning will also be a greater challenge as language is the primary medium of learning. Multisensory teaching and learning approaches and additional visual cues are necessary in order to support some learners with speech and language needs to more effectively access and participate in learning. Speech and language difficulties can show in 'negative' behaviours as students may feel very frustrated. Remember, 'all behaviour is communication'. In some cases, public speaking training can help students who need it most to practise and improve articulation, pronunciation and fluency as well as benefiting from hearing the many examples of their peers presenting too. When they see that their peers all have individual ways of presenting, this too, can help to reduce anxiety about speaking in front of others. They can learn to cleverly use and maximize some of the non-verbal aspects of public speaking and presenting to their advantage. As they practise public speaking and speak about topics of interest and importance to them, they learn to communicate with others more effectively and confidently, which can boost their self-confidence and self-esteem.

In a few cases, these difficulties can be naturally overcome with regular exposure to a language rich environment where children are spoken to face to face, are read to regularly and hear language being used in a variety of meaningful and enjoyable contexts. For some children with more complex expressive (speaking) or receptive (listening and understanding) difficulties, these difficulties can persist and they may require additional specific speech and language therapy and support. Following assessment, speech and language therapists can then put a plan of activities together targeted at addressing the child's identified difficulties. Schools provide a naturally meaningful, social context in which to practise many speech and language activities. What's important is being able to identify difficulties as they occur and provide some necessary support and guidance. Early intervention is key. This is where providing speaking opportunities plays another valuable role as a reluctance to speak may very well flag a possible difficulty a student is experiencing.

Some students may need to be supported to use alternative forms of communication such as sign language, communication devices or specialist language equipment to communicate with others. For children with severe speech difficulties, technology can act as a very effective tool enabling them to express themselves. For some, speech and language difficulties may be lifelong. In these cases, while students will still continue to benefit from specialist support and targeted interventions, it is very important to adapt the learning environment to try to minimize the impact of the child's language difficulties on their access to the curriculum and learning in other areas. Some adaptations may include strategically removing all potential distractions, reviewing seating arrangements, providing more visual cues and appropriate differentiation. The aim is to ensure inclusion and access as best we can.

Supporting children with other categories of special education needs

Not being able to speak is not the same as not having something to say. For children with speech and language challenges, some of the child's speaking tasks can be specifically designed and targeted at achieving specified, agreed goals and communication outcomes for students with communication difficulties. For children with cognitive disabilities, it may be necessary to simplify the language or structure of the presentation. At any rate, simple clear language is a powerful feature of competent and effective public speaking and can ensure a wider reach for a speaker's message. Visual aids and props can be very helpful here for children who struggle with language or comprehension. This also helps to reinforce for all students the power of visual aids. It is important to focus on the child's strengths and interests when selecting the topic or facilitating them to choose the topic, as this can help to keep them engaged and motivated.

For some children with physical disabilities, certain physical accommodations may need to be made to ensure, for example, that all children can access the speaking platform or speaking area. This could involve providing a wheelchair ramp to the stage or podium, lecterns of different heights, or a microphone if the child has difficulty speaking loudly. For children with emotional difficulties, it is essential to create a safe and supportive environment, again an environment that will benefit all, but may require specific additional considerations with certain students' additional needs in mind. Parents, guardians and any professionals, external to school personnel, working with the child should be able to help teachers identify any triggers or issues that could impact the child's ability to speak in public or participate in a public speaking class.

In our school, we embedded the practice of graduating students performing a 'graduation speech' as part of our school's annual graduation ceremony. A few years ago, we wondered how we could support a particular child with complex SEN to present with her peers, at the graduation ceremony. We involved the child in question and the parents in a discussion about this. The parents were happy to go along with what the child wanted and offered to support in whatever way they could. The child, a strong-willed, non-verbal girl with complex physical, mental and medical needs was adamant that she wanted the chance to present like her classmates. The SEN teacher worked closely with her as did some of her classmates to help her prepare. When it came to delivering her presentation on the day on 'Memories of primary school and what moving on to secondary school means to me', she stood, smiled, used hand gestures, gestured towards the PowerPoint she had prepared with the help of her teacher and classmates and held up the uniform of the secondary school she would go to. She got a rapturous applause when she finished her presentation and the pride on her face was undeniable. Her mother remarked afterwards, with tears in her eyes, that she had no idea her daughter had that level of confidence.

In addition to being given opportunities to improve their speaking and presentation skills at a level commensurate with their ability, all children with SEN can listen to and enjoy their classmates' presentations learning something new from each contribution they hear. They can also play an active role in providing feedback to their peers. It will benefit all children to be taught skills required in using alternative methods of communication such as symbols and signs, turn taking and allowing time for others to speak at their own pace. It is necessary to ensure that all students are taught to communicate with each other effectively in a spirit of inclusion and respect for everyone's uniqueness and contribution.

Supporting children from minority groups and for whom English is not their first language

Children from minority ethnic groups may face unique challenges when it comes to public speaking. They may feel more self-conscious. They may feel that their language or accent is different from their peers, which can impact their confidence and willingness to speak in public. When training children from minority ethnic groups in public speaking, it is important to create a culturally open, curious and responsive environment. Open to finding out more about the child's cultural background, teachers may need to be sensitive to cultural differences when facilitating students in selecting the topic and content for their presentation. Providing every child with opportunities to share their own cultural traditions and experiences is a sound inclusive pedagogical approach that not only helps the speaker feel more included and valued but also provides a hugely valuable, meaningful learning experience and opportunity for everybody else in the class in relation to the diverse cultures of their classmates.

In today's globalized world, being able to communicate in English is becoming increasingly more important. Public speaking skill training can support the education of children for whom English is not their first language, by helping them to develop their spoken English language skills, reduce anxiety about speaking in English, build their overall confidence in social situations and help them integrate into their new environment. They will learn a lot also by listening to the multiple speeches of their classmates as they present on the same or a similar topic. Public speaking skill training can also provide non-native speakers of English with a sense of empowerment, as they learn to communicate effectively in a new language and culture.

Mindful of language differences, when an English Additional Language (EAL) student is making the effort to present in their second, or perhaps even third language, teachers can powerfully model and encourage, patience, understanding and support. It's best not to correct or interrupt speakers while they are speaking unless they are visibly struggling and the teacher determines that a little help and encouragement at the right moment might help them to move forward. Providing a child who speaks another language with the opportunity to make a short presentation in their native language can send a very powerful positive message of value for all contributions and all languages. This also presents a unique and powerful learning opportunity for all students as they will gain from listening to another language being spoken fluently, potentially learn something new about another culture and also practise interpreting non-verbal cues when attending to another's presentation. The teacher might also consider letting students who speak the same language, work on presentations together when and where appropriate.

The power of the stories of potential role models

Sharing stories of people from diverse backgrounds, with diverse needs including people who are shy, have SEN or belong to a minority ethnic group and how they have changed the world or made an impact by speaking up or using their voice can serve as motivation and inspiration for other young people and students. If students can relate to these stories and somehow connect, seeing themselves in someone whose story might resemble theirs, students may feel empowered to speak up themselves also. Inspiration and connection can be great motivators. Some inspiring young people who, despite their challenges, have used their voice to change the world include: Malala Yousafzai, Joanne O'Riordan, Mattie Stepanek and Greta Thunberg. I'm sure you can think of many more.

Summary reflection on public speaking support for ALL children

Oral language skills are a significant part of broad and balanced curricula in schools in most countries that **all** children are entitled to access, participate in and benefit from. Public speaking skill training can support the education of shy children, children with speech and language difficulties, special needs and non-native speakers of English. As all children practise public speaking at a level that enables them to make steady progress, they learn to understand their strengths and weaknesses, and develop self-awareness and self-efficacy. A public speaking approach can be empowering, inclusive and future-looking.

In today's world, public speaking skills are essential for success in many areas of life. However, for shy children, children with special needs, children from minority ethnic groups and seldom-heard voices, the process of learning public speaking can be more challenging but not impossible and still necessary. Sometimes, these children may be overlooked and underestimated when this opportunity is being provided. In many instances, it might be even more important for them to learn this skill so as to become empowered advocates, standing up for themselves and others where required. The voice of the loudest, most confident child in the classroom does not represent 'child voice' or 'student voice'. It is simply one child's voice. Being curious about the multiplicity of voices within our classrooms and wanting to genuinely hear them is a wonderful, revelatory adventure. Diverse views and the individual uniqueness of every child can be celebrated through a public speaking approach. When the conditions, the time and the topic are right, that 'shy' child or seldom-heard child in your class might just be the one who blows you away with their input. I promise, this input will be well-worth waiting for. At least, that's been my experience.

Reference List

Alexander, R. (2012, February 20). Improving Oracy and Classroom Talk in English Schools Achievements and Challenges. Presentation given at the DfE seminar on Oracy, the National Curriculum and Educational Standards.

Bourdieu, P. (1991). *Language and Symbolic Power*. Cambridge: Polity Press.

Chaidaroon, S. S. (2003). When Shyness Is Not Incompetence: A Case of Thai Communication Competence. *Intercultural Communication Studies*, 12(4).

Clarke, S., Howley, I., Resnick, L., & Rosé, C. (2016). Student Agency to Participate in Dialogic Science Discussions. *Learning, Culture and Social Interaction*, 10, 27–39.

Cregan, A. (2008). *From Difference to Disadvantage: 'Talking Posh' Sociolinguistic Perspectives on the Context of Schooling in Ireland*. Combat Poverty Agency. Working Paper Services 07/03 ISBN: 978-1-905-48541-1 June 2008

Cregan, A. (2010). From Policy to Practice: The Oral Language Challenge for Teachers.

Cregan, A. (2019). *Promoting Oral Language Development in the Primary School*. NCCA and Primary Developments.

Department of Education and Science. (2005). *Literacy and Numeracy in Disadvantaged Schools: Challenges for Teachers and Learners, An Evaluation by the Inspectorate of the Department of Education and Science*. Government Publications, Dublin.

Fairclough, N. (2001). *Language and Power* (2nd edition). Pearson Education Ltd. London: Longman.

Grice, A. (2014). Old Boys' Club Still Dominates Public Life, According to Major New Report. *The Independent*, 28 August.

Mercer & Mannion. (2018). *Oracy across the Welsh Curriculum. A Research-Based Review: Key Principles and Recommendations for Teachers*. EAS, Education Achievement Service for South East Wales.

Michaels, S., & Cazden, C. (1986). Teacher/child Collaboration as Oral Preparation for Literacy. In B. B. Schieffin & P. Gilmore (eds), *The Acquisition of Literacy: Ethnographic Perspectives*, 132-154. Norwood, NJ: Ablex.

Millard, W., & Menzies, L. (2016). *Oracy: The State of Speaking in Our Schools*, London: Voice 21.

Newcomb A. (1999). Finding a voice. Christian Science Monitor, 91(55), 13.

Stanford, P. (2015). Who Needs a Designer Debating Hall? *The Telegraph*, June 13.

The Communication Trust. (2015a). *Universally Speaking: The Ages and Stages of Children's Communication Development from Birth to 5 Years*. London: The Communication Trust.

Vries, R. D., & Rentfrow, P. (2016). *A Winning Personality: The Effects of Background on Personality and Earnings*.

Wolfram, W., Adger, C. T., & Christian, D. (1999). *Dialects in Schools and Communities*, New Jersey: Lawrence Erlbaum Associates.

11 Examples of 'Student Voice' in Practice

It seems that across the world, schools and teachers are at different points in relation to the promotion of 'student voice'. In an effort to include examples for all schools at various levels of 'student voice' implementation and celebration, in this chapter I'm going to start by looking at where teachers and schools can begin in relation to student voice. I will take a closer look at the role of the teacher vis-à-vis 'student voice' and also explore and present some practical tips and examples regarding how 'student voice' might be effectively facilitated and promoted within the classroom and school. The list of examples I will present is not exhaustive but may help to alert educators to further opportunities within their own school context.

The role of the teacher in relation to 'student voice'

Literature has long informed us that factors involving teachers and high-quality teaching are the most important influences on student learning. Gambrell et al. (2011) point out that teachers should be given the freedom and latitude to use their professional judgement and agency to make instructional decisions that enable students to achieve their full literacy potential. In the Irish context, 'Looking at Our Schools' (LAOS, 2022) acknowledges the pedagogical skills required to enable high-quality learner experiences and outcomes. These include requisite subject knowledge, pedagogical knowledge and classroom management skills; selecting and using planning, preparation and assessment practices that progress all students' learning; selecting and using teaching approaches appropriate to the learning objective and to students' learning needs; and responding to individual learning needs, differentiating teaching and learning activities as necessary.

The teacher's role in relation to 'student voice' and the adult's role in relation to 'child voice' are seen as rooted in the desire to facilitate the child's communicative intent and to develop the child's communicative competence (Bruner, 1983; Snow, 1990). According to NEPS (2015), effective teachers of literacy have been found to have the following characteristics: they have excellent classroom management skills, they establish positive relationships with children, they implement a balanced literacy framework, take a metacognitive approach to instruction, emphasise higher order thinking skills, teach basic skills in meaningful contexts, differentiate instruction, use a range of formative assessment tools, link with parents and the community and have a commitment to continuous professional development (CPD). The teacher assumes a role many may not have received training in, a facilitating role. This

DOI: 10.4324/9781003472063-12

may sound simple but this role requires significant skill, expertise and knowledge on the part of the teacher. In our role as a facilitator of learning, we provide prompts and spark motivation for students to speak.

The word facilitation derives from the word "facile" which is French for "easy". Therefore, to facilitate means to make something easier. Hammerman (1999) suggests that an effective facilitator "recognizes the value of allowing learners to experience the joy and thrill of learning by themselves" (p. 204). This is in-keeping with an enquiry based, discovery and exploratory view of education. The primary responsibilities of a facilitator include setting suitable experiences, posing problems, setting boundaries, supporting learners, ensuring physical and emotional safety, and facilitating the learning process (Ressler, 2012). "An astute teacher plays a vital role in assisting children in their ability to be good conversationalists" (PDST, 2013 p. 3). The teacher's role is to ensure that students develop the confidence to become effective speakers and listeners in order to meet their future needs and be prepared for future opportunities in social, academic, family and community contexts, preparing them for the different types of discourse, e.g., planned and unplanned, formal and informal, dialogue and monologue, public and private (First Steps, 2013, p. 9).

Teachers must challenge themselves to strategically speak less so that students can speak more in classrooms. Let's be honest, it's exhausting to be talking almost all the time anyway. How many times have teachers gone home with a sore throat? Like a conductor in an orchestra, the ideal is to try to bring all voices in and have them speak in harmony. I had a wonderful teacher and school principal in secondary school who spoke significantly less than many of the other teachers. She chose her words carefully and when she spoke, we listened. Her words were like gold dust. I remember once she told us that she would not raise her voice or speak louder to be heard because she said with a smile and a twinkle in her eye, "I fear it would be wasting my sweetness on the desert air".

While playing the role of 'responsive listener' (Hong & Ajex, 1995), teachers are modelling important skills of active listening for their students and must also be intentional in helping children to develop the skills to listen to one another (Deason, 2009). 'Talking Classrooms' (Smith, 2001) recommends the explicit teaching of "School Talk" (extended discourse and decontextualized language), conversational reciprocity (turn taking), eye contact when speaking and listening, awareness of non-verbal communication and how to sustain conversations. When teachers make these matters explicit and provide direct guidance, students have been found to be enthusiastic and effective at grasping 'educated' ways of using language for sharing and constructing knowledge (Mercer, 1995).

Dewey (1938) explains that the teacher's duty is to create "educative" environments that relate to and bring out the student's interests. What's more, teachers who plan and organize instruction around the learning preferences of individual learners, emphasizing special strengths and shoring up underutilized gifts and talents have a better chance of unlocking the full learning potential of their students (Hall Haley, 2005). They create a safe environment, or a 'climate for learning' (Greenaway, 2004) where participants feel safe to share pieces of themselves or push themselves out of their comfort zone without risking their emotional or physical well-being (VanderWey et al., 2014). Kutnick and Colwell (2010) found that the quality of collaboration between students can be enhanced when teachers foster an overall atmosphere of trust and mutual respect in the classroom.

Specific features of adult talk that intentionally facilitate children's language development include repetitions, prompts, expansions, imitation, recasts of what children say, as well as many models of vocabulary in various forms and contexts (Shiel et al., 2012). Alexander (2008, p. 9) claims that the challenge for the teacher lies in consciously resisting habituated teacher-dominated talk behaviours in favour of those that maximise learning and empower learners at all levels, encouraging students to talk more, while teachers talk less. In such dialogic talk episodes, teachers scaffold children to reflect on their contributions, take many turns, give lengthy contributions, listen and build on what has already been said (Reznitskaya, 2012, p. 447). This implies that part of the teacher's role is to intentionally facilitate children's oral language development in skilful ways that elicit engagement and reflection on the part of the student.

Co-creating ground rules

Teachers can significantly enhance the quality of classroom talk by using ground rules for classroom talk. These ground rules can build on students' own awareness of what makes for a productive discussion by explicitly teaching skills and behaviours in empowering and participative ways (Mercer & Littleton, 2007). However, Fisher and Larkin (2008) report that teachers commonly give little priority to their role for guiding and modelling students' effective use of talk, a point also noted by Millard and Menzies (2016). Alexander (2018) points to the importance of teacher talk stating that "it is largely through the teacher's talk that the student's talk is facilitated, mediated, probed and extended" (p. 563). Alexander (2012) explains that teacher agency is more important in relation to talk than in any other aspect of the curriculum or child's learning as talk, by its very nature, is interactive and always dependent on others. Most children can engage silently and independently in reading, writing and maths, but not so with talk. Acknowledging that the teacher's own competence as a speaker and listener contributes significantly to the developing oral competence of the student, Alexander (2012) asserts that in oracy the teacher's agency is critical in unique and uniquely powerful ways.

Providing effective feedback

We all know that effective feedback is important to learning. Feedback is an important part of assessment. In Toastmasters we say that 'feedback is the breakfast of champions'. While students may be particularly used to receiving feedback in writing, verbal feedback from the teacher and peers can be equally and sometimes more beneficial and far less time consuming for the teacher. Effective teachers personalize their feedback and address their questions to the child's conceptual gaps and motivational needs. Wasik and Hindman (2018) suggest that teacher feedback may take the form of an elaboration, corrective guidance on either the meaning or the form of language used, an extended comment or explanation. The subtle interpersonal dynamics of the teacher-student interaction can contribute hugely to student tenacity (Morisano et al., 2010). Skilful questioning is an important feature. Jalongo (2008), reports that 80% of "teacher talk" in classrooms consists of low-level questions that ask children to recall information rather than open-ended questions requiring children to think at higher levels. Attentive body language, expanding children's responses, asking clarifying questions and using reflective listening techniques are ways to support children's continued participation in current and future dialogues (Otto, 2008). Vygotsky was educated by a private tutor, whose pedagogical technique was grounded in a form of Socratic dialogue (Wertsch, 1985), teaching by engaging with the student in extended critical inquiry and philosophical conversations which facilitated the development of critical thinking skills.

Teacher as public speaker

I wonder do many teachers see themselves as public speakers. Petek (2014) points out that for classroom communication to be effective, the teacher needs to observe the principles of successful public speaking. Referring to the responsibility to mediate and facilitate learning, Petek suggests that the ability to communicate effectively is one of the teacher's basic competencies and here, public speaking plays an important role. The teacher in a school is responsible for the initiation, reception and effect of their messages (Petek, 2014). Richmond and McCroskey (1993) acknowledge teachers as professional communicators who communicate with students, students' parents, colleagues, administrators and the general public of the communities where they serve and teach on a daily basis. Teachers are involved in communication all day, every day. Is there any teaching without communication? Richmond and McCroskey (1993) advise that teacher trainers are therefore responsible for preparing prospective teachers to enter the profession equipped with the necessary skills to carry out this role, a role within which communication is a key and significant part.

All four teachers I interviewed as part of my study gave examples of how they engage in public speaking skills every day in front of their students, for example, standing up at the top of the class, using carefully chosen words to try to motivate, inspire and engage student attention, using vocal variety, structuring what they present so that students can better understand, being persuasive, and making sure that they capture the students' attention in the first few moments. In spite of this, one teacher shared that while she has no problem standing in front of a class of children, she would never feel comfortable standing in front of an audience of adults.

Teachers' perceptions and expectations

Teachers' perceptions and expectations matter greatly. Important is their perceptions about language and how important they think it is (Cregan, 2010) and their perceptions of their students' capacity for learning and achievement, which may be influenced by issues of social class, gender and ethnicity (Filer & Pollard, 2000). Rosenthal and Jacobson (1968) reported that teachers with high expectations for their students often produce students who ultimately meet those expectations. Therefore, teachers' expectations for what their students can achieve matter also. Ross and Nisbett (1991) advise that high standards must be perceived as attainable by the students as the effects of any educational intervention depend on its psychological meaning to the students. If students perceive the standards as achievable for themselves, they will be more motivated to work towards them. Sharing high expectations with students conveys the message that the teacher sees potential in them, that they have potential and that greater effort yields greater competence (Dweck et al., 2015, p. 25).

Teachers' confidence

Teachers' own level of confidence is another important factor. According to the Communication Trust (2015a, p. 5), many practitioners report that they're not confident in knowing what children should be doing in terms of speaking skills at different ages and stages, or how to support good language skills and spot those children who might be struggling. First Steps (2013) advises that the role of teachers as reflective practitioners is also key when it comes to speaking, in order to reflect on important, associated questions. For example, do I provide meaningful opportunities for all of my students to talk? Do I regularly timetable oral language lessons? It is clear then that when it comes to nurturing and developing speaking skills so that students may more easily access and use student voice, teachers have an extremely important role to play. Their role consists of listening, planning, explaining, questioning, describing, organising, evaluating, inspiring, challenging, and all of this is done primarily through the medium of talk (Riley et al., 2004). In oral language in the classroom context, the teacher is required to take on a range of roles—facilitator, manager, instructor and assessor (Fisher, 1992) and use a range of strategies such as modelling, demonstrating, supporting and scaffolding (Bruner, 1986).

Reflection, practice and training

'Looking at Our Schools' (LAOS, 2016) highlighted how its quality framework "emphasises the need for pupils to develop a broad range of skills, competencies and values that enable personal well-being, active citizenship and lifelong learning" (p. 6). The updated LAOS (2022) includes references to aspects of learning and teaching that became more significant during and following Covid-19 related lockdowns. These aspects include "the role of assessment and feedback in supporting progression in learning, and the development of students' independent learning skills" (p. 6).

In terms of training in public speaking skills across their lifetimes, 30% of teachers I surveyed said they had received training in public speaking skills. This training, though not always explicit occurred mainly in secondary school by way of debating teams and competitions. Other sources of 'training' mentioned were college debating teams, private elocution lessons or private Speech and Drama classes. One teacher shared, "*I have received advanced facilitation training as part of my prior career in public relations. Confidence in public speaking was a basic requirement of the job*". Two-thirds (67%) of those who had received training opportunities in school indicated that these opportunities were not available to all students in their class. The main type of public speaking training received by survey respondents was through debating followed by formal presentation skills, speech writing, dramatic presentations, group facilitation skills, pitch facilitation, narratives, drama, poetry, negotiation with teams and course delivery. One teacher mentioned that she was trained in *"a variety of public speaking genres"* and another was taught the *"theory of speech"*. Persuasive writing was also mentioned in the responses to the question on public speaking genres.

Almost half (47%) of the teachers I surveyed said they would feel confident in their ability to train children in public speaking skills. Thirty-one percent reported that they weren't sure while 22% stated they did not feel confident. This may be due to not having received training in these skills themselves. However, 70% shared the opinion that a teacher does not have to have excellent public speaking skills themselves to train students in these skills. Teachers surveyed and interviewed thought the most important role of the teacher in training children in public speaking skills in order of the most commonly stated are: *"encouragement"*, *"providing positive, encouraging feedback and reassurance"*, *"creating and fostering a positive classroom environment where children are encouraged to actively participate in all classroom discussions"*, *"facilitation"*, *"making the time, seeing it as important and worthwhile"*, *"knowledge and understanding of skills involved"*, *"being clear in what's expected"*, *"having a step-by-step approach"*, *"supporting the instilling and development of self-belief and confidence"*, *"possess a positive attitude"*, *"enthusiasm"* and *"a willingness to upskill and enable children to enjoy this activity"*.

Additional teacher comments

Additional comments by teachers in my study survey highlighted the need to provide training for teachers in this area. One teacher made the point that *"it's a very difficult area to cover but very worthwhile doing"*. Another teacher shared a passion for wanting today's children to receive what her generation had not. Yet another teacher's opinion was that *"I would personally rate this so much higher than other skill sets we afford so much time to"*. More related comments provided were: *"It gives pupils the skills they need to make presentations in college, interviews and presentations for work in later life. It is a key skill that all young people need going forward"*, and *"as a parent of kids in secondary school doing the Leaving Certificate (LC) exam and new Junior Cycle (JC) exam, I realise now more than ever the need for public speaking in primary school to help with the presentations in secondary schools"*.

The belief that early childhood is the best time to start was specifically expressed in "additional comments": *"Children love the opportunity to speak at an early age, yet we don't capitalise on this opportunity when it would be the easiest time to do so"*, *"I believe this is a crucial life-skill and the younger children are exposed to public speaking, the easier it will be"*. Concern for shy children was expressed by four teachers, and one teacher stated that this skill-set training *"should not involve pressure on nervous or shy pupils"*. Choice for the child with regard to the topic and the size of the audience were also noted as important. Another teacher expressed the concern that currently, in life, only a few have access to this skill set training: *"Unfortunately, it remains the preserve of the more academic and confident pupil"*, she said, *"most will shy away from it"* and *"are allowed to shy away from it"*. One teacher interviewed emphasised how training in public speaking skills is especially beneficial for students with speech and language difficulties and that all students can develop the skills and their confidence at their own rates. For "shy" children, it was suggested that not equipping children with these skills is potentially more detrimental, limiting their options. One teacher spoke about how the process is more important than the product, making the point that even if a child never presented to an audience, they would have learned much through the process, planning and preparation.

How teachers can promote a culture of more 'student voice' in their classroom

One easy way teachers can self-evaluate their practice is to notice how often students literally use their voice in the classroom. Conducting an audit of this over a period of time, for their own information, may help to identify their starting point, what they're already doing well and can build on and areas for improvement and development. It would be helpful to take note of when, where and how students are expressing themselves, their thoughts, ideas and learning. What triggers or prompts these moments? Are they prompted by the teacher or by other students? How are students currently using their voice in the classroom? If it is only in answering teacher's questions that students' voices are heard, are those questions closed or open? Are students given opportunities to ask and explore their own questions? Are they given opportunities to make decisions about their educational experience within their classroom and also the school?

Student voice is connected to choice. Are students encouraged to exercise choice in the classroom? Do students have choice and where is this most evident? This could be evident in a choice of where they sit, choice of topic for study, choice of how they research a topic, choice of who they discuss their ideas with and choice of how they share and demonstrate their thinking and learning. Could the choice and options they already have be extended? Do students have independent processes and activities they engage in throughout the day? Are they facilitated to become as independent as possible? Are they given opportunities to engage in group work with peers where they are encouraged to listen to one another and build on each other's ideas? Are students aware of the importance of their voice and the voice of their peers? Do they have the opportunity to feedback or contribute to discussions about school policies, curriculum design and assessment? Do they have the opportunity to suggest, plan, organize school events? Where these opportunities exist, are they available to all students?

In terms of a classroom or learning environment audit, the following may be helpful. Is the layout of the classroom conducive to 'student voice'? Classrooms that prioritize student voice may not look like traditional classrooms. Students seldom sit in rows but rather in clusters or group formations of tables with a considerable amount of work taking place in circles. The importance of the circle is that everybody is on the same level. Nobody is in front or behind. This set-up is less daunting and more comfortable for students who may be shy or reluctant to speak up. Think seriously about how you want to cultivate a practice and culture of student voice and empowerment in your class. Think about who's voice is heard most frequently in the class. Is there a balance between the teacher/adult voice and students' voices? Are all students facilitated to express themselves in some shape or form? The following are some practical ideas for consideration that may support you to encourage, promote and plan for more 'student voice' in your classroom.

- Become more aware of the different types of talk within the classroom. Cazden (2001) explains that there is a time and place for the different forms of talk, for instructional talk, exploratory talk, recitation, talk in which ideas are explored rather than simple answers to teachers' test questions, talk and discussions in which teachers talk less and students talk more. Students can address one another directly, respectfully and in an orderly manner. Students themselves can decide and/or indicate when to speak rather than always waiting to be called on by the teacher.
- Create or co-create with the students, safe, supportive learning spaces and a positive environment in which students are motivated and feel supported to use, practise and develop their voice, metaphorically and physically.
- Work with students to co-create a classroom vision of success. This could be done when co-creating rules for the class. Engage students in an activity about what a comfortable, learner-centred, successful classroom might look like and what success looks like for them, individually and collectively.
- Work with students to create goals towards that vision. When students have the opportunity to set their own goals, they are more likely to achieve them, since these goals mean something special to them. You can facilitate and support them to set and shape their short- and long-term goals and brainstorm choices they may need to consider and sacrifices they may need to make to reach their goals. Encourage them also to reflect on, acknowledge and celebrate their personal and collective achievements along the way.
- Use templates at the beginning of the school year or a term of work, asking for the students input to inform planning, for example, 'three things I would most like to learn about in this subject/topic/term'.
- Consider providing choice in relation to students' work: choice in learning environment, choice in resources and choice in method of feedback and assessment. Traditionally, assignments set for students have almost always been written assignments. We now know that content can be created and presented in a variety of different ways. Allow and facilitate students to choose ways that are meaningful, interesting, relevant and exciting to them. Allow them also the opportunity throughout the day or class to choose what they want to work or focus on.
- Teach students how to choose. This might sound basic but students need to be aware of their options and be able to weigh them up in order to choose.
- Use a reciprocal model of classroom conversation that encourages, requires and emphasizes student participation which leads to more autonomy and empowerment in classroom interaction.
- Provide and orchestrate opportunities for all students to practise conversations within the class with their peers. Some students may need more guidance and support with this than others but all students will benefit from it on many levels.
- Constantly acknowledge and celebrate the diversity in your classroom and never assume that one child's voice represents all children's voices in the class.

- Provide access to diverse resources for students in a variety of different ways, for example, paper-based resources, physical learning materials and artefacts, digital resources and various multi-media options.
- Encourage, enable and empower students to speak and communicate in a variety of different ways. Traditionally, students' voices may have been heard most when responding to questions. While this is still valuable, especially in relation to responding to open-ended questions, there are multiple other ways in which students can develop and use their voice in the classroom and school. They can share their ideas in small groups, present to small groups or the class or the school, build on other students' ideas, talk about assignments and tasks, tell stories, report, and interview. All of this helps to build their presentation skills as well as their confidence. It also empowers them to feel more involved in their school community. They become known by others for what they say, communicate and share. Not all students need to present in the same way. Some may choose to present live while some may feel more comfortable initially pre-recording their presentations. By facilitating these options, the teacher is ensuring that communication is accessible to all.
- Ensure that students have a voice in shaping the school community. Encourage them to share what they like, dislike, would change about their school and importantly, how they would go about that. Ensure that their suggestions and solutions are acted on where possible and where it is not possible to act on some of students' suggestions, reasons are explained.
- Give them problems to solve that connect closely with and are relevant to their community or better still, students can suggest problems to explore solutions to that form part of their real-life concerns. Encourage and provide opportunities for students to collaborate with peers to come up with possible solutions to real-world problems and issues that affect their lives. They could collect concerns from peers by way of a 'concerns' box in the classroom so quieter, more introverted students can have their input too.
- Use the '5 E model' (Bybee et al., 2006) of inquiry-based learning in your classroom: engage, explore, explain, elaborate and evaluate. This empowering framework facilitates a constructivist, guided-inquiry approach where students are supported to think and work scientifically. They gather and analyse their own evidence, and communicate their ideas, findings and methodologies with others including their peers and the teacher.
- Actively connect with and show an interest in students' home lives. Ensure that family engagement is also encouraged within the school, that school is a place where all parents feel welcomed. Check that various types of communication loops with families are facilitated, for example, through paper forms, texts, calls and online platforms.
- Invite and apply student feedback regularly, not just on a once-off basis, on different aspects of class life and learning by way of surveys, polls and discussion groups. This is preparing young people to continue to actively have their voice heard which prepares them for future situations as voters and active participants in their community. Young people could even be enabled and empowered to administer these surveys and polls themselves.

154 *Examples of 'Student Voice' in Practice*

- Ask more general open questions that would allow students to reveal something of themselves in their answers, e.g., having read a story, instead of beginning with specific, closed questions, you could ask: What was your favourite part of the story? Who's your favourite character and why?
- Offer regular opportunities for project-based learning activities. Incorporate student choice into the selection of topics for research and exploration.
- Kincheloe and Steinberg (1998) note that student voice occurs in classrooms where the focus is on pedagogical strategies that aim to privilege students' own cultural histories and forms of knowing. Search for the work of individuals from backgrounds similar to the student body who reflect common life experiences, struggles and achievements (e.g., stories, poetry, music, presentations, text, blogs). Consider inviting a leader from within their community into the class to speak to the students. Ensure that speakers from diverse backgrounds are invited.
- Model and explicitly teach skills of self-expression and clear, assertive communication.
- Explicitly teach speaking and listening skills and provide a structure that will enable students to take part in various discussions throughout the school day; one-to-one discussions, small group discussions and whole class discussions. Plan 'discussion time' into as many lessons as possible.
- Teach students how to give feedback to peers and to the teacher using 'I' statements referring to what they saw, heard, felt and understood from another's contribution.
- Allow some time for student self-talk and self-reflection on tasks so that they can deepen their own learning and understanding, decide what questions they may need to ask of their peers or teacher to better understand the task at hand while getting used to the sound of their own voice.
- Empower students with strategies such as 'Try 3 before me' so that students develop the habit of effort, trying and exploring different strategies and options themselves before asking the teacher for help and thereby, developing more independence in the process.
- Use language of empowerment that celebrates the uniqueness of each individual student, reassuring them that we all learn differently and that we all have a valuable contribution to make to the world. In short, we all make a difference. Words that teachers and other significant adults in our lives have spoken have stayed with many of us long after the doors of the school years closed, for better and for worse. Be aware that our words have enormous, long-lasting power.
- As recommended by Fielding (2001), take opportunities to engage students as producers of knowledge via, for example, students-as-researchers projects.
- Respond to students' comments with curiosity not judgment and show an interest and desire to understand and find out more.
- Discuss and explore the concept of 'speaking rights' within the class. Who has the right to speak and when? In classrooms in which I was a student in my earlier years, the only person I thought had a right to speak was the teacher, or the principal or another adult when they entered the room. In fact, I remember on one occasion when I spoke up in class, the teacher reprimanded me and said, "You have no right to speak to me like that". Teachers have the right to speak at any time to any person and in any way they choose; they can fill any silence or interrupt any speaker. What about the students?

- Invite student input regarding behaviour management systems within the classroom.
- Incorporate another area of reflection into your daily reflection as a reflective practitioner. Consider "What did I learn from/about my students today?"

The more regularly you engage in these activities, or a combination of them, a culture of 'student voice' will begin to grow and become very evident in your classroom. Embedding these practices will ensure that new students joining your class will be assured and confident that facilitating 'student voice' is one definite and strong aspect of your classroom and your teaching. You'll see from the list of examples above, which is not exhaustive, student voice may include some modes of vocal participation, for example, in classroom discussions, public speaking and debating opportunities and moving on to school-wide representation, in student councils, student advisory panels and student-led school-based research.

How schools can promote a culture of more 'student voice' across the school

Similar for schools, on a whole school basis, staff need to think seriously about how they want to cultivate a practice and embed a culture of 'student voice' and empowerment throughout the school. Where there is clear respect for everyone's views and open communication amongst the adults in the school, students will notice this and it will be easier to ensure that this is extended to students also. On a whole school basis, students can have their voice heard in the following ways:

- Invite student input when updating school policies. When students are invited and facilitated to contribute to school practices and policies, these policies become more relevant and have more buy-in from the student body.
- On the Student Council, in who they elect and the topics they share with the council. All students should be encouraged to participate in the Student Council or become part of another advocacy group. It is a good idea for the school leadership team to have a timetabled time slot when they meet with the leadership of the Student Council for updates and to see how they can collaborate for greater good.
- Seen as potentially more equitable than a student council, a Children's or Student's Advisory Panel model is an alternative to student councils where all students have the opportunity to engage and attend meetings. This is facilitated through whole class meetings where important topics are discussed. Feedback from each class meeting is then brought to a smaller, more focused meeting where a few students from each class attend to present the ideas of their class.
- School-wide and inter-school public speaking events and debating competitions are some concrete ways to support and encourage students in the development of their speaking and critical thinking skills.
- Explicitly teach and show-case the skills of self-expression on a whole-school level.
- Think carefully about how and where students' input is sought and considered in terms of decision-making. Not every idea that students suggest needs to be enacted but students must know that the ideas and feedback they offer are given due and fair consideration in the decision-making process.

- Take every opportunity to gather and give students the practice of sharing their views via surveys, sharing opinions about current events and future plans and projects.
- Students could be supported to lead weekly school assemblies and/or given speaking roles at assemblies.
- Maximize opportunities for younger students to learn from seeing older students, as role models, more vocal and visible.
- When visitors come to the school, assign active roles and responsibilities to students in terms of welcoming them and guiding them around the school.
- Invite students' suggestions regarding speakers to invite to the school.
- Let students decide on school trips. They could suggest some of their preferred options and vote. Students could also be involved in booking some of the activities, liaising with the relevant booking offices regarding prices, times, etc. All of this is really important real-world learning and may be the first and only chance some of your students get to do this.
- Collaborate with a local community group to involve and engage students in a project of interest and benefit to their community and families.
- Assign the task of updating a school or student blog or a section of the school's website to the students, perhaps rotating the role. Another student could be the editor, checking the piece and feeding back on it before it's sent to a staff member for sign-off. The blogs could contain a mixture of pictures, videos and writing. Different students could take responsibility for different sections of the website depending on their individual and collective interests, e.g., students who have a particular interest in sport might take responsibility for updating the school's sport's news on a weekly/monthly/termly basis.
- Put practices in place to intentionally cultivate a culture of listening. Listening to and considering every voice is the true essence of inclusion.
- Taylor and Robinson (2009) point out that student voice 'happens' at the level of the institution, the school in the following ways: through school councils, students as governors, and even students sitting on staff appointment panels (p. 163).

Attempts to listen to young people's voices at a broader level

The EU Parliament is trying to listen to Europe's young voices, for example, 2022 was named the European Year of Youth with the aim of encouraging all young people to make their voices heard. In May that year the 'Voice your vision' platform was launched by the European Commission encouraging young people to upload their thoughts on a range of issues from the future of Europe, inclusion, diversity, education, mental health, climate change and more. The aim? To empower young Europeans from all backgrounds to 'unmute'. Sounds great? But how are **all** young people to do this? How do you unmute when you've been told for so long, in fact generations, to "shh", "be quiet", "stop talking". There is a gap between 'unmute' and 'speak your truth', and here is where we need to focus. This, I believe, is where the Lundy model (Lundy, 2007) of child participation, endorsed widely across the world, for example, by the Irish Department of Children and Youth Affairs, can help organisations and governments endeavouring to promote and facilitate child voice. As mentioned previously, the Lundy model sets out four key elements for listening to young people's voices: space, voice, audience and influence.

All young people must be enabled, encouraged, empowered from a young age to build the skills and confidence to express themselves. If not, launching the 'Voice your vision' platform is like launching the world cup football tournament with teams of players who have never or seldom been given the opportunity to develop and practise the expected skills to play the game. What about youth in poverty and from marginalized communities? What about seldom heard voices? It's not as simple as saying "unmute" and expecting all young people to be willing and ready to heed this call, in the 'European Year of Youth'. Yes, young people are the future. Yes, it is imperative that we hear their voices. President of the EU Commission, Ursula von der Leyen, recognized this when she emphasized that Europe must listen carefully to its young people, to "better shape the Union in their mould". I believe she's right, but it's just not that simple. If Europe and any other continent or country is truly serious about listening to all its young people, it must ensure structures that provide space, voice, audience and influence to uphold the right of every young person to be heard. As Kofi Annan, former Secretary-General of the United Nations, said, "Young people should be at the forefront of global change and innovation. Empowered, they can be key agents for development and peace".

Summary reflection on student voice in the classroom and across the school

Student voice most certainly does not happen incidentally. Incorporating student voice in the classroom and across the school requires clear commitments, deliberate intention and a willingness to deeply listen and share control. To paraphrase an expression that spoke to me, if we don't listen when students whisper, we will be made to listen when they shout. We can intentionally work to promote 'student voice' because of all the benefits that we perceive or simply because we have a duty to do so, or both. Young people have the right to have their voices heard. Lansdown (2011) stresses that governments need to provide sustainable and continuing pre- and in-service training for teachers and all professionals working with and for children on the UNCRC, including Article 12, and how to implement it, learning to listen to and respect children's views, their evolving capacities and their right to freedom of expression.

We hear an increasing amount of talk about child voice and student voice in the education context in recent years but who's doing most of the talking? Ultimately, the goal of encouraging and facilitating student voice is to engage and empower students individually and collectively so that they can talk and communicate more and have their voices heard. It's about increasing students' representation at, and participation in, processes and practices that affect their lives, from which they have historically been excluded. 'Student voice' not only impacts on current students' experience of school, learning and education. It can also help to shape a better, more relevant education for future generations of students.

Student voice and child voice work has the potential to celebrate children's uniqueness from an early stage. When children are being their true authentic selves, they inspire, surprise, teach, make us think and make us smile. What's more, comprising a percentage of the population today, they are one hundred percent the future. Ensuring their voice today is a very wise investment in strong, empowered, active citizens of tomorrow. Young people from all backgrounds and ages can teach us something we don't know if we're brave enough to listen. I am convinced that the world will be a better place when child and student voice are realized and more deeply embedded in our systems. Where do we start? Simple. Just 'shhhhhh' and let the children and students talk while we . . . Listen!.

Reference List

Alexander, R. (2008). *Towards Dialogic Teaching: Rethinking Classroom Talk*, Fourth Edition. York: Dialogos UK.

Alexander, R. (2012, February 20). Improving Oracy and Classroom Talk in English Schools Achievements and Challenges. Presentation given at the DfE seminar on Oracy, the National Curriculum and Educational Standards.

Alexander, R. (2018). Developing Dialogic Teaching: Genesis, Process, Trial. *Research Papers Education* 33(5), 561–598.

Bruner, J. (1983). *Child's Talk: Learning to Use Language*. New York: WW Norton & Co.

Bruner, J. (1986). *Actual Minds, Possible Worlds*. Cambridge, MA: Harvard University Press.

Bybee, R., Taylor, J. et al. (2006). *The BSCS 5E Instructional Model: Origins and Effectiveness*. Colorado Springs, CO: BSCS.

Cazden, C. B. (2001). *Classroom Discourse: The Language of Teaching and Learning*. Portsmouth, NH: Heinemann.

Cregan, A. (2010). *From Policy to Practice. The Oral Language Challenge for Teachers*.

Deason, D. K. (2009). Let's Talk: The Importance of Conversations with Preschoolers. *NHSA Dialog*, 12(4), 374–377.

Dewey, J. (1938). *Experience and Education* (Vol. 10). New York: The Macmillan Company.

Dweck, C. S., Walton, G. M., & Cohen, G. L. (2015). Academic Tenacity: Mindsets and Skills that Promote Long-Term Learning. Paper prepared for the Gates Foundation.

Fielding, M. (2001). Beyond the Rhetoric of Student Voice: New Departures or New Constraints in the Transformation of 21st Century Schooling. *Forum for Promoting 3-19 Comprehensive Education*. DOI: 10.2304/forum.2001.43.2.1

Filer, A., & Pollard, A. (2000). *The Social World of Pupil Assessment*. London: Cassell.

First Steps. (2013). *Speaking and Listening Resource Book FIRST005 | Speaking and Listening Resource Book*. Department of Education, WA.

Fisher, R. (1992). *Early Literacy and the Teacher*. UKRA. Sevenoaks: Hodder & Stoughton.

Fisher, R., & Larkin, S. (2008). Pedagogy or Ideological Struggle? An Examination of Pupils' and teachers' Expectations for Talk in the Classroom. *Language and Education*, 22(1), 1–16.

Gambrell, L. B., Malloy, J. A., & Mazzoni, S. A. (2011). Evidence-based Best Practices in Comprehensive Literacy Instruction. In L. M. Morrow & L. B. Gambrell (Eds.). *Best Practices in Literacy Instruction* (4th ed.), 11–36. New York: Guilford Press.

Greenaway, R. (2004) Critiques of David Kolb's theory of experiential learning.

Hall Haley, M. (2005). *Teachers as Reflective Practitioners Using Multiple Intelligences-Based Instruction*. Graduate School of Education, 4400 University Drive, MSN 4B3 - 2005 Fairfax, VA 22030-4444

Hammerman, D. (1999). Teaching by Inquiry. In J. C. Miles & S. Priest (Eds.), *Adventure Programming* (pp. 201-204). PA: State College.

Hong, Z., & Ajex, N. K. (1995). *Oral Language Development across the Curriculum, K-12*.

Jalongo, M. R. (2008). Putting Children First . . . Literally. *Early Childhood Education Journal* 35, 391–392.

Kincheloe, J., & Steinberg, S. (1998). Students as Researchers: Critical Visions, Emancipatory Insights. In J. Kincheloe & S. Steinberg (Ed.). *Students as Researchers: Creating Classrooms That Matter*, 2–19. London: Falmer Press.

Kutnick, P., & Colwell, J. (2010) Dialogue Enhancement in Classrooms. Towards a Relations Approach for Group Working. In K. Littleton, & C. Howe (Eds.), *Educational Dialogues: Understanding and Promoting Productive Interaction*, 192–215. London: Routledge.

Lansdown, G. (2011). *Every Child's Right to Be Heard, a resource guide on the UN Committee on the Rights of the Child General Comment,* no.12, Gerison Lansdown. Save the Children UK on behalf of Save the Children and UNICEF.

LAOS. (2016). *Looking at Our Schools, a Quality Framework for Primary Schools*, The Inspectorate, Department of Education and Skills. Dublin.
LAOS. (2022). *Looking at Our Schools, a Quality Framework for Primary Schools*, The Inspectorate, Department of Education and Skills. Dublin.
Lundy, L. (2007). 'Voice' Is Not Enough: Conceptualising Article 12 of the United Nations Convention on the Rights of the Child. *British Educational Research Journal*, 33(6).
Mercer, N. (1995). *The Guided Construction of Knowledge: Talk Amongst Teachers and Learners*. Clevedon, Multilingual Matters.
Mercer & Littleton. (2007). *Dialogue and the Development of Children's Thinking: A Sociocultural Approach*.
Millard, W., & Menzies, L. (2016). *Oracy: The State of Speaking in Our Schools*, London: Voice 21.
Morisano, D., Hirsh, J. B., Peterson, J. B., Pihl, R. O., & Shore, B. M. (2010). Setting, Elaborating, and Reflecting on Personal Goals Improves Academic Performance. *Journal of Applied Psychology*, 95(2), 255.
NEPS. (2015). *Good Practice Guide. A Balanced Approach to Literacy Development in the Early Years*. Revised March 2016.
Otto, B. (2008). *Literacy Development in Early Childhood: Reflective Teaching for Birth to Age Eight* (Vol. 3). Upper Saddle River, NJ: Pearson Education Inc.
PDST. (2013). *Five Components of Effective Oral Language Instruction*, Professional Development Service for Teachers, Ireland.
Petek, T. (2014). The Teacher as a Public Speaker in the Classroom. *Studies in Literacy and Language*, 9(1), 124-133 CS Canada.
Reznitskaya, A. (2012). Dialogic Teaching. Rethinking Language Use during Literature Discussions. *The Reading Teacher*, 65(7), 446-456.
Richmond, V. P., & McCroskey, J. C. (1993). Diverse Perspectives on Communication—Communication Overview and Framework.
Riley, J., Burrell, A., & McCallum, B. (2004). Developing the Spoken Language Skills of Reception Class Children in Two Multi-Cultural, Inner-City Primary Schools. *British Educational Research Journal*, 30(5), 657-672.
Ressler, J. D. (2012). Transforming Physical Educators Through Adventure-Based Learning. The Ohio State University ProQuest Dissertations Publishing, 2012.3520577.
Rosenthal, R., & Jacobson, L. (1968). *Pygmalion in the Classroom*. New York: Holt, Rinehart & Winston.
Ross, L., & Nisbett, R. (1991). *The Person and the Situation: Perspectives of Social Psychology*. New York: McGraw Hill.
Shiel, G., Cregan, Á., McGough, & Archer, P. (2012). *Oral Language in Early Childhood and Primary Education (3-8 Years)*, NCCA Research Report No. 14.
Smith, P. (2001). *Talking Classrooms: Shaping Children's Learning Through Oral Language Instruction*.
Snow, C. E. (1990). Development of Definitional Skill. *Journal of Child Language*, 17(3), 697-710.
Taylor, C., & Robinson, C. (2009). Student Voice: Theorising Power and Participation. *Pedagogy, Culture & Society*, 17(2), 161-175.
The Communication Trust. (2015a). *Universally Speaking: The Ages and Stages of Children's Communication Development from Birth to 5 Years*. London: The Communication Trust.
VanderWey, Wallace, & Hansen. (2014). Creating Group Norms by Using Full Value Commitments in Experiential Education Programming. *Journal of Extension*, 57(3).
Wasik, B. A., & Hindman, A. H. (2018). Why Wait? The Importance of Wait Time in Developing Young Students' Language and Vocabulary. *The Reading Teacher*, 72(3), 369-378.
Wertsch, J. V. (1985). *Vygotsky and the Social Formation of Mind*. Cambridge, MA: Harvard University Press.

12 Welcome to the World of Child and Student Voice

Imagine for a moment a world filled with the sweet sound of children's voices and all that those voices represent. A world full of hope, engagement, fun, possibilities and purpose. Imagine a world full of wonder and awe, a world experienced through the eyes of a child, a world where their voices truly matter and make a difference. This is a world where children wake up in the morning looking forward to engaging in their 'wonder-full' world, playing with friends (and maybe some adults too, if we're lucky enough to be invited along) and exploring the magic and magnificence of their surroundings. In this world, children are excited to go to school knowing they will learn something new and meaningful to their lives and have numerous opportunities again, to play, explore and talk to their friends. They will listen and learn from the multitude of voices in their homes, classrooms and communities and contribute from their own unique space of interest and talent. They will see, understand and experience from a young age, diversity and diverse perspectives as the norm. Can this special place exist? For a few minutes, why not reclaim the power of imagination from your childhood, close your eyes and imagine it. Open up all of your senses to see, hear, taste, smell, feel and breathe it in.

How did we get to this brave new world?

So, how did we get to this brave world? Well, it started, as all great things do with a 'dream', a 'vision'. Even as I write, I am aware that it's a dream construed in my 'adult mind' so if it were truly a child's dream, we may have an even more glorious world of possibilities revealed to us. However, I'm very conscious that in order to get to that point, we have to start somewhere. My gaze may be that of an adult but it is the gaze of an adult who has worked with children across the world for thirty-two years as a teacher and school leader and also lived and loved the life of a parent of four beautiful, creative children.

The message of the importance and powerful potential of 'child voice' finally began to filter out, little by little, story by story. A key turning point occurred when adults who had the privilege and good fortune of living and working with children began to actively listen. It was acknowledged widely that children had a unique perspective and a unique body of knowledge in relation to matters that affect them. These insights and knowledge coupled with children's vivid and boundless imaginations were witnessed to be positively changemaking forces for good. Of course, it was initially uncomfortable and unfamiliar for the adults, as all change is, but 'where there's a will, there's a way'. Adults were willing. It required adults to be brave, to step outside their comfort zone. Thankfully, they rose to the occasion because they knew it was necessary and would reap immense benefits for all.

It was also recognized and taken seriously that all children, of all ages and backgrounds have the right to have their views heard and considered. Parents and adults who work with very young babies were already very aware that babies are indeed very capable of expressing needs in a variety of ways when time is taken to observe, listen and notice. Children's ability and readiness to participate was also observed in the many different roles and responsibilities children take on when they play, competently making decisions, collaborating with friends and using many skills and reasoning techniques to solve problems. It was also observed in how they are able to create and problem solve through art, movement, music, drawings and also in creating different worlds online in video games. Their contributions to various social media platforms were also evidence of how they were experimenting with expressing their views.

It also occurred that people of all beautiful, rich, diverse backgrounds woke up one morning to the realization that their families and communities were very under-represented in governing bodies. They wondered how could privileged people who understood little about their challenges and lives adequately advocate for and represent them? Adults also had a 'light bulb' moment when they realized that social policies and school curricula would surely have more relevance if all people, young and old, that they affected most had an input into them and were given opportunities to express their views about and influence them.

Article 12 of the UNCRC was like the alarm clock. There's no doubt that adults woke up more abruptly to the right of every child to have their voice heard when more attention was drawn to Article 12 of the United Nations Convention of the Rights of the Child (UN, 1989) and the legal duty to ensure that this right is implemented and realized. Caring adults accepted that it was their responsibility to find creative and effective ways to provide children and students with opportunities for active citizenship and participation. In an effort to further develop the elusive social concept of 'equality', children were seen as equal citizens, citizens today, in the present moment and not just at some date in the future when they turn 18. As such, they needed opportunities to practise citizenship on a daily basis. Some adults had to be reminded that they are neither superior nor wiser beings simply because of their age. Just because adults previously had the lion's share of social power did not mean that this would always be the case or that it was even the wisest arrangement. What's more, it was clear that the world they were handing on to their children showed many signs that the balance of power was in drastic need of change.

There was a formal ceremony, a handing over of the gavel of power, from the adults, the majority of whom had passively assumed power, to the children who simply wanted to be heard. The dangerous requirement that "children should be seen and not heard" had done untold damage to generations of children, leaving them vulnerable, silenced and in some cases traumatized. And so it was that the children of the world and their respective adult carers met at the 'Bridge of Voice' for the official transfer of power ceremony. What happened next was momentous and would change the world positively and powerfully forever. Child and student voice obviously didn't mean what some had thought.

Home in this brave new world

So, what does home life look like in this brave new world? Parents are very engaged with their children of all ages and lively conversations and discussion warm the homes and hearts. Parents invite their children's views and participation in decision making within the home as they model good listening skills. Children, learning as they always do, from the example of their parents, learn to listen also. They listen to their parents and their siblings while becoming more confident in expressing their own unique individual views. Children are not compared to others, they are allowed and encouraged to be unique. They don't have to win or be 'the best' to prove anything to anyone but get plenty of experience working with others towards a common purpose. They have space to play. From a very young age, children are expected and supported to do what they can do for themselves while given opportunities and support to learn to do even more. They are trusted to help with jobs around the home. In this way, they become gradually more independent and their sense of self-efficacy grows in a real, meaningful way. Jobs might include looking after a pet, making their bed, doing their laundry, tidying their room and a choice of household jobs that will benefit the whole family.

When decisions are being made about renovating or decorating the home, children's opinions are invited. This is sometimes in relation to the colour of paint or new pieces of furniture around the house. Their preference may not always be the one selected but their view is always considered and the reason for going with another option, when that is the outcome, is shared. Children are frequently active outdoors with family members, be it planting a garden or engaging in some type of fun, physical activity. In homes that don't have much outdoor space, mini gardens are planted in a few small pots, and the children take responsibility for looking after them and helping them to grow.

Parents are not vicariously living their dreams through their children's lives but actively encouraging the unique dreams and imaginations of their little ones. Parents accept that the world their children are living and growing up in is very different to the world of their youth. While aware that they adults have valuable life experience to share with children, they also know that their children have expertise in areas that they don't, for example, with regard to technology. Adults show an openness, willingness and interest to learn from children. Parents and children discuss the balance of time and attention regarding technology. Tables have turned slightly and now, instead of bemoaning the detrimental impact of technology, parents have become the curious ones, trying to understand what it's like to be a 'digital native'. Children lead parents through an exploration of the positives and potential of technology while parents lead children through the joys of face-to-face communication and connection. Communication has become more important than ever.

Adults have not forgotten the importance of storytelling and reading to their children. Children, as always, adore stories and are frequently seen cuddling up on their parent's lap asking for yet another story. Sometimes parents introduce new books to their children and often they allow the children to choose the book, the page, the picture themselves. Parents enjoy having wild and wonderful chats about the book becoming playful again, having fun and happily reconnecting with the child inside themselves.

School in this brave new world

Schools very clearly support all students to realise their full potential. The main purpose of schools is learning and educating. Everybody is a learner and teacher, and everybody is a listener in these schools. The doors of the school are open, for all learners to come in and also open to a variety of learning environments and experiences. Inclusive education in these schools celebrates diversity and responds to and celebrates the uniqueness of every child. Opportunities and advantages are provided for children of all backgrounds. The various languages students come to school with are celebrated and approached with curiosity. This richness of diversity is regarded as a wonderful learning opportunity for all. There is a healthy curiosity about people from different backgrounds and a genuine interest in finding out more about others. While most interactions take place through the standard language of the area where the school is located, all children have a chance every day to share something in and about their own language. One language is not perceived to be better than another. All languages are seen as beautiful and acknowledged as the powerful and rich connecting and communicating force that they are.

In these schools, teachers listen and tune in to what's happening in the lives of children and young people. They are acutely aware that children are the only ones who can provide the most accurate and authentic information about their lives, interests and needs. Teachers, themselves, learn a great deal when they incorporate into classroom discussions, information, knowledge and learning that students acquire outside of school in their digital, home and community lives. This is another reason why 'student voice' is more important than ever.

Teachers are not expected to be experts in any particular area but are competent in most. They are reflective practitioners, as they always have been, and very competent in the theory and practice of effective education. However, they are encouraged to share particular passions and expertise they may have with students across the school and sometimes across a cluster of schools. There are periods during the day when the role of 'teacher' is reversed and the 'students' become the 'teachers' teaching certain lessons. As teachers, children teach adults to be more playful and childlike rather than adults always teaching children to grow up. As present beings, children teach the adults at school, the joy and power of presence and mindfulness, how to 'be'. Encouraged to share their expertise, students are a teacher's best resource for supporting better access to and understanding of technology, suggesting the kinds of technology that teachers could be using in classroom, and showing teachers how they can use specific software and hardware tools to teach more effectively. Children grow in confidence as they eagerly share their expertise in relation to technology. They co-construct rules in relation to technology with teachers at school. Children bring their devices to school, be they phones or tablets, and teachers and students learn together how to be optimally smart when using their 'smart' devices. They explore together how to maximise the potential of these devices, especially their mobile phones as students have informed teachers that their mobile phone is their most frequently used device. A strong aim is to learn to use and manage mobile phones in ways that will enrich their own lives as human beings.

Students are supported to increase their confidence and competence in using a range of digital technologies to harness and express their imagination and expand their creative thinking and creative expression. In tandem with developing their critical thinking skills, students develop a wider knowledge and deeper understanding of fact-checking methods in developing media literacy. Teachers regularly engage in dialogue and discussion with students regarding how to stay safe online. However, there is a clear awareness that the internet and 'dark web' trolls that adults once endeavoured to protect their children from were not children but rather 'messed up adults' who probably never had a voice as a child and consequently, do not now know how to use their voice respectfully.

The school seeks students' opinions when a school build is happening or other changes or alterations are taking place. Students live out democratic processes at school and are given opportunities to constructively challenge and question authority. Positive, open and relational school cultures are nurtured. The school corridors are filled with the sweet sound of student voices. Not shouting, but simply communicating. Noise does not signify something bad as it used to. Rather, it is celebrated and embraced as confirmation of participation, engagement and learning.

What students learn

Education in schools starts from a space of acknowledging and celebrating diversity. Before young students engage in sorting activities which involve developing the skills of matching and finding similarities, time is intentionally spent on looking for and marvelling at the natural diversity that surrounds us. Children are encouraged to get comfortable with difference and celebrate the multi-dimensional, beautiful nature of the world around them before they try to sort and order it.

By participating regularly in dialogue, discussion and decision making, students develop and use citizenship knowledge, skills and attitudes. They receive explicit instruction in spoken language skills and are provided with multiple opportunities to practise. Mercer and Mannion (2018) were right when they suggested that spoken language skill development improves cognitive, social and emotional skills and life outcomes for all young people. A deliberate focus on oral language development for all children has been maintained, prioritized and nurtured and as a result, in addition to the benefits Mercer and Mannion (2018) outlined, relationships are flourishing. Students very competently apply their knowledge of communication skills to better interpret, understand and show respect for the perspectives of others. As John Hold suggested in 'How Children Learn', the adults' role is to give children as much help and guidance as they need and ask for, listen respectfully when they feel like talking and then, get out of the way, trusting children to do the rest.

Well-being has become, a primary priority for all schools, well-being of students and teachers, well-being of all. For students to be facilitated to remain positively engaged in new learning, it is acknowledged that their state of well-being—mental, physical, spiritual, academic and social—has to be nurtured and promoted. This is a pre-requisite in order for students to realise their full potential. Teachers are very aware of the role of developing speaking and communication skills vis-à-vis well-being, and put additional supports in place to help children to express themselves in response to the challenges of the Covid-19-related lockdowns of 2020 and 2021.

Project-based learning in school allows for the combining of various topics and subjects, so that students don't just memorise facts, but also understand how things interconnect and affect them in real life. Curriculum content begins with a focus on the child and the child's own community and context. Through constant encouragement to share stories, children gain a deep knowledge and awareness of their own culture and heritage and also a deeper understanding of the different cultures of the classmates they interact with every day. There is a focus on applying acquired knowledge and skills to problem enquiry. Skills and dispositions are prioritised. Skills such as communication, collaboration, social skills, critical thinking, leadership, empathy, teamwork are explicitly developed and nurtured. Students gain skills and insights that will contribute to social growth and mobility rather than social reproduction.

Creative skills are developed not just by engaging in what were traditionally known as creative activities such as Art, Music, Dance and Creative Writing. Children are encouraged to think in lots of creative ways across all of the subjects and curriculum areas when actively engaged in solving problems or as a preferred term, 'solving puzzles'. Effort is encouraged and rewarded. Mistakes are celebrated as an important part of the creative and innovative learning process. Various opportunities are provided for meaningful creative experiences through exploring, clarifying and expressing ideas, new insights and feelings. Teamwork is promoted by actively and effectively working in teams. Collaboration and building on one another's ideas are prioritized and valued over competition. All students develop leadership skills by being supported to take the lead in various areas relevant to their strengths and interests within the classroom and the school.

Public speaking skills are taught to all students as it is recognised that teaching public speaking skills to primary school students can be a fun, playful and engaging way to help students develop important communication and critical thinking abilities empowering them to become the best version of themselves. Having witnessed the transformational power of public speaking instruction and practise, students regularly share their ideas, thoughts and learning more effectively with a range of audiences, and are also empowered to speak up against social injustices when and where they notice them. Students know that they are learning 'public speaking skills' so that they can be very aware that they are well-equipped with concrete skills to mitigate any potential fear of public speaking in their lives as children and in the future. Furthermore, engaging students in public speaking training and activities at their own stage of readiness, is helping teachers to fulfil their duty under Article 12 of the United Nations Convention on the Rights of the Child.

Becoming more confident has been for children, a profound, powerful process of growing into their authentic self and becoming more comfortable in their own skin. Although presenting on a topic ensures that knowledge sticks for longer than when gained through some other means, the confidence and learning students gain from public speaking training has become a part of who they are and often sticks with them long after facts and knowledge learned for particular presentations are forgotten.

Students are also aware that being empowered to speak up and out for themselves and others has a powerful impact on mental well-being, supporting them to communicate their needs, ideas, thoughts and desires, and in so doing, to better understand them. They know, as the animated character Shrek said, words, thoughts, ideas and feelings are "better out than in". Probably one of the most critical skills that underpins mental health and well-being is the confidence and ability to ask for help. Individuals connect with others when their opinion is invited, considered and valued and deep trust has formed. Furthermore, learning and practising how to deal with that proverbial "knot" or "butterflies in the stomach" and manage nerves if experienced before presentations has proven to be a very valuable self-regulating skill for life.

Children are empowered as citizens to take positive actions to live justly, sustainably, and with regard for the rights of others. They learn experientially through active participation about democracy and citizenship. Some adults were initially sceptical wondering how students might best learn about democracy. One suggested, somewhat cynically, that children might simply look at the many bad examples adult leaders in history created and just do the opposite. In 2012, a study that included thirty-one countries across Europe found that citizenship featured somehow in all national school curricula. It was either a subject in its own right or a cross curricular topic or a feature of the school's function as a place where students actively learn citizenship through contribution, experience and practise (Eurydice, 2012).

There are no uniforms in schools. Therefore, time is not needlessly wasted checking who isn't wearing the correct uniform correctly. Students are trusted to wear whatever they choose to school, free to express their individuality. Each school day ends with reflection time, individually and in groups, considering "What did I learn today" as well as "What did I teach or share today". Homework is not such a big issue. Referred to more commonly as 'home learning', it is acknowledged that learning happens everywhere, and children can consolidate anything new they've learned at school, especially that which appeals to their own interests, by sharing it with parents and family when they go home. Well-being and relationships come first so if 'home learning' interferes negatively with these, it's not engaged in. School report cards are based not just on grades but also, on happiness, fun, effort, tenacity and contribution. Students input into their own report cards which contain a comment from the student themselves and also a comment from one or a few of their peers at school. There is no standardised testing. How could there be when it is widely recognized that each student is unique and individual and cannot be standardised. However, teachers, of course, use a variety of assessment tools and methods that include each child's input to evaluate and ensure progress.

Where students learn

Recognizing that there are a lot more fascinating and effective ways and places to learn things than by just sitting in classrooms, many classes are conducted outside the school building: in the outdoors, in the local library, in the local community, in the local sports grounds and in the local theatre. There is time every day for physical activities. Learning, sharing and reflection can happen outside in 'walk and talk' groups, sitting under a tree or in a shelter. Groups of a specified number are organized. Students views are taken into consideration when arranging the groups while the teacher has a very important role to play in ensuring that children of different backgrounds who might not usually get a chance to work together, get this chance during school time.

In the classroom, the seating arrangement is organized into small groups at circular tables with quiet spaces for students to work in pairs or on their own when required. Around these tables, students regularly negotiate and discuss curriculum topics, connecting with the content, sharing their views, listening to other voices and building on one another's ideas. Sometimes views are respectfully debated through the lens and motivation of trying to understand another view and solve a specified problem. All views are considered interesting and worthy of consideration. Students are also more frequently engaged in whole-class 'circle-time' activities and discussions.

How students learn

Pedagogical approaches and strategies used in schools connect with children's life experience, strengths and interests. Students learn mainly through enquiry and exploring, through new knowledge being introduced and applied at the most relevant time, and through lots of experiential opportunities. They learn from everything and everyone around them. They learn from and with their teacher. They learn in various types of groups, with and from one another, supporting and collaborating with peers and teachers. There is time for self and time for others and learning 'balance' through living it, there are plenty of opportunities for work, rest and play.

Children learn with, in and about their local environments. Engaged in active learning with and about the others with whom they share their school and community, deeply promotes children's well-being. It creates a sense of belonging and connection. It contributes to a child's deep sense that who they are and what they do matters. Cultivating collaboration is emphasized. Each child contributes to the learning in class and to the life of the school. Competition is only encouraged for the purposes of improving on one's own personal performance and also to the extent that it increases fun and participation. Schools have come up with a new term, 'complabboration', a combination and merging of the 'old' terms, 'competition' and 'collaboration'. This refers to the potential of collaboration to continuously improve and have winning results. It is acknowledged that collaboration is not always easy and has to be regularly practised. It requires communication, trust and a willingness to negotiate, compromise and work together towards a common goal that has been identified as worth working towards. We are sure that this respectful collaboration, negotiation and 'complabboration' has the potential to bring the world closer to a state of peace and security. These skills will surely change and improve how world leaders relate in the future.

Students have more choice over how they learn. They are supported to discover which method of learning best suits and most benefits them. They access and co-create content on the same topic in a variety of different ways. Some prefer to watch and take notes from videos and documentaries, some learn best from discussions, podcasts or other forms of multi-media, some learn best from reading material, either online or in books or magazines. For some projects and topics, students connect and collaborate with students in classrooms across the world. There are various websites that connect classrooms and schools internationally, e.g., eTwinning. Everybody can find someone in the world to work with, another student or group with common interests. Teachers and administrators play an important role in helping to set this up, ensuring the necessary vetting and safeguarding. Then, they stand back and marvel at how it happens.

A slight departure from role models and heroes of the past, children are motivated and inspired by role models closer to them, amongst their peers, in the form of other students in their classrooms and communities who are excelling in particular areas and overcoming adversities and challenges. Other children and young people further afield but whose influence is easy to access and recognise via the internet also act as role models, anyone brave enough to express who they truly are and use their gifts and strengths to change the world. There are many examples of children around the world following through on innovative new ideas, setting up companies, participating in international projects, speaking up and advocating for their own rights and the rights of others more vulnerable. As children competently collaborate, communicate and contribute in groups, teachers have noticed a very powerful, positive impact on bullying. Through listening to all voices, students have become even more empathetic and aware of when others might need some additional support. They are more inclined to look out for one another.

Questions are always invited, actively encouraged and listened to. The maxim frequently used is: 'There is no such thing as a silly question. The only silly question is the one you don't ask'. Students are encouraged to ask questions to clarify what they don't understand. In fact, there are weekly prizes and acknowledgement in schools for the best questions. Students know that it's okay to say, 'I don't know' in response to a question as it signals a gateway into exploration. 'I don't know' is followed closely with 'How can I find out?' Students are used to being asked, 'What do you think?' They face new challenges, motivated with a 'can do' attitude and mindset, beginning by asking themselves, 'What can I do here?', developing into 'What can I do for the good of the team here?' All children's talents and contributions are valued and celebrated. Exploratory talk is heard in use in classrooms, school yards and corridors and students have become really proficient at 'interthinking', a concept named by Mercer (2000) which refers to actively building on one another's ideas collaboratively.

The school provides multiple opportunities for citizenship education. Student voice very obviously leads to the development of numerous participation and democratic skills in students. Schulz et al. (2010) had noted that Citizenship Education had, by 2010, become an international movement. Now, it is most definitely a global phenomenon. All children are empowered to act and make decisions in relation to specific learning, experiences, events, and situations. There is a period of every school day when students and teachers engage in something they deeply love. They can teach someone else what they love. In these schools, with teacher and student agency to the fore, while policy-informed practice is still greatly respected, good practice and ideas that clearly work well on the ground, also solidly inform policy. The line between academic and every day is not so defined. Education is for everyone, not just the most academic. Learning is strongly encouraged as a life-long endeavour. It neither starts nor stops in the school building.

Teachers, like parents accept that the world their students are living and growing up in is very different to the world of their youth and they have long acknowledged that today's students will face challenges unique to their generation. However, students continue to learn so much from the teacher who constantly models active listening, curiosity and open communication skills. Teachers know that it's only by listening to and valuing the ideas of students that relevant solutions to current problems may be found. Teachers recognize that student empowerment is key. Very cognisant of the difference between equality and equity, teachers know that some individual students and some groups may require additional support to more fully participate and be involved. Aware of how difficult it is to prepare children for a world that adults didn't experience, teachers support one another through support groups. They also avail of regular and relevant, continuous professional development (CPD) and sometimes this CPD is given by students.

School buildings may eventually become 'centres of learning', places where everybody can drop in to learn and teach something new. However, it is thought that in time, there may be fewer classrooms. Instead of sitting inside in unnatural postures and unnatural, man-made surroundings, students will choose to be outside, under trees and shelters without walls. Rather than going outside to experience nature, they will, at times, go inside to experience History. Some of this may seem fanciful and somewhat unrealistic. The world is in a constant state of change and as we've often heard, everything new seems impossible until it is done. We've learned that student voice is not just one initiative or collection of initiatives. It has become an integral part of the school culture. It is simply a way of life now, a way of being, a significant part of how we do things around here.

Community in this brave new world

Communities have also benefited from more child input. More parks and gardens have been developed in community areas, places where people can go out with their families and friends and take quiet walks or where they can 'walk and talk' with their neighbours. These are places where local children plant flower beds and vegetable patches, play together and spend some time with older citizens on the park benches, reading or talking together. Touching the soil in these shared, recreational areas helps to keep everyone grounded. Elders share their gardening skills with children, deepening their love and appreciation of the earth. Children have set up outdoor shelters in these parks where they can reciprocate and help older citizens understand and better use their technological devices. Some people have begun to question the concept of owning land at all on an individual and national level. They realize that if we looked at the world as 'ours', 'all of ours', there might be less war, less possessions to fight about and more people to care for the shared spaces.

People who speak different languages wave at one another, trying to use as much of the language of the person they are greeting and meeting as possible. As the community is made up of such a rich tapestry of diversity, it is in the process of developing its own common language which consists mainly of open, welcoming, inclusive body language. Local libraries regularly consult with children and young people regarding book choices and facilities for their engagement and enjoyment. They host weekly 'communication corners' where young people come to share their thoughts and ideas on current affairs and they also host monthly 'soap box' events on topics young people have suggested, to which parents, grandparents and other members of the community are invited. The library podcast run by local adult and child volunteers, 'Young Voices Aloud' interviews young people on a wide variety of topics including their favourite books, videos, social media influencer, and 'tip of the week' for adult listeners. Libraries have storytelling corners. There is a corner called 'Everyone has a story' where children can read and speak to older people and another corner called 'Tell me a story', where older people read to or tell their story to younger people who listen and ask questions. There are also many other corners for quiet reading, silence and reflection. These are, indeed, also regarded by children and adults alike, as very important activities.

Having listened to and taken on board, young people's preferences, there are more restaurants serving healthier food options in the area instead of the usual fast-food chains. The community shares out vegetables they have grown in the community garden. Local restaurants buy some of these vegetables for their healthy recipes and the money received is reinvested into the further development of the gardens. Community festivals, celebrating music, song, theatre, dance and life, continue and have become more sustainable. Those who can't walk or cycle to these events tend to share lifts. All the materials used to serve food are reused or biodegradable and citizens are very mindful of how to take care of any additional waste that is created. Sporting organisations have begun to ensure that child voice is listened to within their structures and this has led to some very interesting changes in sports events and competitions.

There are lawyers and solicitors in the community with specific expertise in Child Law and Children's Rights. The community has ensured that they are available to talk to children in less formal settings to answer their questions and provide information on their rights and responsibilities. Within the community, young people are encouraged and given opportunities to volunteer in areas, shops and businesses of interest to them, helping out where they can, asking questions and learning from those older, more experienced and qualified. People have learned over time to work smarter not longer and spend more time with their families, surrounded by nature. The local roads are lined by trees and every celebratory event is marked by the community planting yet another tree together. There is a community sense of joint environmental responsibility, action and purpose. People of all ages in the community work together to look after the trees and people are regularly seen walking mindfully amongst the trees, sometimes even hugging them, following the Japanese tradition of 'shinrinyoku'.

Many walls have blank white boards where people are encouraged to draw or write a motivating, inspiring message to brighten someone else's day. When the weather washes them away, new drawings and messages can be added. Museums also have a section of blank white walls for young people's contemporary art, where the pieces on display are changed every day. This not only facilitates young people's expression but informs and updates older people, through the medium of art, of what is going on in the hearts and minds of young people.

What life in this brave new world looks and feels like

Young people in this brave new world are considered and celebrated as 'changemakers'? They feel safe, empowered, listened to, respected and trusted. Children, not yet tainted with detrimental inflated egos, take part openly and honestly in many decision-making processes and everyone benefits. This is a peaceful world where it is recognised that we do not assume to know everything (as unfortunately they did in generations past) about, for example, another country and its people. It is widely acknowledged that we, in fact, know little, if anything at all, unless we have lived amongst other cultures and people, asked questions and communicated openly with them. We engage in respectful dialogue and discussion which was taught and practised in our homes, schools and communities. Since the world is viewed as 'ours', there is less to fight for, only something beautiful to share.

Some people had thought that society would be ruined if young people were given more of a voice. They equated it, with neither reason nor proof, to everyone doing whatever they wanted to do on a whim. They had underestimated the innate goodness, empathy and wisdom of our children. Since the beginning of so-called 'civilization', the voices of millions had always been silenced in the pursuit of power and control by a few (adults). For too long, this untrue narrative was spread that innate human instinct was to be distrusted. However, we remembered and believed the words of Nelson Mandela, that "love comes more naturally to the human heart than its opposite".

There are robots and artificial intelligence (AI) doing many of the jobs that used to take up so much of human beings' time. The potential of AI is not feared but cleverly, competently and creatively managed. Much and all as our children love and have embraced technology, they are careful to ensure that the jobs robots do are only the ones that humans ought not be doing. This leaves more time and space to really tune in and develop 'human' jobs where people work with people in a spirit of empathy, solidarity and collaboration. Young people connect and collaborate with peers from across the world and are encouraged to voice and share their vision and provide a youth lens on all major events. Because they have become proficient at questioning, young people are applying their critical thinking skills to cut through, as best they can, misinformation, disinformation and propaganda. Used to questioning almost everything, they reflect and explore by probing with the simple question, "how do you know?" Our young people are, no doubt, the most affected by and aware generation on issues such as technology, climate change, mental health challenges and well-being.

In this brave new world, children feel free to use their untethered imaginations. It is okay and even encouraged not to 'know' everything as certainty is seen as the enemy of curiosity. It is recognized that nobody knows everything about everything and everybody knows something that we can all learn from if we take the time to listen and interact with curiosity and openness. Mahatma Gandhi said, "In a gentle way, you can shake the world". We have become more aware that simple, seemingly small actions can make a big difference. For example, imagine if we got to the stage where everybody in this world planted a tree, a single tree per person. In this gentle way, we might not just shake the world but make the world a better, brighter, healthier place.

A day in this brave new world

People live more mindfully and in the moment in this brave new world. The concept of time is slightly but noticeably different. People are less guarded and more spontaneous. Like children when they are most at ease, people do what brings them joy. In this way, they have a better idea of what they want for the rest of their lives. Days are 'adventure-full' as all children engage in inclusive made-up games (weren't all games and sports made up once?). The sound of laughter, joking and music fills the air. Children play their own music on musical instruments before they are taught the music of others. Children choose the clothes to wear for the day and frequently 'dress-up'. They love to mix and match their clothes, recycling styles. They run, dance, play, fall and get back up again. Willing and brave adults get to play and dance along too. Days are filled more with 'day-doings' than 'daydreaming' although periods of 'daydreaming' are encouraged too.

Birthdays are not so commercial as they were before. In fact, there is no one day for a birthday. There is not the same practice of celebrating such days as: 'Valentine's Day', 'Mother's Day', 'Father's Day', 'Grandparents' Day', when, where and how commercial entities tell people to. Love, family and people are celebrated and appreciated every day. People are not asked, "How old are you?" but rather, "how long have you truly lived?" For children, one day may be the equivalent of one adult week, given the amount of learning they pack into it.

The future in this brave new world

With empathetic, confident young people brimming with a strong sense of self-efficacy at the helm, the future looks very hopeful indeed for all of us. Young people will openly communicate and freely consult with wise elders on certain issues. They are very comfortable collaborating as this is how they grew up. Leadership is shared but most often, youth-led. There is no more space for mad, ego-driven, individualistic people to make decisions on their own, as happened too often in the past. Knowing from experience how to address large audiences, use a range of rhetorical techniques to persuade, inspire and motivate others, communicate effectively with confidence, empathy and flair with people from all different backgrounds who live in their community has proven to be a powerful investment in a brighter future for all. A future where people actively and deeply listen to others and where young people having their voices heard is a very normal and natural part of life.

The child in this brave new world

Young people are ambitious, energetic creative, positive and dream big. Many young people are already courageously working for change, seeing change as normal, a constant feature of their world. Empowered and facilitated by the caring adults in their lives to become the best version of themselves, they are becoming more self-actualized by the day, confident, calm and engaged with life and the world. It was Bourdieu (1991, p. 37) who had stressed that "one must not forget the relations of communication 'par excellence' are also relations of symbolic power". Speaking is power. It always has been but now power is shared amongst adults and young people in a spirit of collaboration for a better world for all. Speaking empowers and liberates. It continues to allow people to challenge any injustices that may arise.

Being able to speak well and with purpose continues to be transformative, for the individual speaking and for the audience listening. Students continue to learn and practice the different aspects of being a clear communicator and how these skills can benefit not only their presentation abilities, but their personal confidence, relationships and career opportunities as well. Young people speak out, reach out and learn with and from others.

Summary reflection on this brave new world of child and student voice

Governments finally took heed and provided sustainable and continuing pre- and in-service training for all professionals working with and for children on the UNCRC, including Article 12, and how to implement it. All have benefited from learning to listen, hear, and respect children's views. This world, now, co-ruled by children with the adults who listen to them, is deeply democratic and truly compassionate at the core. Children want to do and explore more. When trusting adults step aside and lovingly let their little ones lead the way, amazing things have been seen to happen. This does not mean that there is no role for adults to play. Adults have also been busy, upskilling as facilitators, encouragers, enablers, supporters and young people's loudest cheerleaders. Inspired by what they have seen young people achieve, they too have begun to more openly share their knowledge and authentic stories, giving their own 'inner child' who was silenced for way too long, permission to emerge.

This is a world of listeners, a world of speakers but with everybody listening first, just as babies do when they first come into the world. It is less binary as that beautiful grey area in-between extremes is the space that children love to explore most. In fact, it's no longer called 'grey area' but rather 'various shades of rainbow'. There is no doubt but that a world with more child voice and student voice is a better world for everyone. It's certainly hard to imagine how it could be worse.

Welcome to the world of child and student voice

"Once upon a time, it was mainly adults who wrote and told the stories", an adult said to a child. The adult turned to the child and said, "now, it's your turn. We trust you. Here's the pen. Can we write the story together with you as the lead author?" The message is clear. Children are the future, but prior to the emergence of this brave new world, their opinions were rarely, if ever, taken into account when planning for them. Over the last few decades, their contributions have begun to be listened to and it continues to make a huge, significant, changemaking difference on many levels. It has proved hugely beneficial to allow young people to learn to be active citizens by being active citizens.

The age of children being seen and not heard is well and truly over, and that is something for all of us to celebrate. Unblemished by the manipulation and madness of previous adult societies, children and students have become strong authentic advocates, representing themselves, their families, their communities, on education issues, social issues, health issues, on matters that affect them. So much of this has depended on parents, teachers and the communities in which young people grow up and how willing they were to listen and share power with the younger generation. This brave new world, co-created with children is brimming with acceptance, fun, hope and potential. It is a space intent on building inclusive, empowering, more equal environments ensuring support is always available to those who need it. Be prepared to be intrigued and inspired. We adults might consider ourselves lucky and privileged if young people, tomorrow's leaders, invite us in to their world to play along. We will be their guests and they will listen to our voices (we hope).

And so it was that the children of the world and their respective adult carers met at the 'Bridge of Voice' for the official transfer of power ceremony. What happened next was momentous and would change the world positively and powerfully. Child and student voice obviously didn't mean what some had thought. When the gavel of power was handed from the adult to the child, the child didn't remove it completely from the adult's hand but smiled and said, **"Let's share it"**.

Reference List

Bourdieu, P. (1991). *Language and Symbolic Power*. Cambridge: Polity Press.

Mercer, N. (2000). *ICT and Interthinking, Occasional Paper*. Milton Keynes: Centre for Language and Communications, Open University.

Mercer & Mannion. (2018). *Oracy across the Welsh Curriculum. A Research-Based Review: Key Principles and Recommendations for Teachers*. EAS, Education Achievement Service for South East Wales.

Schulz, W., Ainley, J., Fraillon, J., Kerr, D., & Losito, B. (2010). *Initial Findings from the IEA International Civic and Citizenship Education Study*. International Association for the Evaluation of Educational Achievement. Herengracht 487, Amsterdam, 1017 BT, The Netherlands.

United Nations. (1989). United Nations Convention on the Rights of the Child.

13 Concluding Chapter

As a shy child, personally, I understand deeply the daily challenges of trying to speak out and have your voice heard. Professionally, having taught children from a range of different backgrounds in a range of different school contexts, I have witnessed the powerful potential of empowering children and students to express themselves and improve their communication skills. I agree with the advice of Mannion (2023) that "the development of knowledge and skills relating to spoken language and communication should be considered the beating heart of the curriculum, and everything else should revolve around that."

Reminder of our obligation as educators and parents

Child and student voice is not just a privilege but an ethical imperative and important fundamental right as set out by the United Nations Convention on the Rights of the Child (UNCRC, 1989, Article 12), critical to improving the nature and quality of the childhood children experience (Lansdown, 2011). This right, carries with it a responsibility for those who work with children to support and prepare them to claim their rights. While there is an increasing awareness and understanding of the concepts of child and student voice, it appears that Article 12 of the UNCRC has proven a difficult article to implement. Article 12 safeguards children's protection, expression and participation in various different ways in matters that affect their lives. It is through Article 12 that children can more easily access their other rights. Importantly, children while not obliged to express their unique view, have the right to. What can be done to support the enactment and realization of child and student voice? What good practices already happening in schools can be leveraged to hear and realize more student voice?

Probably the most obvious and least-often talked about way to hear student voice is to hear students' voices. No matter where any of us end up in life, communication skills are a must, personally and professionally. Because someone's not speaking doesn't mean they don't have something to say. As educators, parents and professionals working with children, it is helpful to consider the space, voice, audience and influence of children's contributions. Do they feel comfortable in that space? Has their voice been invited and shown value? Is it clear who the audience is or what the influence may be?

Historically in schools, we have too often heard the admonition, "Stop talking". Why? Did you ever consider why that might be so, why students might be told to "stop talking"? Yes, we can understand how a teacher needs to establish some kind of order and discipline in a busy classroom. But what if the message received is different to the message intended? Once we have successfully silenced our students, we later hear that efforts are being made to hear student and child voice. The contradictions here are obvious and the gap between policy, rights and practice, evident.

Some years ago, while living abroad in a country where corporal punishment in schools was still legal, I witnessed a teacher kick a teenage student in the stomach for dying his hair. As corporal punishment in schools had been illegal in Ireland since 1982, thankfully I had never witnessed anything like this before. The incident deeply impacted me. I tried to imagine how the student, hurt and humiliated in front of other students and teachers might feel and penned the following poem:

> "The impact of your hand,
> You didn't understand,
> You knocked me to my knees to beg you please,
> Please listen to me.
> You asked me why
> But didn't wait for answers,
> Fighting raging silence,
> To escape this troubled heart.
> You asked again, struck again,
> Between the blows you answered for me
> With unfounded accusations.
> For dying my hair, you coloured my character,
> Black, orange, grey and blue, you mixed them too.
> I only cared that someone showed attention.
> If my parents knew, they'd beat me too, just like you
> Into submission.
> They too may not listen
> To the mere, imploring cries
> Of a confused, congested, teenaging heart.
> The impact of your hand,
> Reinforcement, no-one can understand.
> You kick me in my gut
> But only hurt
> My soul
> And you scream, red-faced, wild-eyed and shaking that
> I
> Am out of control."

Corporal punishment in schools has been illegal in Ireland since 1982 and in the UK since 1986. There are, however, some countries where it is still legal to hit students as a form of punishment. The example in the poem of the incident I observed shows how messages and intentions can be misunderstood with a disastrous impact and how not being listened to can lead to deep pain. For some, this may sound radical but just imagine, instead of telling our students and children to 'stop talking', if we said, "talk, and keep talking and we'll give you the skills, the structure and the safe, supportive environment in which to plan, prepare and practise talking. Talk with intention, talk to investigate, talk to learn."

Reminder of the benefits of developing children's speaking and communication skills

The ability to communicate clearly has many benefits for individuals themselves, opening the door to many opportunities and also for wider society. There are many terms used to refer to the area of communication skill development in school curricula. In chapter 2, terms such as communication skills, oral language, oracy, speaking and listening, and public speaking are briefly described and explored. Also detailed is the importance of competence and confidence in these areas for children's lives as children, for children's experience of learning in school, for life outcomes and employability and as a skill to mitigate disadvantage. Knowing about these skills is not enough. The bottom line for our children and students is doing, developing and understanding them.

Focusing on the explicit teaching of public speaking skills fosters empathy and connection for all students as they listen to and learn about the stories, lives and interests of their peers. Studies also show that it leads to enhanced self-efficacy and has a positive impact on vocabulary development. It provides students with periods of uninterrupted speech exploration which they may not be used to getting anywhere else. Public speaking is more than just a necessary skill-set. It's a skill with the potential to mitigate disadvantage and enhance social mobility and personal and social growth.

The ability to listen and to speak are also critical components in the development and maintenance of mental health and well-being. Speaking is a door to power that can remain closed to many people simply because of lack of opportunity and training. A leading character in Irish history, Jim Larkin, famously said, "The great appear great because we are on our knees. Let us arise". Nobody was born a great speaker. Great speakers may appear great to us simply because we ourselves have not yet been given the opportunity to learn or practise the required skills to become a great speaker.

Reminder of how child and student voice can be facilitated in homes, schools and the community and how public speaking and communication skills can be taught

Chapter 3 explores how parents, guardians, carers, child-care professionals and teachers can facilitate an increased focus on child voice and student voice in homes, communities and schools. The duty of adults to facilitate children's realization of their right to be heard, is reiterated and the connection between student voice and public speaking training is also explored. Detail is provided of some of the well-known, widely-used support models that can support, guide and scaffold parents and practitioners to facilitate and explore different levels of child and student voice.

Following on from chapter 4 which details the author's research on public speaking in primary school, chapters 5 and 6 explore the why and what of public speaking in primary school detailing where it sits on the curriculum, the benefits and related challenges. Examples are provided of playful and engaging ways to initially engage students in public speaking activities, some of which are already being implemented in classrooms across the world. The importance of the explicit teaching of public speaking skills is emphasized. This builds up then to a discussion on supportive, empowering pedagogies in chapter 7. The analysis of the pedagogies contained in this chapter should support teachers to begin and/or develop their teaching of public speaking skills so that all students may be empowered to have their voice and voices heard.

Reminder of the ongoing important role of the teacher

Student voice does not diminish the role of the teacher. It may just require slightly different skills. Teachers are constantly innovating, upskilling and overcoming various challenges as they arise. They are seldom given credit for the complexity and ever-evolving nature of the job they do. They are agentic professionals who constantly use their professional judgment to adapt their teaching to the learning needs and contexts of their students. By cleverly co-creating ground-rules, creatively co-designing the safe space, providing effective feedback, building on students' strengths, and of ultimate importance, listening, the teacher's role in facilitating (Elam & Duckenfield, 2000), modelling openness and encouraging student voice is key to the learning and teaching process. Teachers giving themselves credit for being the confident, effective public speakers they already are, is important. We can't forget that as Mercer and Mannion (2018) note, schools and teachers are uniquely positioned and empowered to act and teach in ways that are likely to have significant benefits on the life outcomes of future generations. By providing more examples of 'student voice' in action, the aim in chapter 11 is to encourage and empower teachers to build and broaden a culture of more 'student voice' in their classrooms and schools.

Reminder of how to overcome the fear of public speaking

We took a closer look in chapter 9 at the commonly experienced fear of public speaking, its origins, reasons, effects, how it manifests, how it can be overcome and how we can support students to self-regulate and manage nerves. The main reasons offered for this fear were no training and lack of opportunity to practise public speaking. A first initial negative experience of public speaking and a negative experience of speaking in childhood were noted by some, as contributors to this fear. The number one and most obvious and effective antidote to fear of public speaking is public speaking skill training in a safe, supportive environment. When students are supported to develop confidence and competence in communicating, this naturally leads to them being able to speak out clearly on matters that affect them, confidently sharing their thoughts, feelings, experiences and individual stories.

Public speaking skills can be taught, and assessed and can prove a powerful tool for realizing the wonders and principles of democracy when embedded across the whole school. Chapter 7 provides teachers with some helpful tips and techniques as to how to begin to train students in public speaking skills. The primary school years is a time when children typically have fewer inhibitions and to the contrary, seem to revel in the attention of others.

Out of all of the common fears, fear of public speaking might be one of the most difficult to ignore as there are definite occasions in life and throughout education on which we are called to speak in front of others. Various emotions have the potential to overwhelm us on these occasions, but if we can fall back on a habit of learned and practised public speaking skills, we may be more empowered to face, challenge and overcome our fear.

Reminder of WAITing to debate

While debating may be recognized as an important skill to develop, it is 'debatable' how effectively this skill has historically served the world. For one side to be right when debating, the other side has to be made wrong, at all costs. As you will have noted from the discussion in chapter 8, debating, while having the potential to develop some very valuable skills, also has the potential to be polarizing. It too often puts people into defensive or offensive mode rather than opening them up to listen to the views and experiences of others, engaging in dialogue rather than debate. At a time when our world would seem to need more empathy practitioners, debating may not be the answer.

Furthermore, debating is only one genre of public speaking and may not be the most effective place to start in terms of public speaking skill training. The prevalence of debating clubs in schools may not be serving all students. Before we launch into competitive debating, it may be more helpful for students to have been introduced to public speaking and on an incremental basis '**W**eaving **A**spects of debate **I**n and out of **T**opics' (WAIT) explored from a multitude of viewpoints. Debate is great, but my advice is: WAIT.

Reminder of how child and student voice initiatives are for all children

In chapter 10, the importance of neither overlooking nor underestimating any children when facilitating child and student voice is emphasised. Rather, ways of supporting all children are explored. Specific reference is made to children who are shy, come from disadvantaged backgrounds, children with speech and language difficulties, children with special education needs (SEN) and children for whom English is not their first language. All children should be empowered to participate in and benefit from opportunities that will enhance their life chances, on a par with their peers. It's about meeting children where they're at, building on their unique strengths and providing training and support at a level that will allow all children to make progress and have their voice heard. There is a possibility that some students who have not been given the opportunity to develop, find and use their voice are being labelled as 'shy', lacking in confidence or otherwise. Cregan (2012) states that scaffolding the development of requisite oral language skills in students for whom they may not be immediately accessible is mandatory.

Reminder that child and student voice is not something new

Prioritizing student voice is not about introducing something new. It's about bringing to the fore, showing value for and developing something that has always been there. Students have always had their opinions and ability to engage in dialogue, whether educators have leveraged or shown explicit value for student voice or not. Public speaking skills in schools is also not a new idea. The explicit teaching of public speaking skills to all students and labelling these skills as 'public speaking' may be. In addition to fitting relevantly into language instruction, many public speaking skills fall under other areas, for example, nurturing 'self-confidence', 'sense of self-efficacy' and 'helping children to acquire a range of communication skills'. Every subject on the curriculum very naturally provides rich content for public speaking presentations allowing content to come to life in a real, meaningful and interactive way while promoting the participation of all children.

Concluding thoughts

Everybody will need to use speaking, listening and communication skills throughout their lives. Anderson (1997) makes the point that no matter where a child is on the developmental continuum, they will ultimately prosper and benefit if they can handle the anxiety of speaking in public. It's a fact of life, he writes, that every day people, young and old, face the prospect of speaking in some type of a public forum. The question for him is whether or not we are prepared for this fact of life and how we prepare the young people entrusted to our care.

McIntyre et al. (2005) are optimistic that students can become "the catalysts for school-wide change" by confidently contributing their opinions and ideas and experiencing those contributions being valued. Current policy initiatives in education seem to situate student voice in pedagogy and as dialogic consultation at classroom and whole-school level. It's important to consider where this empowerment begins and how it can be facilitated to benefit all students. It doesn't just happen incidentally.

Considering the Lundy (2007) model of child participation, by continuing to consult and collaborate with young people who have been enabled and empowered to develop their speaking voice and communication skills, we can ensure that the participation we facilitate with and for our students is neither tokenistic nor manipulative, that authentic contributions when invited are taken seriously. In this book, the concepts of 'child voice' and 'student voice' have been explored, referring to not only the legal requirement enshrined in the UNCRC, Article 12 but also their powerful potential and positive impacts for relationships and contribution, for learning and teaching, for the individual and indeed for the benefit of us all.

From my study we discovered that 'public speaking' is a term that is not widely used within schools but "the art of effective communication with an audience" is an art that is taught explicitly and practised in some schools with very positive outcomes. Every area of the curriculum requires talk. Every interaction in the school day requires talk. Overcoming the fear of public speaking is of serious social significance as there are many known occasions in life on which we'll all be called on to speak. On these occasions, many of which can trigger the deepest and rawest emotion, we need to have something to fall back on, a habit that's been formed over years and especially in our younger years, a time when we most wanted to talk.

There is no denying that public speaking is closely connected with power. It's how world leaders share their messages and vision and motivate, inspire and communicate with the masses. Today, we still have a system of public representatives who speak on behalf of others. Perhaps it is still deep within society that public speaking is not something that everyone could or should do. Perhaps there is a fear of what empowering the majority with competent skills of public speaking might lead to. The paucity of research in the area of public speaking in primary school would suggest that it is even less likely that public speaking is an activity associated with children. My research provides evidence revealing how explicit public speaking training can positively impact children's self-efficacy and vocabulary development and more, at a time when they have fewer inhibitions, having not yet passively inherited a fear.

The Children's Commissioner (2015) states that handing the power over to children to tell their stories freely and democratically, whilst also knowing that someone is listening and cares, helps them become capable, confident, included and responsible members of our broader society, increasing their sense of belonging in the community, and promoting good citizenship, agency and self-advocacy skills. Prensky (2005) cautions that if we do not stop and listen to the children we serve, value their opinions, and make major changes on the basis of the suggestions they offer, we will be left in the 21st century with school buildings to administer but with students who are physically or mentally somewhere else. Encouraging, enabling and empowering student and child voice begins with listening and a willingness to see children and young people for the unique, competent individuals that they are.

Who knows the thoughts of a child better than themselves? Every heart has a story to tell. Our students, who are empowered in so many ways outside their schools today, too often, have little or no meaningful voice in their own education or school, a place where others decided they must spend a large proportion of their time. Let's not forget that the school exists for our children and students, all of them. This is their education, not ours, yet if we're wise enough, we too might realize the many learning opportunities that surround us every day in our homes, schools, work places and communities.

Finally, in chapter 12, we delved into our adult imaginations to conjure up what a brave and beautiful world of child and student voice might look like. We embraced change to imagine the impact on the individual, home, school, communities and to dare to dream for a better, braver and brighter future for all of us. What are we waiting for? It's time to stop wasting time. We discovered through our visualization and exploration that child and student voice didn't actually mean what some who had resisted it for so long had thought it would but rather something more special and powerful.

Imagine a world of people confidently and competently sharing their stories and compassionately listening to others as they do the same. Imagine a world where every voice is equally valued and celebrated. Imagine a world of effective 'complabboration'. I hope I'm lucky enough to be invited to play along in this world and observe our younger generation as they play, develop and grow together. Imagine a world of child and student voice. That's a world that's on my travel 'bucket list'. How about you? We adults might consider ourselves privileged if young people, tomorrow's leaders, invite us in to their world to play along with them. We will be their guests and having learned from our example, they will listen to our voices (we hope).

When children are involved in active learning through discussion, they are not simply listening but are developing skills in handling and understanding concepts and ideas in an atmosphere of trust, love, curiosity (TLC) and support. "By giving high priority to the rights of children . . . we serve the best interest of all humanity" (UNICEF, 2008). The Dalai Lama said, "when you talk, you are only repeating what you already know. But if you listen, you may learn something new". 'Listening' is a word that's so much easier said than done. It surfaces repeatedly across discussions of child and student voice efforts and refers to a wide range of practices.

Empowering child and student voice and then, listening, is a small thing that we can do today that would have a huge impact on tomorrow. Jane Goodall, English primatologist and anthropologist, said, "young people, when informed and empowered, when they realise that what they do truly makes a difference, can indeed change the world". We adults cannot control this change and are limited in how we can contribute to it so, in my view, it's probably wise to go with the flow, cheerlead and empower our children, partner with them and support them. . . . . and LISTEN!

Reference List

Anderson, L. (1997). *Public Speaking Opportunities for Elementary School Students*.

Cregan, A. (2012). Empowering Teachers to Promote Oral Language in Culturally Diverse Classrooms in Ireland. *Journal of Multilingual Education Research*, 3(Article 5).

Elam, K. G., & Duckenfield, M. (2000). *Creating a Community of Learners: Using the Teacher as Facilitator Model*. National Dropout Prevention Center. ERIC.

Lansdown, G. (2011). *Every Child's Right to Be Heard, a resource guide on the UN Committee on the Rights of the Child General Comment*, no.12, Gerison Lansdown. Save the Children UK on behalf of Save the Children and UNICEF.

Lundy, L. (2007). 'Voice' Is Not Enough: Conceptualising Article 12 of the United Nations Convention on the Rights of the Child. *British Educational Research Journal*, 33(6).

Mannion, J. (2023). *The Transformative Power of Oracy*. Blog. https://oracycambridge.org/oracy-at-the-heart-of-the-curriculum/

McIntyre, D., Pedder, D., & Rudduck, J. (2005). Pupil Voice: Comfortable and Uncomfortable Learnings for Teachers. *Research Papers in Education*, 20, 149-68.

Mercer & Mannion. (2018). *Oracy across the Welsh Curriculum. A Research-Based Review: Key Principles and Recommendations for Teachers*. EAS, Education Achievement Service for South East Wales.

Prensky, M. (2005). Learning in the Digital Age. Listen to the Natives. *Educational Leadership*, 4, 8-13.

UNICEF. (2008), A World Fit for Children. The United Nations Children's Fund, Children's Commissioner. 'State of Care–2015: What We Learnt from Monitoring Child, Youth and Family', Office Children's Commissioner, August 2015.

Index

A

Accent 142
Access, access to appropriate information 5, access to skill-set training 150, accessing the speaking area 142
Action research 50, 53, 54, 56, 58, 102
Active citizens 2, 4, 5, 8, 13, 35, 40, 66, 158, 173 active citizenship 5, 8, 13, 35, 108, 115, 149, 161
Active participants 7, 153, Active participation 5, 13, 16, 33, 66, 166
Adults, adult bias 43, 'adult gaze' 42, adult initiated, shared decisions 40, adult imaginations 181, adult-led or adult-led participation 12, adult negotiations 13, adult talk 147, caring adult 8, spaces between adult and child 62, trusted adults 136
Advocacy 35, 36, 40, advocacy group 155, advocates 35, 70, 108, empowered advocates 144, 173, self-advocacy skills 181
Agency 9, 35, 36, 62, 73, 86, 97, 145, 147, 168, 181
Agreeing and disagreeing respectfully 101
Affirmations 42, 122, 125
Akhtar, (2005) 53, 59
Albert Einstein 134
Alexander (2003) 63, 70, 71, 73, 92, 104, Alexander (2008) 16, 22, 28, 61, 73, 92, 104, 147, 158, Alexander (2010) 26, Alexander (2011) 40, 44, 71, 73, Alexander (2012) 25, 27, 28, 70, 71, 73, 88, 89, 94, 104, 137, 144, 147, Alexander (2018) 23, 28, 147, 158
Alford (2016) 72, 73, 100, 104
American Psychiatric Association (2013) 120, 129
Amy Gaunt, Head of Oracy in School-21 43, 132
Anderson (1997) 62, 63, 69, 70, 73, 87, 89, 180, 182

Andrew Fitch 112
Andrews (1994) 37, 44
Anxiety 22, 23, 48, 49, 52, 62, 65, 68, 70, 72, 97, 119, 120, 121, 124, 125, 126, 127, 132, 136, 141, 143, 180, Public Speaking Anxiety (PSA) 48, 119, 120, 123, 124, 125, social anxiety 72, 120, 126, 135, social anxiety disorder 120
Argument 23, 63, 76, 78, 79, 80, 81, 83, 106, 107, 108, 109, 110, 111, 117, student voice arguments 10
Aristotle 20, 63, 77, 123
Article 12 of the UNCRC 1, 2, 3, 4, 5, 6, 13, 15, 28, 36, 37, 38, 48, 49, 68, 73, 157, 159, 161, 165, 173, 175, 180, 182
Article 13 of the UNCRC 4
Article 29 of the UNCRC 4, 29, 36
Articulation 78, 139, 140
Ashley et al. (2015) 25
Ashlock et al. (2015) 124, 129
Assemblies 71, 116, school assemblies 56, 88, 100, 156, speaking assemblies 99
Assertiveness skills 33, 136
Assessment 29, 30, 49, 53, 74, 84, 85, 86, 87, 89, 103, 104, 105, 125, 130, 141, 145, 147, 149, 151, 152, 158, 166, assessment of oral language and public speaking skills 69, 83, 84, 85, 86, 125, Cambridge Oracy Assessment 85, Class-Based Assessments (CBA) 126, 128, formative assessment 145, self-assessment 85
Audience 1, 19, 20, 22, 23, 24, 28, 39, 42, 44, 47, 49, 54, 55, 56, 62, 64, 70, 76, 77, 78, 80, 81, 82, 83, 86, 87, 88, 90, 97, 98, 99, 101, 102, 106, 109, 110, 117, 120, 122, 123, 124, 126, 127, 131, 135, 136, 148, 150, 151, 157, 165, 172, 175, 180
Authenticity 24, 42

Index

Awards ceremonies 128
'A world Fit for Children' 6, 15, 183
Ayres et al (1995) 125, 129

B

Babies and toddlers 3, 21, 34, 161, 173
Backlund & Morreale (2015) 20, 28, 63, 73, 86, 89
Bailey (2019) 20, 28
Baker (2008) 66, 73
Bandura (1977) 51, 52, 59, 128, 129, Bandura (2008) 51, 52, 59, Bandura's Social Learning Theory 51, Bandura's theory of self-efficacy 51, 52
Barlow (2002) 121, 129
Barnes & Todd (1995) 68, 73
Beatty 1988 125, 126, 129
Behaviour 18, 19, 22, 25, 33, 36, 37, 66, 68, 78, 83, 86, 95, 96, 99, 101, 115, 121, 123, 124, 125, 128, 130, 133, 138, 140, 147, 155
Belonging 22, 34, 167, 181
Bennett (1984) 125, 130
Bercow '10 Years On' Report 64
Berman (2004) 69, 74
Biemiller (2010) 53, 59, 72, 74
Bippus & Daly (1999) 120, 130
Black & William (1998) 101, 104
Blote et al (2009) 119, 130
Bodie (2010) 120, 130
Body language 17, 19, 22, 34, 47, 53, 67, 78, 82, 83, 95, 97, 148, 169
Bourdieu (1991) 20, 26, 29, 137, 138, 144, 172, 174
Boyce et al. (2007) 64, 81, 89
Brice-Heath (2012) 108, 118
Brink and Costigan (2015) 18, 26, 29, 71, 74
Bruner (1983) 92, 94, 104, 145, 158, Bruner (1986) 92, 94, 104, 149, 158
Building on others' ideas 35, 76, 92, 111, 165, 167, 168
Bullock Report (1975) 93, 105
Bullying 9, 33, 108, 133, 168
Bybee et al (2006) 153, 158

C

Cambridge University (2014) 19, 29, 84, 89, 100, Cambridge University (2018) 103
Cameron (2003) 95, 104
Catts et al (2002) 72, 74
Cazden (2001) 92, 104, 152, 158
CBI (2016) 72, 74
CCEA (2007) 64, 74, 80, 89, 99, 101, 104
Centre of attention 57, 62, 127, fear of being 'the centre of attention' 67, 120
Chaidaroon (2003) 134, 144
Change 2, 4, 5, 9, 10, 11, 14, 34, 39, 43, 44, 50, 52, 58, 59, 111, 113, 115, 125, 133, 143, 153, 157, 160, 161, 167, 168, 169, 172, 174, 180, 181, 182, changemakers 43, 53, 59, 170, climate change 108, 156, 171, School 21, a 'changemaker' school 43, 'Speak for Change' 27, 29, 49, 60, 64, 74, Wheel of Change 45
Chesebro et al (1992) 126, 130
Child advisory panels (CAPs) 88
Child-led play activities 56
Child Protection 9, 44
Children's Commissioner (2015) 181, 182
Child voice 2, 3, 6, 7, 8, 9, 14, 21, 31, 32, 39, 44, 144, 145, 156, 157, 160, 170, 173, 176, 177, 180, 181
Choi 1998 123, 130
Choice 2, 9, 33, 36, 37, 39, 40, 41, 42, 54, 73, 86, 97, 98, 100, 134, 136, 150, 151, 152, 154, 162, 167
Christopher Nolan 138, 139
'Circle-time' discussions 37, 115
Citizens / citizenship 1, 2, 3, 4, 5, 7, 8, 10, 13, 14, 15, 27, 35, 40, 44, 63, 66, 78, 87, 100, 108, 115, 149, 158, 161, 166, 169, 170, 173, 174, 181, citizenship education 10, 11, 168, citizenship knowledge 164, citizenship skills 10, 13, global citizenship 40
Civic awareness 107
Clark & Tree (2002) 121, 130
Clarke et al. (2016) 137, 144
Classroom 9, 10, 11, 22, 24, 26, 34, 36, 40, 41, 42, 43, 50, 54, 56, 59, 61, 65, 66, 68, 69, 70, 71, 76, 77, 80, 87, 89, 93, 96, 99, 102, 107, 115, 120. 124, 125, 126, 137, 139, 140, 144, 145, 149, 150, 151, 152, 153, 155, 157, 163, 165, 176, 180, classroom management 145, classroom organization 40, 93, 166, classroom talk 26, 28, 30, 64, 70, 73, 74, 89, 92, 93, 94, 99, 104, 105, 144, 147, 148, 150, 152, 155, 158, 159, 163, classroom vision of success 152
Cognitive behavioural therapy (CBT) 124
Cognitive restructuring 124, 125, 130
Collaboration 9, 10, 17, 29, 61, 79, 107, 114, 147, 165, 167, 171, 172

Collectivity 92
Collins III & O'Brien (2003) 96, 104
Collins dictionary 19
Combes et al (2008) 49, 59, 76, 89
'Comfort zone' 101, 103, 107, 146, 161
Common Core State Standards Initiative (2010) 66, 74, 76, 89
Communication 1, 2, 10, 13, 14, 16, 17, 18, 19, 20, 21, 22, 24, 25, 26, 27, 28, 29, 30, 31, 33, 34, 35, 48, 50, 54, 62, 63, 64, 66, 7-, 73, 74, 75, 77, 78, 83, 89, 90, 94, 95, 96, 100, 105, 107, 114, 115, 122, 126, 132, 134, 136, 137, 138, 140, 144, 148, 154, 155, 162, 164, 165, 167, 169, 172, 180, alternative forms of communication 141, 153, communication apprehension 48, 49, 59, 74, 119, 120, 124, 125, 129, 130, 131, communication as power 1, 92, communication avoidance 120, 123, 129, communication difficulties 22, 141, communication skills 1, 16, 17, 18, 19, 20, 23, 24, 25, 26, 27, 28, 36, 37, 43, 46, 47, 48, 49, 53, 59, 61, 63, 64, 65, 66, 72, 78, 83, 93, 97, 103, 114, 126, 164, 168, 175, 177, 180, excessive communication 123, non-verbal communication 17, 67, 146, oral communication 17, 18, 24, 26, 29, 48, 58, 71, 72, 74, 79, 91, 99, 109, 120, written communication 17, 107
Community 6, 8, 10, 13, 15, 21, 22, 24, 31, 32, 36, 38, 40, 43, 44, 47, 66, 87, 88, 99, 114, 131, 145, 153, 154, 156, 163, 165, 166, 167, 169, 170, 172, 177, 181
Competencies 13, 19, 24, 25, 76, 78, 86, 96, 148, 149
Competing response training 124
Competition 56, 58, 79, 100, 107, 108, 110, 111, 112, 114, 116, 149, 155, 165, 167, 170
"Complabboration" 114, 167, 181
'Concerns' box 153
Confidence 1, 2, 4, 5, 7, 11, 13, 14, 16, 18, 19, 20, 22, 25, 32, 35, 40, 43, 44, 50, 51, 53, 55, 56, 57, 58, 64, 65, 66, 67, 68, 70, 73, 77, 79, 80, 87, 88, 95, 97, 100, 101, 103, 106, 107, 113, 116, 117, 123, 124, 126, 127, 131, 132, 133, 135, 136, 140, 142, 143, 146, 150, 151, 153, 157, 163, 165, 172, 177, 178, 179, self confidence 31, 64, 133, teacher confidence 149
Conflict 32, 28, 66, 74, conflict resolution 40, 66, 99, 105
Constructivist learning 101
Consultation 31, 97, 102, 136, 180

Content craftsmanship 86
Continuous professional development (CPD) 44, 145, 169
Conversations 21, 23, 43, 80, 84, 86, 146, 152, 158, 162, philosophical conversations 148, phone conversations 116, 133
Corden (2000) 93, 104, Corden (2007) 101, 104
Cornwell et al. (2006) 125, 130
Covid- 19 22, 23, 27, 49, 71, 164
CRC (2001) 4, 6, 37, 44
Creativity 10, 13, 16, 100, 107, 113, 134
Cregan (2008) 26, 71, 74, 138, 144, Cregan (2010) 16, 22, 23, 25, 26, 29, 44, 63, 39, 70, 74, 99, 101, 104, 109, 118, 137, 144, 148, 158, Cregan (2012) 16, 29, 179, 182, Cregan (2019) 16, 18, 22, 29, 95, 104, 137, 144
Critical thinking 10, 23, 24, 66, 70, 81, 100, 107, 114, 115, 148, 155, 163, 165, 171, criticality 92, constructive criticism 94
Cronin (1990) 22, 29
Cultural capital 26, 138
Curaclam na Bunscoile (1971) 62
Curriculum 6, 10, 16, 18, 19, 23, 26, 27, 28, 29, 38, 43, 44, 45, 47, 48, 49, 52, 53, 54, 55, 57, 58, 59, 60, 61, 62, 63, 64, 65, 67, 69, 71, 73, 74, 75, 76, 77, 78, 79, 80, 81, 82, 83, 84, 89, 91, 92, 93, 95, 97, 98, 99, 100, 101, 103, 104, 105, 107, 115, 118, 127, 130, 131, 137, 141, 144, 147, 151

D

Dalai Lama 182
Daly et al (1997) 121, 130
Davey et al. (2010) 11
DCU Changemaker Schools Network (2020) 53
Deason 2009 146, 158
Debate 19, 28, 31, 62, 78, 81, 82, 83, 88, 94, 100, 104, 106-113, 116, 117, 118, 179, alternatives to debating 115-116, debating 27, 54, 58, 64, 72, 82, 88, 91, 99, 100, 104, 106, 107, 108, 109, 110, 111, 112, 113, 116, 117, 118, 133, 144, 179, debating clubs 65, 114, 138, debating competitions 79, 100, 109, 112, 155, 179, debating skills 25, 36, 37, 47, 55, 58, 100, 108, 112, 138, debating team 47, 79, 91, 111, 112, 117, 149, drawbacks of debating 109-111
Decision-making 2, 5, 7, 10, 11, 12, 13, 15, 34, 38, 39, 40, 66, 108, 134, 139, 155, 162
Déclaration des Droits de l'Homme et du Citoyen' 14

Index

Deihl et al (1970) 125, 130
Delivery dynamism 86
Democracy 6, 8, 37, 38, 44, 166, 178, democratic participation 32, 36, 40, democratic processes 1, 5, 34, 164, democratic structures 36, 38
Department of Education and Skills (DES) 25, 29, 137, 144, 159
Describing 41, 70, 72, 76, 99, 149
DeVito (2009) 126, 130
Dewey (1938) 10, 15, 146, 158
DfES (2003) 71, 74
Diagnostic and Statistical Manual of Mental Disorders (DSM-5) 120, 129
Dialect and accent 42, 102, 142
Dialogue 5, 10, 22, 31, 34, 35, 36, 92, 93, 94, 104, 105, 113, 114, 115, 146, 148, 158, 159, 164, 171, 179, dialogic talk 92, 147, dialogic teaching / pedagogy 28, 73, 92-93, 104, 158, 159
Differentiation 67, 100, 102, 141
'Digital native' 162
Disadvantaged contexts 22, 25, 29, 35, 48, 52, 53, 55, 84, 137, 144, 179
Discourse 76, 92, 104, 105, 146, 158
"Discursive tradition" 63
Discussion 22, 27, 28, 35, 44, 79, 80, 81, 84, 93, 112, 113, 134, 147, 153, 162, 164, 171, 178, 179, 181, 'discussion time' 154, panel discussion 88, student-led discussions 71
Diversity 11, 38, 40, 68, 152, 156, 161, 163, 164, 169
Divorce 32
Donaldson (2015) 19, 29, 63, 74, 85
Drama 32, 36, 64, 71, 79, 81, 92, 99, 100, 149, dramatic presentations 78, 149, dramatic role-playing 19, 116, Speech and Drama 65, 149
Drawings 36, 138, 161, 170
Dweck et al. (2015) 51, 59, 130, 149, 158

E

Early intervention 126, 141
Earnshaw (2016) 99, 104
Education Department of Western Australia (1997) 84, 89
Education Endowment Foundation 29, 85
Edward De Bono's 'Thinking Hats' 116
Edwards and Mercer (1987) 68, 74
Edwards and Westgate (1987) 93, 104

Effort 10, 35, 47, 51, 107, 109, 124, 126, 128, 143, 146, 149, 154, 165, 166
Eisenhart (1990) 95, 104
Elaborating 77, 159
Elam & Duckenfield (2000) 178, 182
Ellen Notbohm 139
Elocution 149
Empathy 13, 16, 17, 27, 66, 70, 81, 113, 165, 171, 172, 177, 179
Employability 2, 21, 24, 117
Empowerment 9, 37, 40, 143, 151, 152, 154, 155, 169, 180
Encouragement 32, 42, 67, 70, 83, 101, 113, 115, 136, 143, 150, 165
Engel et al (2017) 99, 104
English 25, 30, 32, 64, 74, 76, 79, 89, 91, 100, 137
English Additional Language (EAL) 26, 42, 55, 142, 143, 179
English Speaking Union (ESU, 2016) 25, 26, 29, 35, 43, 44, 59, 62, 68, 69, 71, 74, 81, 89, 100, 101, 103, 104, 109, 112
Enunciation 80
Equity 35, 126, 138, 169, social equity 48
Erythrophobia 47
ESRI (2017) 88, 89
Ethos 20, 103, school ethos 69
EU Parliament 156
Euphemisms 80
European Commission 15, 156, President of the EU Commission 157
European Year of Youth 156, 157
Eurydice (2012) 10, 11, 15, 166
Evaluating 24, 41, 42, 53, 54, 56, 76, 77, 94, 149
Evans & Jones (2007) 26, 29
Every Child's Right to be Heard 4, 5, 15, 44, 158, 182
Expansions 147
Explaining 79. 99, 101, 149
Explicit approaches 23, 24, 25, 26, 37, 43, 54, 55, 58, 66, 68, 72, 97, 113, 146, 180, explicit public speaking training 40, 50, 52, 56, 57, 59, 67, 73, 79, 83, 91, 181, explicit teaching of skills 82, 83, 91, 95-96, 99, 103, 146, 164, 177, 178, 180
Exploring 108, 116, 136, 154, 160, 165, 167, exploring and using language 73, 77, 100
Expression 4, 5, 9, 13, 16, 28, 35, 47, 59, 63, 77, 86, 110, 115, 117, 136, 140, 163, 170, 175, freedom of

expression 157, self-expression 2, 22, 139, 154, 155
Extra-linguistic knowledge 22, extra-linguistic skills 78
Eye contact 22, 34, 53, 67, 78, 79, 82, 83, 97, 121, 125, 146

F

Facial expressions 17, 34, 41, 47, 54, 56, 80, 82, 85, 97
Facilitation 5, 38, 146, 149, 150, facilitating 14, 15, 22, 23, 31, 32, 34, 36, 38, 39, 40, 44, 45, 88, 102, 115, 128, 134, 141, 142, 145, 146, 153, 155, 157, 178, 179
Fail-safe environment 38
Fairclough (2001) 26, 29, 137, 144
Family Ch 1 p2, 4, 6, 7, 8, 13, 20, 24, 32, 33, 34, 41, 44, 50, 102, 103, 118, 128, 129, 135, 146, 153, 162, 166, 172, 182
Fear 4, 5, 23, 42, 46, 114, 127, 128, 130, 131, 181, fear of judgement 30, 120, 127, fear of being the centre of attention 67, 120, fear of public speaking 1, 42, 47, 48, 49, 50, 52, 54-55, 57, 58, 60, 62, 65, 67, 70, 73, 82, 96, 102, 107, 104, 119, 120, 121, 123, 124, 125, 126, 127, 128, 129, 130, 165, 178, 179, 180, fear of making a mistake 120, 126, 128
Feedback 7, 8, 33, 38, 39, 41, 42, 50, 51, 54, 56, 62, 65, 67, 69, 70, 71, 72, 82, 85, 86, 87, 94, 95, 96, 97, 99, 100, 102, 103, 114, 123, 124, 125, 126, 133, 134, 136, 139, 142, 147, 149, 150, 151, 152, 153, 154, 155, 178
Field et al (2003) 123, 126, 130
Fielding 2001 154, 158, Fielding 2004 31, 44
Filer & Pollard (2000) 148, 158
First Steps (2006) 86, 87, 89, First Steps (2013) 52, 53, 59, 80, 81, 86, 89, 95, 96, 97, 104, 146, 149, 158
Fisher (1992) 149, 158
Fisher and Larkin (2008) 147, 158
'5E model' 153
Frederickson & Collins (1989) 87, 89
Fremouw & Scott (1979) 125, 130
Funerals 56, 128, 129
Furmark et al (2000) 120, 130

G

Gambrell et al (2011) 145, 158
Gandhi 134, 171

Gap, gap between policy and practice 26, 49, 70-71, 176, gap between speaking and being listened to 4, 156, language gap 23, 26, 137, learning gap 94, gap between what employers require and what is being prioritised in schools 26, 71
Geoff Barton 109
George Bernard Shaw 17
Gestures 17, 21, 34, 140
Governments' responsibility 3, 5, 6, 14, 19, 44, 156, 157, 173
Gradual Release of Responsibility Method (GRR) 54, 60, 95, 96, 105
Grandparents 2, 32, 100, 169, 172
Greenaway (2004) 146, 158
Greta Thunberg 143
Grice (2014) 112, 118, 138, 144
Grief 23
Group work 17, 49, 50, 65, 67, 76, 81, 86, 101, 102, 114, 120, 132, 153, 166, 167, 168
Grounding 42, 122
Gschwend (2000) 85, 89
Guardians 31, 142, 177

H

Habermas (1989) 14, 15
Habit reversal 124, 130, nervous habits 121, 124, unhelpful habits 125
Halbhuber (2005) 66, 74
Hallet et al (2003) 13
Hall Haley (2005) 146, 158
Hammerman (1999) 146, 158
Hand gestures 22, 47, 54, 56, 67, 82, 83, 97, 142
Harris et al (2009) 53, 59
Hart (1992) 40, 44, Hart's Ladder of Participation 39
Hart and Risley (1995) 52, 59, 72, 74
Hawthorne effect 42, 45
Hayes & Marshall (1984) 125, 130
Helen Keller 139
Henry Waldsworth Longfellow 98
Hewitt and Inghilleri (1992) 63, 74
Hibbins (2016) 69
Home 5, 6, 10, 15, 22, 25, 31, 32, 33, 34, 46, 58, 72, 81, 83, 137, 146, 153, 162, 163, 166, 181
Honeycutt et al (2009) 125, 130
Hong and Ajex, (1995) 18, 29, 146, 158

Howe (2013) 71, 74
Howe and Abedin (2013) 101, 104
Human rights 3, 4, 40
Humour 41, comedy 116, telling a joke 47, 87, 116
Hunt et al (2014) 66, 74
Huryn (1986) 100, 104
Hyperbole 81

I

Identity 8, 16, 22, 31
Idioms 80
'Ignite programme' 43
Imagery 80, 125
Imaginal experiences 52, imagination 13, 56, 64, 82, 116, 161, 163 181, untethered imaginations 160, 171
Imitation 51, 147
Inclusion 10, 12, 15, 25, 38, 42, 59, 89, 102, 108, 112, 116, 117, 139, 141, 142, 143, 156, 162, 163, 169, 171, 173
Influence 1, 6, 7, 9, 16, 24, 38, 39, 44, 51, 52, 71, 78, 80, 88, 93, 108, 134, 157, 161, 168, 175
'Initiation-Response-Evaluation' (IRE) interactions 101
Inquiry 37, 49, 50, 148, 153, 158
Inspection regime 9
Interests (child's) 8, 9, 12, 14, 31, 33, 35, 41, 52, 54, 81, 97, 135, 136, 141, 146, 156, 163, 165, 166, 167, 177
'Intermental development zone' (IDZ) 93
'Interthinking' 24, 29, 168, 174
Interviews / interviewing 19, 24, 36, 42, 50, 73, 80, 82, 86, 116, 133, 150, 153, 169
Intonation 22, 78, 85
Introducing and thanking 47, 78, 80, 115
Introversion 120
Involvement 4, 7, 36, 37, 38, 40
'IRF' or 'initiation, response and feedback' 7
Irish Department of Children and Youth Affairs 156
Isolation 22, 23, 27, 135

J

Jaffe (2015) 20, 29
Jalongo (2008) 148, 158
James Maddux (2012) 52, 59
Jane Goodall 182

Jehanzeb Khan 3
Jim Larkin 177
JK Rowling 134
Joanne O' Riordain 138, 139, 143
Joe et al (2015) 86, 89
John Bridges, Bishop of Oxford 20
Junior Cycle 128, 150, Junior Certificate 126
"Junior Entrepreneur Programme" 79
Justice 46, social justice 40
Justification / justifying 10, 52, 77, 79

K

Kahlil Gibran 7
Kalesnikava et al (2019) 107, 118
Keenan Fitzgerald (2018) 126, 130
Key words 41
Killen and Nucci (1995) 66, 74
Kincheloe & Steinberg (1998) 154, 158
Knowledge 4, 5, 10, 11, 12, 14, 18, 19, 20, 23, 35, 38, 52, 59, 62, 63, 68, 73, 74, 76, 77, 83, 89, 99, 100, 104, 128, 146, 154, 159, 160, 163, 164, 165, 167, 173, 175, pedagogical knowledge 53, 103, 145, subject knowledge22, 69, 94, 145, 150
Kofi Annan 157
Kostić-Bobanović, (2006) 123, 125, 130
Kutnick and Colwell (2010) 146, 158

L

Lansdown (2011) 3, 4, 6, 14, 15, 36, 44, 157, 158, 175, 182
LAOS (2016) 149, 159, LAOS (2022) 145, 149, 159
Lawy & Biesta (2006) 10, 15
Leadership 8, 15, 37, 46, 47, 73, 105, 114, 134, 135, 155, 165, 172, 182
Leaving Certificate exam (LC) 150
Lecterns 56, 102, 142
Lefstein (2006) 92, 104
Le Loup and Pontero (2007) 18, 29
'LET's Stand' Public Speaking Programme 97, 'LET's Stand' (2018) 59, 89, 104, LET's Stand (2021) 97, 104, 'LET'S Stand' public speaking assessment rubric 85
Life outcomes 2, 21, 24, 35, 164, 177, 178
Lippman et al (2015) 24, 29
Listening 1, 3, 16, 18, 19, 21, 23, 24, 25, 26, 27, 28, 29, 33, 34, 35, 42, 53, 54, 59, 64, 66, 70, 73, 74, 77, 80, 81, 83, 84, 86, 87, 89, 92, 93, 95, 96, 97,

99, 104, 107, 110, 115, 116, 122, 140, 141, 143, 146, 148, 149, 154, 158, 162, 172, 173, 177, 178, 180, active listening 17, 19, 21, 113, 117, 146, 168, listening to children 1, 2, 8, 11, 12, 13, 14, 33, 34, 35, 37, 39, 58, 156, 157, 167, 168, 181, 182
"Literate language" of schools 26, 42, 55, 67, 109
Littleton and Mercer (2013) 24, 29
'Logical fallacies' 110
Logos 20
Lopez (2008) 96, 104
Louden (2010) 107, 118
Lucas (2007) 86, 89, 126, 130
Lundy (2007) 39, 44, 156, 157, 159, 180, 182

M

Malala Yousafzai 143
Mancuso (2014) 119, 124, 125, 130
Mannion (2023) 175, 182
'Mantle of the Expert' 99, 105
Marcotte (2006) 85, 89
Marginalised groups 5, 8
Mark Twain 119, 121
Martin-Lynch et al (2016) 119, 123, 126, 130
Martin Robinson, ESU (2016) 71, 81
Mastery experiences 51, 56, 66, 88
Mattie Stepanek 138, 139, 143
McAlinden 59
McCroskey (1970) 48, 59, 120, 130, McCroskey (1977) 119, 120, 123, 130, McCroskey (1984) 18, 29, McCroskey et al (1981) 57, 59, 72, 74
McIntyre et al (2005) 10, 15, 36, 43, 45, 180, 182
McKenzie and Saunders (2007) 126, 130
Media literacy 164
Mental health 22, 23, 156, 165, 171, 177, mental illness 22, mental wellbeing 48, 154, 165, 177
Mentors for younger children 37
Mercer (1995) 94, 104, 146, 159, Mercer (2000) 168, 174, Mercer (2016) 22, 29, 95, 104, Mercer & Littleton (2007) 147, 159, Mercer et al. (1999) 94, Mercer and Mannion (2018) 19, 22, 23, 24, 25, 27, 29, 35, 45, 50, 58, 59, 68, 70, 72, 74, 79, 83, 84, 85, 89, 91, 95, 96, 99, 100, 104, 133, 137, 144, 164, 174, 178, 182, Mercer and Wegerif (1999) 68, 104
Merriam Webster dictionary 1, 20, 28, 29, 49, 54, 60, 64
Metaphor 80

Mezuk and Ko (2021) 104, 107, 118, Mezuk et al (2011) 99, 112, 118
Michelangelo 48
Michaels & Cazden (1986) 26, 29, 137, 144
Michaels et al (2008) 101, 105
Millard and Menzies (2016) 16, 19, 29, 43, 45, 62, 65, 68, 69, 70, 71, 72, 74, 99, 103, 105, 108, 118, 132, 138, 144, 147, 159
Miller and Gildea (1987) 52, 53, 60
Miltenberger (2012) 125, Miltenberger et al (1998) 121
Mind-maps 41, 68, 86
Mindset 43, 68, 7118, 168
Minority group 47, 87, 88, 142, 143, 144
Modelling 13, 21, 22, 51, 56, 57, 68, 93, 95, 96, 99, 125, 143, 146, 147, 149, 154, 162, 178, 'Model, Share, Guide and Apply' 96, 97
Model United Nations 99, 104
Monologue 72, 146
Moorghen 100
Morisano et al (2010) 148, 159
Morreale et al (2000) 97, Morreale et al (2007) 20, 29, 86, 89, 104
Motley (1997) 119, 130
Mulac & Sherman (1974) 121, 130
Munro (2009) 18, 29
Mutual respect 5, 31, 147
'"My News"' 79, 81

N

Narration / narrate 18, 76, 78, 92, 94
Nash et al (2016) 119, 125, 130
National Curriculum in the UK 63
National Literacy Strategy 71, 75
NCCA (1999) 65, 74, 78, 89, NCCA (2007) 83, 89, 103, 105, NCCA (2012) 95, 105, NCCA (2015) 77, NCCA (2017) 62, 74, NCCA (2019) 16, 22, 29, 47, 49, 52, 53, 60, 77, 78, 79, 83, 89, NCCA (2023) 49, 60, 63, 74
Negotiating 8, 46, 61, 114
NELP (2008) 18, 29, 53, 60, 99, 105
NEPS (2015) 145, 159
Nerves 42, 47, 55, 102, 107, 121, 122, 123, 124, 125, 127, 133, 136
Newcomb (1999) 76, 89, 132, 144
Nicosia (1997) 125, 131
Niedermeyer and Oliver (1972) 26, 29, 72, 74

Nonverbal cues 18, 134, 143
Northern Ireland Commissioner for Children and Young People 4
Northern Irish primary school curriculum 80, 99
Nystrand et al (1997) 92, 105

O

Ó Duibhir and Cummins (2012) 83, 89
Office of the Ombudsman for children 38
Ofsted (2005) 9, 15, 64, 74
Ontario (2007) English Curriculum 64, 74
Opportunities 5, 7, 8, 10, 13, 14, 15, 22, 24, 26, 28, 32, 33, 34, 36, 37, 38, 40, 42, 45, 47, 51, 52, 53, 54, 55, 57, 58, 59, 62, 64, 65, 66, 70, 71, 73, 77, 78, 79, 82, 83, 87, 88, 89, 92, 93, 95, 96, 99, 100, 101, 102, 103, 108, 109, 111, 112, 113, 116, 117, 119, 120, 126, 133, 135, 136, 137, 141, 142, 146, 149, 151, 152, 153, 154, 155, 156, 160, 161, 162, 163, 164, 165, 167, 168, 170, 172, 177, 179, 181, 182
Oracy 2, 16, 19, 23, 26, 27, 28, 29, 35, 43, 44, 45, 48, 49, 52, 59, 60, 62, 64, 65, 68, 69, 70, 71, 73, 74, 79, 83, 84, 85, 89, 95, 99, 101, 103, 104, 105, 112, 118, 123, 132, 144, 147, 158, 159, 174, 177, 182
Oracy All-Party Parliamentary Group (OAPPG, 2021) 23, 25, 27, 29, 49, 60, 64, 71, 74
Oral language 16, 18, 21, 22, 23, 24, 25, 26, 27, 28, 29, 30, 44, 47, 48, 49, 50, 52, 53, 54, 55, 62, 63, 64, 65, 68, 69, 70, 71, 73, 74, 75, 77, 79, 80, 81, 83, 84, 87, 88, 89, 90, 91, 95, 99, 100, 103, 104, 105, 113, 118, 132, 137, 143, 144, 147, 149, 158, 159, 164, 177, 179, 182
Oral lessons, rarity of entirely oral lessons 71, wholly oral lessons 64
Osborn et al (2009) 126, 131
Otto (2008) 148, 159

P

Pabst-Weinschenk (2005) 76, 90
Pace 3, 22, 76, 78, 83, 86, 97, 109, 113, 114, 142
Participation 2, 3, 5, 6, 8, 9, 10, 11, 12, 13, 16, 31, 32, 33, 36, 37, 38, 39, 40, 44, 45, 66, 92, 93, 104, 107, 112, 118, 132, 148, 152, 155, 156, 157, 159, 161, 162, 164, 166, 167, 168, 175, 180
Parents 2, 3, 4, 8, 11, 14, 21, 31, 32, 38, 44, 48, 50, 51, 52, 53, 54, 55, 56, 59, 61, 65, 66, 67, 69, 71, 77, 81, 87, 91, 103, 127, 128, 129, 135, 136, 138, 139, 140, 142, 145, 148, 153, 161, 162, 166, 168, 169, 173, 175, 177
Pathos 20
Pause 22, 54, 78, 83, 97, 124
PDST (2013) 62, 74, 80, 90, 96, 105, 146, 159
Pearson & Gallagher (1983) 53, 54, 60, 95, 96, 97, 105
Pearson et al (2007) 46, 60, 120, 131
Pedagogy 28, 73, 74, 92, 93, 104, 105, 158, 159, 180
Peers 22, 35, 37, 42, 49, 53, 54, 55, 56, 57, 64, 65, 66, 72, 73, 79, 96, 99, 116, 133, 140, 141, 142, 147, 151, 152, 153, 166, 167, 168, 171, 177, 179, peer counselling 37, peer education, 12, 36, 37, peer evaluation 41, 86, 97, 102, 142, 154, peer mediation 105, 115, peer pressure 33, 127, testing ideas with peers 76, 132
Pellegrini (2002) 26, 29
Persistence 35
Personification 80
Persuading / persuasion 20, 46, 51, 70, 86, 107, 109
Pertaub and Barker (2002) 119, 121, 123, 131
Petek (2014) 148, 159
Philosophical dialogue 115, philosophical discussions 79, 100, philosophy for Children (P4C) 115
Phobias 119, 126
'Picture prompts' 41
Pitch 22, 24, 78, 79, 80, 82, 83, 97, 149
Play 5, 7, 8, 13, 21, 22, 32, 33, 34, 37, 46, 55, 56, 63, 67, 70, 73, 80, 82, 87, 93, 99, 100, 116, 118, 157, 160, 161, 162, 167, 169, 172, 173, 181
Poetry 7, 46, 47, 79, 87, 99, 132, 138, 149, 154
Policy 2, 5, 6, 12, 14, 15, 26, 27, 29, 39, 44, 48, 49, 59, 63, 70, 71, 74, 103, 104, 108, 144, 158, 176, 180, police-informed practice 168, practice-informing policy 168
Politics 23, 106, 112, 138
Positive psychology 51, 59, 104, 105
Pouteaux and Berg (2013) 20, 49
Power 1, 4, 6, 7, 9, 10, 13, 15, 24, 26, 29, 39, 40, 43, 44, 45, 47, 59, 62, 70, 78, 88, 89, 92, 98, 106, 115, 127, 137, 138, 141, 143, 144, 154, 159, 160, 161, 163, 165, 171, 172, 173, 174, 177, 180, 181, 182
Practise / practicing 13, 16, 26, 35, 36, 37, 40, 51, 52, 53, 54, 55, 56, 57, 58, 64, 65, 66, 67, 69, 70, 73, 77, 78, 81, 82, 87, 91, 94, 95, 96, 98, 100, 101, 103, 107, 108, 113, 114, 115, 116, 117, 122, 123,

124, 126, 127, 128, 135, 136, 140, 141, 143, 152, 157, 161, 164, 165, 166, 177, 178
Praise 71, 136
Predicting 99
Prensky (2005) 11, 15, 181, 182
Preparation 29, 41, 67, 66, 77, 95, 99, 111, 112, 117, 120, 123, 127, 128, 144, 145, 151
Presentation / presentations 6, 20, 23, 24, 27, 28, 40, 41, 42, 43, 47, 53, 54, 56, 57, 59, 62, 63, 64, 65, 66, 67, 68, 73, 74, 75, 76, 77, 78, 79, 80, 81, 82, 84, 86, 87, 89, 94, 96, 98, 99, 100, 101, 102, 103, 104, 119, 120, 121, 122, 123, 124, 126, 128, 133, 136, 141, 142, 143, 144, 149, 150, 153, 154, 158, 165, 166, 172, 180
Primary Language Curriculum (PLC) 47, 49, 52, 53, 60, 73, 77, 80, 84, 89, 130
Primary National Strategy (2003) 71
Primary Curriculum Framework 49, 60, 62, 74
Problem solving 19, 23, 38
"Project-based learning" 79, 154, 164
Project Soapbox 99
Prompts 34, 41, 146, 147, 151
Pronunciation 82, 83, 140
Props 54, 56, 83, 136, 141
Proverbs 80, 81
Proximity 22, 83
Public relations 24, 30, 131, 149
Public representatives 35, 108, 180
Public speaking 1, 2, 16, 19, 20, 21, 24, 26, 27, 28, 29, 30, 35, 36, 37, 40, 41, 42, 43, 46-91, 94-103, 105-107, 109, 111-132, 135, 140-144, 148-150, 155, 165, 177-182, public speeches 23, 66, 86, 103, 120

Q

Quaglia (2016) 35, 45
Questioning 4, 2, 70, 80, 86, 93, 100, 115, 148, 149, 171
Quinn & Owens (2014) 11, 15
Quotations 99

R

Rankin et al (2015) 23, 30
Rating scales 85
Reading, reading aloud 84, reading at Mass 46, 127, 128
Reason and Bradbury (2008) 50, 60

Reasoning 23, 95, 104, 107, 110, 115, 116, 117, 161
Recalling 72, 99
Recasts 147
Reciprocity / reciprocal 77, 92, 146, 152
Recitation 47, 63, 64, 93, 152
Recount 65, 78
Reflection 16, 24, 39, 50, 92, 109, 115, 147, 154, 155, 166, 170
Reflective practitioner 26, 149, 155, 158, 163
Rehearsal 82, 125
Relationships 17, 22, 36, 66, 73, 77, 92, 93, 135, 145, 164, 166, 172, 180
Relaxation techniques 122, 125
Repetition 57, 80
Reporting 25, 40, 48, 72, 76, 83, 88, 95
Representation 5, 9, 36, 88, 155, 157
Research 4, 5, 8, 9, 11, 12, 16, 25, 26, 27, 28, 35, 39, 40, 42, 46, 48, 50, 53, 54, 56, 58, 59, 63, 65, 66, 68, 70, 71, 76, 81, 85, 86, 88, 91, 94, 96, 100, 102. 107, 108, 109, 110, 112, 119, 123, 126, 133, 136, 137, 151, 154, 155, 178, 181
Resilience 35, 51, 52, 107, 129
Resistance to change 5
Respect 3, 4, 5, 11, 12, 31, 32, 33, 34, 36, 92, 101, 113, 116, 117, 142, 147, 155, 157, 164, 173
Ressler (2012) 146, 159
Restorative Practice 37, 115
Retelling 72, 77, 78, 102, 116
Reznitskya (2012) 147, 159
Rhetoric 20, 24, 63, 70, 71, 77, 106, 110, 116, 119, 158, rhetorical 17, 18, rhetorical techniques 19, 72, 79, 80, 94, 98, 117, 172
Rhythm 80, 139
Richmond and McCroskey (1993) 17, 30, 148, 159
Rights and Responsibilities 8, 170
Riley et al (2004) 149, 159
Robinson (1997) 124, 131
Robinson and Taylor (2007) 10, 15, 36, 45
Role play 33, 73, 82, 96, 101, 116
Role models 6, 51, 88, 143, 156, 168
Rosenthal and Jacobson (1968) 148, 159
Ross and Nisbett (1991) 148, 159
Roulstone et al (2011) 72, 75
Royal College of Speech and Language Therapists (2012) 22, 30
Rubrics 85, 86, 87, 89, 103, Public Speaking Competence Rubric (PSCR) 86, 90, 105

Rudduck (2006) 31, 45
Rudduck and McIntyre (2007) 6, 15
Rules 8, 31, 33, 54, 83, 123, 152, 163
Ruscio et al (2008) 119, 131

S

Safe space 5, 12, 14, 51, 87, 93, 115, 164, 170, 178, safe supportive environment 4, 23, 31, 32, 37, 38, 40, 54, 56, 58, 62, 69, 92, 95, 96, 97, 114, 124, 126, 129, 135, 136, 142, 146, 152, 177, 178
Salim and Joy (2016) 20, 24, 30, 46, 60
Save the Children's Practice Standards in Children's Participation (2005) 12, 15
Scaffolding 41, 82, 88, 94, 99, 102, 147, 149, 177, 179
School 2, 4, 5, 6, 9-15, 17, 18, 21-23, 25-29, 31, 33-38, 40, 42-51, 53-59, 61-76, 76-81, 83-85, 87-89, 91, 95, 97, 100, 102-109, 111, 112, 114, 116, 117, 118, 123, 126, 128, 129, 132, 135-137, 142, 145, 146, 148-157, 160, 161, 163-169, 175, 177, 178, 180, 181
'School 21' 43, 72, 79, 85, 132
Schreiber et al (2012) 86, 90, 103, 105
Schulz et al (2010) 168, 174
Scotland's Curriculum for Excellence (CfE) 84
Scottish Survey of Literacy Curriculum for Excellence (CfE) 84, 90
Seldom heard voices 8, 10, 87, 144, 157
Seligman (2002) 96, 105
Self-awareness 70, 143, self-belief 116, 150, self-conscious 127, 133, 140, 142
Self-efficacy 13, 16, 35, 41, 50-52, 55-57, 59, 66, 73, 78, 106-108, 116, 129, 143, 162, 172, 177, 180, 181
Self-esteem 4, 22, 43, 120, 126, 135, 141, self-fulfilling prophecy 132, self-limiting belief 13, self-monitoring 124, self-regulating 70, 166, self-talk 19, 154, self-reflection 39, 154, self-worth 35
Sellman (2011) 99, 105
SEN – Special Education Needs 37, 55, 57, 102, 132, 139, 142, 143, 179
Shafer (2010) 49, 60, 65, 72, 75, 96, 105
Shannon-Weaver (1949) 18
Sherrington (2016) 99, 105
Shiel et al (2012) 23, 71, 72, 147
Shier (2001) 39, 45, Shier's Pathways to Participation (2001) 40

'Shinrinyoku' 170
'"Show and Tell"' 79, 81, 91, 116
Shy / shyness 40, 42, 46, 47, 53, 55, 57, 68, 70, 76, 102, 103, 126, 127, 128, 129, 130, 132, 133, 134, 135, 136, 137, 140, 143, 144, 150, 175, 179
Silence 9, 59, 154, 170, 176
Similes 80
Skidmore (2000) 92, 105
Skills 1, 2, 10, 11, 13, 16-30, 32-38, 40-43, 46-51, 53-56, 58-66, 68-70, 72-79, 81-85, 87-89, 91, 93-97, 99-101, 103-108, 112-117, 123-132, 135-140, 142-151, 153-155, 157-159, 161-165, 168, 169, 171, 172, 175, 177-181
Slater et al (1999) 124, 131
Slavin (1988) 101, 105
Smith (2001) 146, 159
Smith & Foley (2015) 99
Smith et al. (2004) 70, 75
Snow (1990) 72, 75, 145, 159
Social and emotional wellbeing 19, 22, 43, 107, 164
Social constructivism 93
Social awareness 18, 19, 22, 58, 62, 64, 66, 80, 101, 120, 131, 132, 133, 135, 136, 141, 143, 144, 165, social awkwardness 134, social capital 20, social control and power 26, 137, social equity 48, 138, social exclusion 8, 25, social growth and mobility 2, 25, 28, 35, 43, 58, 109, 165, 177, social justice 40, social modelling 51, social or verbal persuasion 51, social reproduction 165, social responsibility 10, 78
Socrates 100, Socratic circles 100, Socratic dialogue 148
'Speak for Change' 27, 29, 49, 60, 64, 74
Speaking 1, 4, 16, 17, 19, 22, 24, 27, 29, 42-46, 54, 58, 59, 74, 89, 102, 107, 113, 137, 141-144, 149, 155, 156, 158, 159, 164, speaking and listening 19, 21, 23-25, 27, 28, 73, 113, 116, 146, 154, 180, 'speaking rights' 154, speaking up 2, 168, 172, 177
Speech 2, 18-20, 22-25, 27-30, 36, 41-43, 53-56, 59, 60, 62-65, 68, 74, 77, 80, 82, 83, 86-89, 94, 95, 97-99, 101-103, 105, 114, 116, 117, 119-122, 125, 129, 130, 136, 137, 139-143, 149, 150, 177, speeches 20, 23, 41, 43, 56, 62, 63, 66-68, 72, 76, 79, 82, 86-88, 94, 98, 101, 103, 116, 120, 121, 124, 126, 136, 143
Speculating 79, 92, 94
Spohr (2009) 24, 30, 121, 131

SSLN (2014) 84, 90
Stage fright 119, 130
Stahl (2005) 52
Standing up 56, 65, 97, 128, 148, standing up for others 24, 108, 144
Stanford (2015) 112, 118, 138, 144
States of Physiology 51
Stein et al (1996) 119, 123, 131
Stewart and Tassie (2011) 119
Stories 7, 20, 22, 41, 46, 66, 72, 73, 78, 79, 82, 99-101, 104, 106, 138, 143, 153, 154, 162, 165, 173, 177, 178, 181, storytelling 61, 73, 78, 80, 97, 98, 100, 104, 162, 169
Stothard et al (1998) 25, 30
Strahan (2003) 126, 131
Strengths 12, 35, 40, 59, 84, 85, 87, 96, 100, 136, 138, 141, 143, 146, 165, 167, 168, 178, 179
Structure 19, 41, 42, 52-54, 67, 80, 85, 94-98, 107, 109, 141, 154, 177
Student advisory panels 38, 155
Student agency 9, 97, 144, 168
Student councils 9, 11, 37, 38, 88, 100, 155
Students as governors 156
Student-led school-based research 155
Student voice 2, 3, 6, 7, 9-12, 14, 15, 31, 34-46, 49, 54, 58, 87, 115, 144, 145, 149, 151, 152, 154-159, 161, 163, 168, 169, 173-175, 177-182
Stuttering 121, 139
Support 1, 2, 5, 6, 8, 14, 25, 28, 32, 38-41, 43, 44, 47, 48, 50, 51, 54, 55, 58, 64, 65, 67, 69-71, 81, 84, 87-89, 91, 92, 94, 95, 97, 102, 103, 113, 116, 122-124, 126, 127, 129, 132, 135-143, 148, 149, 152, 155, 162, 163, 168, 169, 173, 175, 177-179, 182
Suskie (2009) 85, 90
Sustainability 14, 44, 114, 157, 170, 173
Swanson (2016) 99, 105

T

Talents 4, 13, 25, 36, 136, 146, 161, 168
Talk 2, 3, 7, 17-19, 23-27, 29, 43, 71, 70, 71, 79, 84, 95, 97, 99, 101, 123-125, 127, 136, 139, 147-149, 152, 180, accountable talk 101, 105, classroom talk 28, 64, 70, 73, 89, 104, 144, 147, 158, dialogic talk 92, disputational talk 94, evaluative talk 92, exploratory talk 35, 94, 152, 168, expository talk 78, 92, expressive talk 92, formal talk contexts 78, informal talk contexts 78, instructional talk 152, rich talk experiences 72, 137, school talk 146, talk as content 94, talk as pedagogy 93, talk-based activities / lessons 68, 69, 103, transactional talk 92, 'walk and talk' 166, 169
Taylor and Robinson (2009) 9, 15, 43, 45, 156, 159
Teamwork 17, 24, 33, 107, 114, 165
Teacher 2, 6, 10, 14, 23, 29, 30, 34, 35, 38, 40-43, 46, 47, 49, 50, 53-57, 61, 65, 67, 68, 70-72, 81, 84, 86, 89, 91, 92-95, 99, 102, 103, 112, 116, 127, 128, 130, 133, 136, 140, 142-154, 158-160, 163, 166, 167, 168, 176, 178, 182
Technology 11, 13, 17, 29, 45, 51, 71, 83, 141, 162, 163, 171
'TED Talks' 63, 82
Temple Grandin 138, 139
Tenacity 135, 28, 148, 166, academic tenacity 51, 59, 130, 158
The Bercow Report in the UK in (2008) 18
The Cambridge Primary Review 16, 44, 73
The Communication Trust (2015) 18, 25, 30, 137, 144, 149, 159
The Prophet 7, 15
Thinking 9, 10, 16, 18, 19, 23-25, 29, 34, 51, 64, 66, 70, 76, 81, 92, 94, 95, 99, 100, 104, 107, 110, 111, 113-117, 127, 145, 148, 151, 155, 159, 163, 165, 171
Thomas (2007) 120, 131
Thomson and Rucker (2002) 86, 90
Time and space 33, 140, 171
Toastmasters International 46, 47, 53, 114, 147
Topping & Trickey (2007) 99, 105
Toshalis & Nakkula (2012) 35, 45
Training for adults 12, 38, 43, 44, 49, 50, 55, 57, 67-69, 78, 91, 128, 145, 149, 150, 157, 173
Travelling community 47, 88
'Try 3 before me' 154
Turn taking 31-32, 77, 83, 115, 142, 146
21st century skills 10, 13, 23, 24, 61, 76, 107

U

Understanding 5, 8, 12, 13, 16, 18, 21-23, 25, 27, 28, 34, 39, 40, 49, 52, 59, 63, 64, 67, 76-78, 83, 92-94, 98, 99, 103, 109, 113, 115, 117, 129, 137, 139, 141, 143, 150, 154, 163-165, 175, 177, 181
UN (1989) 4, 10, 39, 49, 161
UNCRC 1, 2, 3, 4, 14, 15, 28, 36, 38, 44, 48, 49, 58, 70, 73, 157, 161, 172, 175

UN General Assembly Special Session on Children in 2002 - 6
UNICEF (2004) 32, 45, UNICEF (2008) 6, 15, 182, UNICEF (2011) 155
UNICEF review of the impact of child participation in South Asia in 2004 - 32
Unique / uniqueness 2-9, 11, 12, 14, 32, 36, 47, 48, 62, 67, 68, 87, 88, 113, 116, 132, 136, 138, 139, 142-144, 147, 154, 157, 160, 162, 163, 166, 168, 175, 178, 179, 181
United States Office of International Development (USAID, 2015) 24
Universal Design for Learning (UDL) 135, 139
Ursula von der Leyen 157

V

Van der Veen (2017) 22, 30
VanderWey et al (2014) 146, 159
Van Ginkel et al (2015) 66, 75
Vicarious experiences 51
View / viewpoints 3-7, 11, 12, 14, 16, 31, 37, 39, 41, 63, 64, 66, 68, 71, 78, 80, 92, 94, 101, 108, 109, 110, 111, 113, 114, 117, 132, 144, 155-157, 161, 162, 166, 167, 173, 179
Virtuous circle 36
Visual aids 81, 83, 86, 97, 136, 140, 141, visual cues 140, 141
Visualisation 122, 124
Vocabulary development 50, 53, 57, 78, 127, 177, 181
Voice (metaphorical) 1-15, 21, 28, 31-46, 48, 49, 54, 58, 62, 66, 73, 77, 87, 89, 91, 108, 112, 115, 117, 132, 138, 139, 143-145, 149, 151-161, 163, 164, 168-171, 173-182
Voice (physical) 1, 4, 14, 17, 19, 22, 35, 43, 47, 54, 59, 64, 73, 80, 82, 83, 85, 86, 91, 95, 97, 100, 106, 113, 116, 121, 122, 125, 146, 152, 154, 175
Voice 21 - 29, 71, 74, 101, 105, 118, 144, 159
Vries and Rentfrow (2016) 132, 144
Vygotsky (1978) 93, 94, 105

W

Wasik and Hindman (2018) 147, 159
Well-being 2, 3, 17, 22, 48, 49, 56, 64, 126, 146, 149, 164, 165, 166, 167, 171, 177
Welsh school curriculum 29, 45, 59, 63, 74, 89, 104, 144, 174, 182
Wertsch (1985) 148, 159
Wickström & Bendix (2000) 42, 45
Wilkinson (1965) 19, 30
Woolfram et al (1999) 26, 30, 137, 144
Workplace 24, 29, 74, 128

X

Xie & Dong (2017) 23, 30

Y

Youth groups 38

Z

Zenger and Folkman (2017) 96, 105
ZPD, Zone of proximal development 87, 94

For Product Safety Concerns and Information please contact our EU
representative GPSR@taylorandfrancis.com
Taylor & Francis Verlag GmbH, Kaufingerstraße 24, 80331 München, Germany

www.ingramcontent.com/pod-product-compliance
Lightning Source LLC
Chambersburg PA
CBHW082100230426
43670CB00017B/2902